Intellectual Property Valuation and Innovation

With the recent global economic crisis, attitudes and practices in relation to intellectual property valuation are changing as exemplified by the dichotomy explained in this book, which makes it unique. While there has been a move towards global harmonisation in terms of valuation of both tangible and intangible assets that are based on innovation, there is also a tendency against global harmonisation because of cultural attitudes and practices of different countries. This can be seen most acutely in relation to intellectual property valuation in Asia, especially East Asia, which often differs from the West's perception of valuation. The book is written by experts in intellectual property, valuation and innovation who are mainly practitioners covering innovators, marketers, accountants, social innovators and business and management academics. The breadth and practitioner background of most of the contributors make the material relevant to those involved in valuation, economics, business, management, accounting and finance, law and maritime insurance. This book takes an interdisciplinary approach that cross-cuts all the above-mentioned disciplines and takes the understanding of intellectual property valuation to a new level.

Ruth Taplin is Director of the Centre for Japanese and East Asian Studies, UK, which won Exporter of the Year in Partnership in Trading/Pathfinder for the UK in 2000. She received her doctorate from the London School of Economics and is the author/editor of 17 books and over 200 articles. She is Editor of the *Interdisciplinary Journal of Economics and Business Law* (www.ijebl.co.uk), holds a Graduate Diploma in Law and is a featured author of Routledge.

Routledge Studies in the Growth Economies of Asia

1. **The Changing Capital Markets of East Asia**
   Edited by Ky Cao

2. **Financial Reform in China**
   Edited by On Kit Tam

3. **Women and Industrialization in Asia**
   Edited by Susan Horton

4. **Japan's Trade Policy**
   Action or reaction?
   Yumiko Mikanagi

5. **The Japanese Election System**
   Three analytical perspectives
   Junichiro Wada

6. **The Economics of the Latecomers**
   Catching-up, technology transfer and institutions in Germany, Japan and South Korea
   Jang-Sup Shin

7. **Industrialization in Malaysia**
   Import substitution and infant industry performance
   Rokiah Alavi

8. **Economic Development in Twentieth-Century East Asia**
   The international context
   Edited by Aiko Ikeo

9. **The Politics of Economic Development in Indonesia**
   Contending perspectives
   Edited by Ian Chalmers and Vedi R. Hadiz

10. **Studies in the Economic History of the Pacific Rim**
    Edited by Sally M. Miller, A.J.H. Latham and Dennis O. Flynn

11. **Workers and the State in New Order Indonesia**
    Vedi R. Hadiz

12. **The Japanese Foreign Exchange Market**
    Beate Reszat

13. **Exchange Rate Policies in Emerging Asian Countries**
    Edited by Stefan Collignon, Jean Pisani-Ferry and Yung Chul Park

14. **Chinese Firms and Technology in the Reform Era**
    Yizheng Shi

15. **Japanese Views on Economic Development**
    Diverse paths to the market
    Kenichi Ohno and Izumi Ohno

16. **Technological Capabilities and Export Success in Asia**
    Edited by Dieter Ernst, Tom Ganiatsos and Lynn Mytelka

17. **Trade and Investment in China**
    The European experience
    Edited by Roger Strange, Jim Slater and Limin Wang

18. **Technology and Innovation in Japan**
    Policy and management for the twenty-first century
    Edited by Martin Hemmert and Christian Oberländer

19. **Trade Policy Issues in Asian Development**
    Prema-chandra Athukorala

20. **Economic Integration in the Asia Pacific Region**
    Ippei Yamazawa

21. **Japan's War Economy**
    Edited by Erich Pauer

22. **Industrial Technology Development in Malaysia**
    Industry and firm studies
    Edited by Jomo K.S., Greg Felker and Rajah Rasiah

23. **Technology, Competitiveness and the State**
    Malaysia's industrial technology policies
    Edited by Jomo K.S. and Greg Felker

24. **Corporatism and Korean Capitalism**
    Edited by Dennis L. McNamara

25. **Japanese Science**
    Samuel Coleman

26. **Capital and Labour in Japan**
    The functions of two factor markets
    Toshiaki Tachibanaki and Atsuhiro Taki

27. **Asia Pacific Dynamism 1550–2000**
    Edited by A.J.H. Latham and Heita Kawakatsu

28. **The Political Economy of Development and Environment in Korea**
    Jae-Yong Chung and Richard J. Kirkby

29. **Japanese Economics and Economists since 1945**
    Edited by Aiko Ikeo

30. **China's Entry into the World Trade Organisation**
    Edited by Peter Drysdale and Ligang Song

31. **Hong Kong as an International Financial Centre**
    Emergence and development 1945–1965
    Catherine R. Schenk

32. **Impediments to Trade in Services**
    Measurement and policy implication
    Edited by Christopher Findlay and Tony Warren

33. **The Japanese Industrial Economy**
    Late development and cultural causation
    Ian Inkster

34. **China and the Long March to Global Trade**
    The accession of China to the World Trade Organization
    Edited by Alan S. Alexandroff, Sylvia Ostry and Rafael Gomez

35. **Capitalist Development and Economism in East Asia**
    The rise of Hong Kong, Singapore, Taiwan, and South Korea
    Kui-Wai Li

36. **Women and Work in Globalizing Asia**
    Edited by Dong-Sook S. Gills and Nicola Piper

37. **Financial Markets and Policies in East Asia**
    Gordon de Brouwer

38. **Developmentalism and Dependency in Southeast Asia**
    The case of the automotive industry
    Jason P. Abbott

39. **Law and Labour Market Regulation in East Asia**
    Edited by Sean Cooney, Tim Lindsey, Richard Mitchell and Ying Zhu

40. **The Economy of the Philippines**
    Elites, inequalities and economic restructuring
    Peter Krinks

41. **China's Third Economic Transformation**
    The rise of the private economy
    Edited by Ross Garnaut and Ligang Song

42. **The Vietnamese Economy**
    Awakening the dormant dragon
    Edited by Binh Tran-Nam and Chi Do Pham

43. **Restructuring Korea Inc.**
    Jang-Sup Shin and Ha-Joon Chang

44. **Development and Structural Change in the Asia-Pacific**
    Globalising miracles or end of a model?
    Edited by Martin Andersson and Christer Gunnarsson

45. **State Collaboration and Development Strategies in China**
    The case of the China–Singapore Suzhou Industrial Park (1992–2002)
    Alexius Pereira

46. **Capital and Knowledge in Asia**
    Changing power relations
    Edited by Heidi Dahles and Otto van den Muijzenberg

47. **Southeast Asian Paper Tigers?**
    From miracle to debacle and beyond
    Edited by Jomo K.S.

48. **Manufacturing Competitiveness in Asia**
    How internationally competitive national firms and industries developed in East Asia
    Edited by Jomo K.S.

49. **The Korean Economy at the Crossroads**
    Edited by MoonJoong Tcha and Chung-Sok Suh

50. **Ethnic Business**
    Chinese capitalism in Southeast Asia
    Edited by Jomo K.S. and Brian C. Folk

51. **Exchange Rate Regimes in East Asia**
    Edited by Gordon de Brouwer and Masahiro Kawai

52. **Financial Governance in East Asia**
Policy dialogue, surveillance and cooperation
Edited by Gordon de Brouwer and Yunjong Wang

53. **Designing Financial Systems in East Asia and Japan**
Edited by Joseph P.H. Fan, Masaharu Hanazaki and Juro Teranishi

54. **State Competence and Economic Growth in Japan**
Yoshiro Miwa

55. **Understanding Japanese Saving**
Does population aging matter?
Robert Dekle

56. **The Rise and Fall of the East Asian Growth System, 1951–2000**
International competitiveness and rapid economic growth
Xiaoming Huang

57. **Service Industries and Asia-Pacific Cities**
New development trajectories
Edited by P.W. Daniels, K.C. Ho and T.A. Hutton

58. **Unemployment in Asia**
Edited by John Benson and Ying Zhu

59. **Risk Management and Innovation in Japan, Britain and the United States**
Edited by Ruth Taplin

60. **Japan's Development Aid to China**
The long-running foreign policy of engagement
Tsukasa Takamine

61. **Chinese Capitalism and the Modernist Vision**
Satyananda J. Gabriel

62. **Japanese Telecommunications**
Market and policy in transition
Edited by Ruth Taplin and Masako Wakui

63. **East Asia, Globalization and the New Economy**
F. Gerard Adams

64. **China as a World Factory**
Edited by Kevin Honglin Zhang

65. **China's State-Owned Enterprise Reforms**
An industrial and CEO approach
Juan Antonio Fernandez and Leila Fernandez-Stembridge

66. **China and India**
A tale of two economies
Dilip K. Das

67. **Innovation and Business Partnering in Japan, Europe and the United States**
Edited by Ruth Taplin

68. **Asian Informal Workers**
Global risks local protection
Santosh Mehrotra and Mario Biggeri

69. **The Rise of the Corporate Economy in Southeast Asia**
Rajeswary Ampalavanar Brown

70. **The Singapore Economy**
An econometric perspective
Tilak Abeyshinge and Keen Meng Choy

71. **A Basket Currency for Asia**
Edited by Takatoshi Ito

72. **Private Enterprises and China's Economic Development**
    Edited by Shuanglin Lin and Xiaodong Zhu

73. **The Korean Developmental State**
    From dirigisme to neo-liberalism
    Iain Pirie

74. **Accelerating Japan's Economic Growth**
    Resolving Japan's growth controversy
    Edited by F. Gerard Adams, Lawrence R. Klein, Yuzo Kumasaka and Akihiko Shinozaki

75. **China's Emergent Political Economy**
    Capitalism in the dragon's lair
    Edited by Christopher A. McNally

76. **The Political Economy of the SARS Epidemic**
    The impact on human resources in East Asia
    Grace O.M. Lee and Malcolm Warner

77. **India's Emerging Financial Market**
    A flow of funds model
    Tomoe Moore

78. **Outsourcing and Human Resource Management**
    An international survey
    Edited by Ruth Taplin

79. **Globalization, Labor Markets and Inequality in India**
    Dipak Mazumdar and Sandip Sarkar

80. **Globalization and the Indian Economy**
    Roadmap to a convertible rupee
    Satyendra S. Nayak

81. **Economic Cooperation between Singapore and India**
    An alliance in the making
    Faizal Yahya

82. **The United States and the Malaysian Economy**
    Shakila Yacob

83. **Banking Reform in Southeast Asia**
    The region's decisive decade
    Malcolm Cook

84. **Trade Unions in Asia**
    An economic and sociological analysis
    Edited by John Benson and Ying Zhu

85. **Trade Liberalisation and Regional Disparity in Pakistan**
    Muhammad Shoaib Butt and Jayatilleke S. Bandara

86. **Financial Development and Economic Growth in Malaysia**
    James Ang

87. **Intellectual Property and the New Global Japanese Economy**
    Ruth Taplin

88. **Laggards and Leaders in Labour Market Reform**
    Comparing Japan and Australia
    Edited by Jenny Corbett, Anne Daly, Hisakazu Matsushige and Dehne Taylor

89. **Institutions for Economic Reform in Asia**
    Edited by Philippa Dee

90. **Southeast Asia's Credit Revolution**
    From moneylenders to microfinance
    Aditya Goenka and David Henley

91. **Economic Reform and Employment Relations in Vietnam**
Ngan Thuy Collins

92. **The Future of Asian Trade and Growth**
Economic development with the emergence of China
Linda Yueh

93. **Business Practices in Southeast Asia**
An interdisciplinary analysis of Theravada Buddhist countries
Scott A. Hipsher

94. **Responsible Development**
Vulnerable democracies, hunger and inequality
Omar Noman

95. **The Everyday Impact of Economic Reform in China**
Management change, enterprise performance and daily life
Ying Zhu, Michael Webber and John Benson

96. **The Rise of Asia**
Trade and investment in global perspective
Prema-chandra Athukorala

97. **Intellectual Property, Innovation and Management in Emerging Economies**
Edited by Ruth Taplin and Alojzy Z. Nowak

98. **Special Economic Zones in Asian Market Economies**
Edited by Connie Carter and Andrew Harding

99. **The Migration of Indian Human Capital**
The ebb and flow of Indian professionals in Southeast Asia
Faizal bin Yahya and Arunajeet Kaur

100. **Economic Development and Inequality in China**
The case of Guangdong
Hong Yu

101. **The Japanese Pharmaceutical Industry**
Its evolution and current challenges
Maki Umemura

102. **The Dynamics of Asian Labour Markets**
Balancing control and flexibility
Edited by John Benson and Ying Zhu

103. **Pakistan – The Political Economy of Growth, Stagnation and the State, 1951 to 2009**
Matthew McCartney

104. **Korean Women Managers and Corporate Culture**
Challenging tradition, choosing empowerment, creating change
Jean R. Renshaw

105. **Trade Liberalisation and Poverty in South Asia**
Edited by Prema-Chandra Athukorala, Jayatilleke S. Bandara and Saman Kelegama

106. **Pro-poor Growth and Liberalization in Developing Economies**
The case of Nepal
Sanjaya Acharya

107. **China and the Global Economy in the 21st Century**
 Edited by John Saee

108. **State Structure and Economic Development in Southeast Asia**
 The political economy of Thailand and the Philippines
 Antoinette R. Raquiza

109. **An Economic History of Indonesia**
 1800–2010
 Jan Luiten van Zanden and Daan Marks

110. **Taxation in ASEAN and China**
 Local institutions, regionalism, global systems and economic development
 Edited by Nolan Cormac Sharkey

111. **Macroeconomic and Monetary Policy Issues in Indonesia**
 Akhand Akhtar Hossain

112. **Economic Reform Processes in South Asia**
 Toward policy efficiency
 Edited by Philippa Dee

113. **Manufacturing Enterprise in Asia**
 Size structure and economic growth
 Dipak Mazumdar and Sandip Sarkar

114. **Managers and Management in Vietnam**
 25 years of economic renovation (*doi moi*)
 Vincent Edwards and Anh Phan

115. **New Models of Human Resource Management in China and India**
 Alan R. Nankervis, Fang Lee Cooke, Samir R. Chatterjee and Malcolm Warner

116. **Sustaining Development and Growth in East Asia**
 Edited by Timo Henckel

117. **Small and Medium Enterprises in India**
 Infirmities and asymmetries in industrial clusters
 Satyaki Roy

118. **Workforce Development and Skill Formation in Asia**
 Edited by John Benson, Howard Gospel and Ying Zhu

119. **Understanding Management in China**
 Past, present and future
 Malcolm Warner

120. **Reform and Productivity Growth in India**
 Issues and trends in the labour markets
 Dibyendu Maiti

121. **Intellectual Property Valuation and Innovation**
 Towards global harmonisation
 Edited by Ruth Taplin

Intellectual Property Valuation and Innovation

Towards global harmonisation

**Edited by
Ruth Taplin**

LONDON AND NEW YORK

First published 2014
by Routledge

2 Park Square, Milton Park, Abingdon, Oxon OX14 4RN
711 Third Avenue, New York, NY 10017, USA

Routledge is an imprint of the Taylor & Francis Group, an informa business

First issued in paperback 2016

Copyright © 2014 selection and editorial material, Ruth Taplin; individual chapters, the contributors.

The right of Ruth Taplin to be identified as author of the editorial material, and of the authors for their individual chapters, has been asserted in accordance with sections 77 and 78 of the Copyright, Designs and Patents Act 1988.

All rights reserved. No part of this book may be reprinted or reproduced or utilised in any form or by any electronic, mechanical, or other means, now known or hereafter invented, including photocopying and recording, or in any information storage or retrieval system, without permission in writing from the publishers.

Notice:
Product or corporate names may be trademarks or registered trademarks, and are used only for identification and explanation without intent to infringe.

British Library Cataloguing in Publication Data
A catalogue record for this book is available from the British Library

Library of Congress Cataloging in Publication Data
Intellectual property valuation and innovation: towards global harmonisation / edited by Ruth Taplin.
pages cm.—(Routledge studies in the growth economies of Asia; 121)
Includes bibliographical references and index.
Summary: 'Intellectual property is an increasingly key element in business worldwide. Methods for valuing intellectual property however vary widely. Moreover, issues surrounding the ownership and valuation of intellectual property give rise to a wide range of ethical issues, which apply especially in developing countries as they are increasingly integrated into the world economy. International agreement on how intellectual property should be valued is urgently needed. This book provides an overview of the issues surrounding the valuation of intellectual property, and assesses the steps being made towards harmonization'—Provided by publisher.
1. Intellectual property—Valuation. 2. Intellectual property—Valuation—Asia. 3. Commercial law—International unification.
I. Taplin, Ruth, editor of compilation.
K1401.I579 2013
338.4'3 – dc23
2013017513

ISBN 978–1–138–65716–8 (pbk)
ISBN 978–0–415–53215–0 (hbk)
ISBN 978–1–315–88151–5 (ebk)

Typeset in Times New Roman
by Swales & Willis Ltd, Exeter, Devon

Contents

List of illustrations		xiii
Notes on contributors		xv
Acknowledgements		xix
List of abbreviations		xx
1	**Overview and introduction** RUTH TAPLIN	1
2	**Future of innovation and intellectual property** TIM JONES	22
3	**Creating value in health care through social innovation** NEIL REEDER	54
4	**The financial reporting of research and development costs and its signalling effects on firms' market values** CHIN-BUN TSE AND ANDREW EKUBAN	73
5	**Value–energy interrelationship and dynamic added value taxation** VICTOR BARTENEV	84
6	**Residual value insurance in the maritime sector** STEPHEN ALLUM	113
7	**From co-creation to entrepreneurialism: mobile apps and other examples** VALERIA CORNA	135

8	**Big Data and innovation**	148
	DAVID RANKIN AND ADRIAN FRY	
9	**Innovation, valuation and crisis**	163
	ALOJZY Z. NOWAK AND BERNARD AROGYASWAMY	

Index 173

Illustrations

Figures

1.1	A back-test of the Innovation Leaders Fund against S&P 500 shows a clear outperformance over ten years (2002–12)	14
1.2	Although the Innovation Leaders Fund outperforms the BCG/*Businessweek* Fund, both provided better returns than the major cross-industry indexes over ten years (2002–12)	15
2.1	US patents granted	36
3.1	Different stages of health	56
3.2	Stages of social innovation	60
3.3	Seven core capabilities in coping with uncertainty	62
3.4	Possible pathways to success	63
5.1	US electricity prices, 2009	87
5.2	The current scheme of world economy energy sources	88
5.3	Primary and secondary energy sources of the world economy	89
5.4	The world production of the grain basket	91
5.5	Comparative dynamics of economic efficiency and the average US electricity price	93
5.6	The growth of primary energy consumption per capita in the world economy	94
5.7	The dynamics of the US and the world economy efficiency	94
5.8	The dynamics of the grain basket world price	98
5.9	The magnitude of "useful energy" component of oil price and observed prices	99
5.10	Two different economies	102
5.11	Opposite trends of the optimal profitability magnitudes in the DAVT- and VAT-using economies	105
6.1	The decline in freight rates from 2008 to 2012	115
6.2	Containerised volume growth	116
6.3	Container supply growth	117
6.4	Fair market value	124

Tables

2.1	US patents granted	36
5.1	The R_0 magnitudes for world and US economies in 2010	89
5.2	Efficiency R and primary energy consumption magnitudes in the world, US, EU, Japan and China economies, 2010	92
5.3	The VAT and DAVT comparative features	107
9.1	Innovation ratios in selected countries in 2010	169

Contributors

Stephen Allum is Principal Consultant at Renaissance Risk, a company that he founded in 2007 to provide risk management consulting, expert witness and interim management services to the energy and maritime sectors. Prior to that he was with Aon, initially as a Management Consultant on Risk, and in 2000 joined their Global Practice Groups; first as Global Manager for the Energy and Marine Practices and then as Chairman of the Marine Global Practice. Steve has been involved with the insurance industry for over 20 years, and has focused on Residual Value Insurance since 2009 when he joined JLT Specialty Limited as Head of Residual Value in the Financial Risks Team, and latterly as a consultant to those working in such markets and investors endeavouring to break into this niche area. Steve has an unusual career DNA, which combines extensive technical skills, sound commercial and financial exposure and a deep understanding of risk and project management. Steve has a BSc (Hons) in Physics and an MSc (Tech) in Process Safety and Loss Prevention, both from the University of Sheffield. He is a Chartered Environmentalist and a Chartered Engineer, and is a member of the Energy Institute and the Institute of Risk Management.

Bernard Arogyaswamy is Professor of Global Strategy and Entrepreneurship at the Madden School of Business in Syracuse, New York. He has served as a Fulbright Professor and is also a Visiting Professor at the University of Warsaw in Poland. His most recent publications are in the areas of entrepreneurship and innovation, particularly in the context of policy and institutions. Professor Arogyaswamy also provides consulting services in his areas of expertise.

Victor Bartenev was born in the Russian Federation. In 1981, he graduated from the Moscow Physical-Technical Institute and, as a graduate of the Institute, defended his thesis for a doctor's degree in Biophysics. Before the collapse of the Soviet Union in 1991, he was involved in research of biological nanostructures in the USSR Academy of Sciences. In 1991–2000, he served as the Director and Chief Accountant at firms that developed computer accounting programs. In the early 2000s he began independent research on physical and bio-evolutionary foundations of economy and its tax system, which is now merged under the name of 'physical macroeconomics'. Victor Bartenev is a member of the Editorial Board of the *Interdisciplinary Journal of Economics and Business Law* and lives in Moscow.

Valeria Corna holds a BA in Economics from Bocconi University in Italy and an MRes in Management from IESE Business School in Spain, where she specialised in marketing and innovation. Prior to joining KAE, she was a Marketing Researcher and Lecturer at Bocconi University in Milan. In recent years, Valeria has been a consultant with several global corporations to improve their application developer marketing programmes. She is also retained to identify new opportunities for product and service innovation in both developed and emerging markets.

Andrew Ekuban is Senior Lecturer and Course Leader for Undergraduate Accounting at the University of Bedfordshire. Prior to this, he was Head of (Financial and Regulatory) Compliance for a commodity brokerage firm based in the City of London. He is a fellow of the Association of Chartered Certified Accountants.

Adrian Fry holds a BSc Econ from the University of Wales and an MA in International Political Economy from the University of Newcastle-upon-Tyne. He is an experienced research consultant with over a decade's experience with KAE, where he has specialised in international financial services. Adrian has been retained by several of the world's leading financial institutions to provide in-depth market intelligence, including scenario planning on the impact of emerging themes and new corporate opportunities.

Tim Jones is Programme Director of Future Agenda, Head of Research of the Innovation Leaders analysis, Founder of Innovaro, London, and Co-founder of a new global expert network, the Growth Agenda, which helps organisations around the world to identify and exploit emerging opportunities. For over 20 years Tim has been active in the conception, development and introduction of a wide range of products, services and businesses; he has worked with many of the world's leading companies, building new innovation spaces, developing new ideas, leading development teams, defining new business models, designing new organisational structures and creating innovation-centric cultures to build new and improved innovation capability. Tim is a recognised leader in innovation and growth and has specific expertise in helping organisations to identify new growth platforms and opportunity spaces, highlight emerging technology areas and define new innovation strategies. He advises a number of public bodies on these topics, is the author of numerous articles and eight related books. Tim is a regular speaker at corporate events focusing on such topics as innovation leadership, innovation strategy and future trends in society and technology. He recently co-authored the book *Growth Champions* (Wiley, 2011).

Alojzy Z. Nowak is currently Chairman of the Department of Economics in the School of Management at the University of Warsaw and Vice Rector of the University of Warsaw, teaching and researching in Poland, Europe, America and Asia. Previously he was Dean of the University of Warsaw Faculty of Management and is a member of the Research Committee of the Polish National Bank. He is Associate Editor of the *Interdisciplinary Journal of Economics and Business Law*. He was educated at the Warsaw School of Economics and at the University of Illinois Urbana-Champaign, the University of Exeter, England, and the Free University of Berlin. Professor Nowak has authored/edited a number of books and many articles internationally.

David Rankin is Managing Director of KAE. He is a career consultant with over 25 years' experience and access to corporate decision-makers and their advisors throughout the world. David has developed a series of approaches to design, prioritising and modelling the commercial potential of new developments alongside the revenue impact of changes to existing operations. Amongst his commercial engagements, he is currently working with Research UK on the application of citizen science. David has been published in the *Journal of Financial Services Marketing*, *Journal of Brand Strategy*, *Admap*, *Financial Marketing* and *The Banker*. He holds a BSc in Management Science (1st class) from Warwick University.

Neil Reeder is Director of Head and Heart Economics, a fellow of the Young Foundation, a researcher at the London School of Economics, and a trustee of the Poetry Society. Since studying Mathematics and Economics at the London School of Economics, his posts have included Head of Analysis to the Gershon Review of Efficiency; Programme Leader on public service innovation at the Young Foundation; Economic Adviser to the Department of Trade and Industry on the impact of European Monetary Union on British industry; and Team Leader on local government efficiency at the Department for Communities and Local Government, where his team won a Deputy Prime Minister's 'Excellence in Delivery' award. Neil's publications include *Embedding Innovation: Tightly Coupling the Demand and Supply of Better Health Care* (with Geoff Mulgan) (Young Foundation, 2009); *Valuing Service Innovation in Health* (with Sarah Hewes) (Young Foundation, 2010); *Public Service Productivity in the UK – What Went Wrong? What Could go Right?* (Young Foundation, 2011); and *Strengthening Social Innovation in Europe – Journey to Effective Metrics and Assessment* (with Carmel O'Sullivan) (European Commission, DG Enterprise and Industry, 2012).

Ruth Taplin is Director of the Centre for Japanese and East Asian Studies, which won Exporter of the Year in Partnership in Trading/Pathfinder for the UK in the year 2000. She received her doctorate from the London School of Economics and has a Graduate Diploma in Law. She is the author/editor of 17 books and over 200 articles. She wrote freelance for *The Times* newspaper for nine years on Japan, Taiwan and Korea, and was a consultant to the Federation of Electronics Industry for nine years. Professor Taplin studied Japanese at Durham University over 20 years ago as part of a special course for future leaders in the Japanese field in the UK. Her most recent books are *Decision-making* *and Japan – A Study of Japanese Decision-making and its Relevance to Western Companies* (reprinted by Routledge in 2003, first published by The Japan Library in 1995); *Exploiting Patent Rights and a New Climate for Innovation in Japan* (Intellectual Property Institute, 2003); *Valuing Intellectual Property in Japan, Britain and the United States* (RoutledgeCurzon, 2004); *Risk Management and Innovation in Japan, Britain and the United States* (Routledge, 2005); *Japanese Telecommunications: Market and Policy in Transition* (co-edited with Masako Wakui) (Routledge, 2006); *Innovation and Business Partnering in Japan, Europe and the United States* (Routledge, 2007); *Outsourcing and Human Resource Management: An International Survey* (Routledge, 2008); *Intellectual Property and the New Global Japanese Economy* (Routledge, 2009); *Intellectual Property, Innovation and Management in Emerging Economies* (co-edited with Alojzy Z. Nowak) (Routledge, 2010); and *Mental Health Care in Japan* (co-edited with Sandra J. Lawman) (Routledge, 2012). She is Editor of the *Interdisciplinary Journal of Economics and Business Law* (www.ijebl.co.uk). Professor Taplin is also a Visiting Professor at institutions around the world and has been interviewed on radio and television globally.

Chin-Bun Tse has extensive academic experience, having previously worked at the Universities of Leicester, Coventry and Bedfordshire. He is currently Professor of Finance and Accounting, and Head of Academic Unit (International Finance, Accounting and Economics) at Salford University Business School, Manchester. Before his academic career, Chin-Bun was working in accounting practices in both Hong Kong and London at a senior level, dealing with complicated cases and working with CEOs, CFOs and Directors of companies of all sizes. His research interests are mainly corporate finance, market-based accounting research, investment and value relevance of accounting choices. He has published a book and numerous papers in international academic journals and professional journals/magazines. Many of his publications are widely cited globally.

Acknowledgements

I would like to acknowledge the support of David Rankin of KAE and his colleagues Valeria Corna and Adrian Fry for their sponsorship and contribution to making this book a reality. Thanks also goes to the contributors for their original analyses and hard work as well as to James Brewer who was Insurance Editor of Lloyd's List for ten years. Thanks is also given to Peter Sowden, Asian Editor at Routledge for his continuing support and advice concerning my series of books with Routledge.

Abbreviations

ASB	Accounting Standards Board
AWS	Amazon Web Services
BIMCO	Baltic and International Maritime Council
CDO	collateralised debt obligation
DAVT	dynamic added value taxation
DCF	discounted cashflow
DWT	deadweight tonnage
FMV	fair market value
FRS	Financial Reporting Standards
GAAP	General Accepted Accounting Principles
GDP	gross domestic product
GT	gross tonnage
HSA	Hamburg Shipbrokers Association
IAS	International Accounting Standards
IASB	International Accounting Standards Board
ICAEW	Institute of Chartered Accountants in England and Wales
IFRS	International Financial Reporting Standards
IP	intellectual property
IPR	intellectual property rights
JAL	Japan Airlines
KG	*Kommanditgesellschaft*
LDT	light displacement tonnage
LED	light-emitting diode
LTAV	long-term asset value
LTV	loan-to-value
M&A	merger and acquisition
NCVO	National Council for Voluntary Organisations
NGO	non-governmental organization
NHS	National Health Service
OECD	Organisation for Economic Co-operation and Development
OS	operating system
PC	personal computer
R&D	research and development

RV	residual value
RVI	residual value insurance
S&P	Standard and Poor
SFAS	Statement of Financial Accounting Standards
SLA	service-level agreement
SME	small and medium enterprise
SPA	Software Publishers Association
SSAP	Statement of Standard Accounting Practice
TEU	twenty-foot equivalent unit
ULCV	ultra-large container vessel
USPTO	United States Patent and Trademark Office

1 Overview and introduction

Ruth Taplin

Valuation

Valuation has always been a difficult concept and in my edited volume *Valuing Intellectual Property in Japan, Britain and the United States*[1] it became clear that valuation is an art not a science.

This is becoming more true with a move away in recent years from too rigid accounting standards or too lax ones such as fair value for insurance valuation and a move towards more flexible negotiation in tune with the economic climate. Valuation increases in complexity according to field such as residual value in the maritime industry or value attached to products and services in the financial services sector, whether it is tangible or intangible assets to be valued such as fine art or patent/trademark respectively and depending on the national, regional and cultural perceptions of value. What has emerged, which we will address in this book, is a dichotomy in which valuation, innovation and intellectual property (IP) are moving towards a global harmonisation while at the same time being limited in this direction by specific countries cultural practices.

There are many dimensions to the valuation of both tangible and intangible assets and the recent stresses that the banking sector put on capital markets through the fiasco of subprime lending and other questionable practices that distorted and then slowly but surely degraded the value of banking products had a knock on effect throughout the world economies leading to a shortage in liquidity and loans to businesses and for the housing market. This economic shock has led in this book to a re-visit of the subject of value in relation to not only tangible but also largely intangible assets and the processes of innovation that can be used to promote growth and re-balance economies. While a re-think is taking place as to what can add real value to both tangible and intangible assets it must be done within the context of some sort of global harmonisation, for national markets are becoming so interdependent through global business and banking that there is an imperative for ideas of innovation and valuation of both tangible and intangible assets on a global basis.

Tangible assets

If we begin with tangible assets such as *objets d'art*, the value is often in the eye of the beholder. Michael Findlay, for example, notes in his book *The Value of*

Art: Money, Power, Beauty[2] that the valuing of fine art may be defined at three levels that are inextricably linked. These are the commercial level in which art is valued as an asset, the social level in which art is valued as a status symbol and the aesthetic level in which the value may be described as beauty in the eye of the beholder. The first is relatively quite straightforward in that the market price that the fine art can fetch determines its tangible asset value. The second has to do mainly with trends, with some art being valued socially at a higher level than other *objets d'art* at certain periods of time. Trends are often cyclical. As to the value that accrues to a piece of artwork depending on the individual tastes of the buyer, this is often completely random and is influenced by the psychology of the individual. Innovation is often involved in terms of fine art in, for example, a picture innovating in terms of style or form. Valuation in its tangible form can also occur within the global context of trade such as in the maritime industry.

In Chapter 6 Stephen Allum assesses residual value in relation to the maritime industry of shipping and shows how new ways of valuation must be forged for ship owners to plan in the future for, among other activities, buying new ships. The maritime industry, one of the earliest industries to operate globally on a cross-border basis to facilitate maritime trade, which constitutes 90 per cent of world trade, can teach us a good deal about innovation and valuation. Of all industries it is the maritime industry that can give us clues of how value is created, mainly in terms of tangible assets within the framework of global harmonisation.

Allum notes that when loans were used to buy assets, these loans pushed up the value of assets. This rise in the value of assets sparked yet more lending, which in turn pushed up asset prices further.

After 2007, with the impending financial crisis, assets depreciated and lending fell because ship owners were no longer able to pay their debts. Allum argues that this has led to a new paradigm, that of residual value.

Lease financing is an important tool for acquiring durable goods and it accounts for nearly a third of the new industrial and commercial equipment sold annually.

Generally, a lease contract transforms a risky new real asset into two components, a front-end financial asset with fixed periodic payments over a known term, and a back-end residual physical asset that covers its economic life beyond lease termination.

Therefore, the residual value refers to the expected value of the used physical asset at the end of the lease. The main source of uncertainty embedded in the back-end residual asset is the risk that the future market value of the underlying asset at lease termination will vary from the projected residual value. This price fluctuation is commonly known as residual value risk. A lease is thus a loan of a physical asset that depreciates over time: it exposes the lessor (lender) to not only default risk on the contractual lease payments but also to fluctuations in the lease-end residual value of the underlying asset.

Residual value risk is the greatest uncertainly in lease financing because forecasting residual value several years in advance is fraught with difficulty.

Intangible assets

As this form of valuation for tangible products can be so complex it follows that intangible assets of IP are even more sophisticated. However, in recent times valuation of IP has been further complicated by what some believe is the impending demise of copyright, perhaps trademarks and even patents. It may be argued that patenting is on the wane but it is perhaps more accurate to state that there are good patents and bad patents. The former will ensure the continuation of patents especially in sectors such as pharmaceuticals, which by necessity relies on patenting to protect the enormous sums needed for research and development (R&D) for new innovative products to be created. This does not mean however that even when patenting remains a good positive necessity, the form will continue to be the same. Moves towards open source and open innovation, which will be defined by Tim Jones of Future Agenda in Chapter 2, emphasise cooperation, which will mean more patent pools and other forms of knowledge sharing that may not involve intellectual property rights (IPR).

However, it may be seen in the case of the bankruptcy of a former world-leading firm Kodak that IP does retain its value and can be used for collateral purposes. In December 2012 Eastman Kodak sold its digital imaging patents to a consortium of bidders for US$525 million (£322 million). The company, which was a pioneer of photography, sold roughly 1,100 patents to pay off its creditors after it filed for bankruptcy in January 2013. Among those participating in the consortium led by Intellectual Ventures and RPX, who are both patent aggregators that dedicate themselves to buying and then licensing out rights to patents, included Samsung, Apple, Google, Amazon, Research in Motion (BlackBerry) and Chinese Huawei Technologies. Kodak decided to pull out of the digital camera business because, some argue, they did not exploit effectively development in this field, which allowed East Asian firms in particular to develop this area, taking the business from Kodak. Kodak has now exited bankruptcy and will become a much smaller digital-imaging company.[3]

What is certain is that the link between IP and innovation and the need for new forms of valuation to understand the true market value of intangible assets will not be diminished in the future anytime soon.

It is possible to see how innovation, IP and the need for more flexible, negotiated methods of valuation are required to deal with future ways of ascertaining market value for intangible assets, for services and the creation of products based on knowledge and information technology.

Good and bad patents?

East Asia, like the US and Europe, makes a conscious link between IP and innovation.[4] These countries see that this linkage leads to economic growth and business success. This emphasis can be seen very clearly in the high-profile dispute between Samsung (which is a South Korean company) and Apple (which is US based). This dispute has led to the re-emergence of the underlying definition of what constitutes good and bad patents.

4 *Ruth Taplin*

It is possible to argue that the patent system has failed in the Samsung–Apple case because it is monopolistic, which has bad connotations. This is because the patents involved award a limited duration to the inventor or those who have bought or own the patent. This means that the value is diminished for the inventor especially when the company they work for offers them a limited sum of money and then goes on to exploit the inventor's idea for vast sums of money. The consumer also loses in terms of value as the mark up is very high and not based on the quality and importance of the idea.

The patent, however, is both good and necessary because the inventor explains the details of the invention instead of keeping it secret for fear of not being given credit or remunerated properly. The patent is awarded in exchange for a monopoly for exploiting the invention.

Are many, including a number of inventive creative people, against patents because a lot of employees have to sign their rights to their invention away to the company? Or is it because inventors are rewarded directly but in lesser amounts than they deserve by the company? Without innovative and creative people there is no innovation, or the need for patents. When patenting deprives inventors of the rewards they richly deserve patents become a negative experience for the inventors. Conversely when it rewards and safeguards their ideas and livelihood then it becomes a positive experience. This is all part of the dual perspective of good and bad patents.

Employees rights to compensation

Japan was woken collectively in both the business and judicial world by the then unheard of case of an inventor suing his company from California where he took up residence after feeling cheated by not receiving proper remuneration for a groundbreaking invention. This was, of course, the Nakamura Shuji case in which he was instrumental as an inventor in developing the two-way light-emitting diode (LED) semiconductor, which glows blue when electricity is passed through it. This invention netted his employer Nichia Corporation a great sum of money through the invention becoming a 404 patent. Judge Shitara Ryuchi made one of the most important decisions in relation to patents and IPR in the history of the Intellectual Property Division of the Tokyo District Court in the form of a new employees rights to compensation law, which had not changed substantially in content since the Patent Law of 1960.

In awarding the inventor Nakamura Shuji proper compensation by taking into account that he created this invention himself and the actual invention was originally assessed negatively by a Nichia representative, Judge Shitara added value to the inventor's creative idea.

In calculating the compensation due to Nakamura Shuji, the Tokyo District Court itself decided that half of the sales amount was due to the exclusive right of the two-way invention; that the profit due to this patented invention would be calculated by multiplying half of the sales amount by 20 per cent, which is a hypothetical running royalty rate of the invention; and that US$1.09 billion was the amount of profit that Nichia obtained from the two-way invention. Nakamura settled with

Nichia Corporation in 2005 for 844 million yen (US$8 million) as the Tokyo High Court overturned the decision of the District Court, which had initially awarded the inventor 20 billion yen (US$187 million). This made the Japanese Business Federation pleased as it realised that employees were not to be given too great a reward for their inventions that would become too costly for employers to afford. The Tokyo District Court found that Mr Nakamura was solely responsible for the invention, contrary to the statement issued by Nichia that the invention was a joint effort. The fact that Nichia had bought the invention for US$2.7 million and had assessed the potential value of the blue LED in a negative light, at one point even ordering Mr Nakamura to cease further research of this highly important invention was why the contribution to the employer was deemed to be only 50 per cent.[5]

The signs here were very clear that standard accounting methods such as royalty rate were too limited and rigid to assess the value of a highly important invention that had been at first incorrectly assessed negatively, then turning into a massive money-spinner for the corporation employing the inventor. The company would have fared much better if it had been flexible and negotiated with the inventor acknowledging the real value of his invention. What could have been a good patent became a toxic point of dispute that placed the employer in a negative light damaging its brand value. Value, as we shall see in this book, comes in all different forms and intensities and cannot just be assessed by accounting methods. Brand, the value of public relations, continued good will of the inventor and public, and consumer perception all comprise valuation. Culture does as well, for what may have a certain value in one country or region of the world may have another value somewhere else even for the same product.

For example, a well-known fizzy drink such as Coca-Cola may be drunk in much greater amounts and have higher sales revenue in such countries as India and South Africa than in, say, Britain or other parts of Europe but be valued higher in the latter than in the former because the currency and price is greater in the latter.

In the example below, despite the multitude of lawsuits between Samsung and Apple over the iPhone and patent infringements, East Asian IP courts have tended to award the same amount of damages to both companies taking the dispute and negative publicity out of the court proceedings, which shows culture impacting on value.

The continued importance of patents and the arguments surrounding good and bad patents were therefore brought to the fore during the massive lawsuit between Samsung and Apple in September 2012. Samsung and other chaebols in South Korea are no strangers to being sued for patent infringement, much of it by Japanese companies. Samsung was found by a California court to have infringed six patents of Apple in relation to smart phones by Judge Lucy Koh, of North Korean derivation herself. The initial fine was for 1 billion US dollars and the amount was eventually halved. In real economic terms, however, Samsung contributes over 20 per cent of gross domestic product (GDP) to the South Korean economy so even a fine of 3 billion US dollars will not destroy it. However, it may have a positive effect in that Samsung will become inspired to become more inventive on its own and create even better products.

Good public relations?

This particular lawsuit was the largest one in history and Samsung and Apple have 50 lawsuits pending against each other around the world. This is obviously good news for IP lawyers globally but has it really benefited Apple in terms of creating extra value for its products in dispute such as the iPhone, and did Apple win in real terms? Brand and good public relations can add and detract value from a product. In this case, although Apple was the financial award winner, it created a good deal of antagonism against its brand. Consumers wanted to know if Apple took advantage of suing on its home territory. It has been questioned whether Apple suing Samsung over the shape of a frame similar to the iPhone or using the same colour was petty and money-grabbing. Surely, there are only so many colours or shapes of frame that can be used that it does not take an inventive person to create this and makes a mockery of patents?

It has recently been reported in January 2013[6] that Apple share prices were lowered in early pre-market trading by nearly 4 per cent to below US$500 (£310). This was lower than a year ago and it was because iPhone sales have been less than expected and demand is slowing.

Therefore, despite Apple being the world's most highly valued technology firm, other smart phone makers have been eating into what Apple seems to have thought was a safe market for the company.

What shows the importance of valuation is that Samsung has now overtaken Apple as the world's largest smart phone seller with 50 per cent greater unit movement, and its Galaxy range recently outsold the iPhone for a fourth straight quarter. Apple still has a slightly larger market share in the US, its home territory, with 34 per cent to Samsung's 32.3 per cent, according to the most recent figures. The newest Samsung smart phone was introduced in New York on 14 March 2013. It has pioneering features such as a handset that allows users to control the screen using their eyes, can take two pictures at once and 'smart pause', which lets users pause a video by looking away from the screen and a 'smart scroll' allowing users to browse through emails without touching the screen, as the S4 detects the movements of the eyes and wrist. Samsung is expecting 10 million sales of the new handsets per month. J.K. Shin, President and Head of IT and Mobile Communications at Samsung, stated he believed technology and innovation assists people with becoming closer to what matters in life, bringing us a richer, simpler and fuller life.

In my estimation, the perception by many consumers that Apple was being greedy in its lawsuit against Samsung by trying to sue for such a large amount; petty in challenging Samsung on the grounds of patent infringement in terms of size and colour, which was not particularly based on invention or special innovative ideas; and had the court proceedings in California on its home ground, which will inevitably be seen within the context of bias, all affected the value of its products.

Additionally, Apple has not foreseen that more and more consumers are questioning the conditions under which products are made and the conditions of workers who produce them. There was recent criticism of the condition of workers in

China in huge production facilities operated by Taiwan's Foxconn. In the final analysis neither Apple nor Samsung can rest on their laurels for, in March 2013 at the Barcelona World Mobile Congress, other companies have launched new devices that offer the consumer even greater value. Chinese company Huawei has offered what it claims is the world's fastest smart phone: the Ascend P2 has download speeds up to 150 megabits per second.

HTC and Blackberry have also launched their newest innovative products with the HTC One debuted in February 2013, while the Blackberry 10 was launched in January 2013.

It is not all about high-end phones however; demand still exists for cheaper handsets with Nokia announcing a 15 euro (£13) handset, the Nokia 105, aimed at emerging markets such as China and India.

The value that can be given to products or taken away by consumers, which can be positive or negative, for brands is too often taken for granted by the largest companies, which often seem to believe they can do whatever they want without corporate responsibility. Perhaps many consumers have been dismayed by the vast sums of money spent on litigation by many companies in the US rather than on what consumers require, a fair-priced product that does not damage the environment or the people who produce the goods.

The courts in Japan and South Korea, which have tried to take the negativity out of patent infringement by making equal awards to both sides, realise that the unnecessary disputes caused by patent infringement in many cases not only lower the valuation of the product but also make patents seem bad and unnecessary. Cultural perception can affect valuation.

Asian and Western cultures

Another example of the cultural interpretation may be linked to how IP, value and competition is viewed by Asian and Western cultures.[7] It is noted that Asian businesses are conducted both on the basis of family and long-term relationships that often do not involve law to settle disputes. The main reason for the Asian businesses is to keep the family together, honour ancestors and make income, providing the family with jobs. There is a lack of transparency with highly complex corporate structures so it is difficult for family members to leave the company. This can be seen in Japan where the changes to company law in recent years have tried to relinquish any family connection to Japanese business but the complexity, lack of transparency and certain family ties remain despite these efforts. Such vested interests work against the rule of law and the laws of economics, which are central to an open democratic working of the economy.

Open knowledge

This does not mean that open source or open knowledge as discussed in Tim Jones' chapter in this book is not without problems or could ever replace the patenting system.

Tim Jones writes in Chapter 2 that there is open source and open innovation. Apart from emphasising sharing and cooperation both are fundamentally different from one another. Open source is akin to those who do not see the need for IP as it refers to no one owning the intellectual property and if they do they should give their IPR royalty free licences to anyone to use and develop. Open source, it could be argued, is positive for those with few ideas or mediocre ones who can then benefit freely from the ideas of creative inventive people leaving the latter with little income and no rewards.

Henry Chesbrough's idea of open innovation is still in its nascent stage and has a good deal of potential with many companies holding the capabilities to have ideas flow into their company from numerous ecosystem partners including consultants, universities, entrepreneurs, customers and so forth. Open innovation has raised the idea of taking IP trading out of the R&D process and going straight into the boardroom. However, Chesbrough estimates that only 10 per cent of such potential is used to create value not for process reasons but for cultural ones.

Chin-Bun Tse and Andrew Ekuban's Chapter 4, like open innovation, does not dismiss the importance of IPR such as patents but looks at the idea of signalling to open markets the value of a product based on the money spent during the R&D stages rather than the usual way of after the product is on the market through share prices and dividend level changes. As the amount of money spent on R&D is huge it can give an indication of the value of the product. They ask how such R&D expenses should be reported in financial statements. Do investors react to the spending on R&D, do they wait until they see the realisation of cash after the products are on the market or do they react right away when they know a company has spent a great deal of money on R&D? As accountants they ask ultimately whether capital markets react differently to different ways of reporting R&D costs. Therefore, can capitalisation of a product be used as a signal of the potential value of such a product?

How does culture affect valuation especially cross-border IP valuation? Just as brand, public perception of a company's integrity and attention given to the customer affects the value of its products and services, as does the cultural perception and interpretation.

JAL turnaround

Sometimes innovation and increased value for a company can be brought about by a more flexible yet rigorous management style based on a sense of moral obligations to the company and its staff. This is what happened when Mr Kazuo Inamori, founder of Kyocera, at 78 years old, was requested by the Japanese government to turn around Japan Airlines (JAL), which had filed for bankruptcy and delisted from the Tokyo Stock Exchange on 20 February 2010. It was the largest non-financial bankruptcy in Japanese history with roughly US$25 billion (£16 billion) of debt.

JAL's turnaround was due in part to a US$6 billion debt waiver, a US$4 billion capital injection from a state-backed fund and future tax exemptions. However, it was Mr Inamori's innovative restructuring methods that added real value to the company. He did this in 3 ways, discussed below.

First, he used a post-war (a time when Japanese company culture was thriving), decision-making idea[8] of involving all those working for JAL in the restructuring. This included *nemawashi* (the process of building company cohesion from the bottom up by consulting those at all levels of the company). JAL issued a booklet soon after Mr Inamori's appointment based on his philosophies, which were influenced by his having been ordained as a Buddhist priest. Buddhism emphasises harmony, cooperation and working together for the greater good. All company staff were required to carry this booklet, which caused some resistance early on in addition to his compulsory training sessions that staff had to attend. He also used another method that Japanese bosses have used traditionally since the post-war period that is a great leveller, facilitating the process of *nemawashi* in using alcohol, in this case cans of beer, to relax with staff after the training sessions with those working late so that staff will open up and be more honest with their boss. There was an understanding that anything offensive said will be forgiven the next morning as such openness was due to alcohol. Information obtained from such sessions was used by Mr Inamori to improve relations and cohesion throughout the company staff, which provided a more positive and supportive working environment. Underpinning all this was an insistence by Mr Inamori that a caring, moral culture should prevail at the company so everyone would work together more effectively for a greater goal, Japanese social values, which have become increasingly lost in recent decades.

The second innovation that Mr Inamori introduced was a rapid understanding of monthly settlement of accounts. Mr Inamori termed this Amoeba Management, which meant not a rough picture of accounting but detailed and precise daily accounting. He was surprised to learn that JAL was so slow to understand its revenue and expenditure as well as its financial data. It was even practising imprecise bookkeeping with revenue and expenditure by department and section (*bu* and *ku*) being reported 2–3 months later. This, Mr Inamori believed was a deterrent to employees understanding the current financial situation. He ensured that employees closed accounts at the end of each month knowing their profit and loss situation at the beginning of the next month.

This practice had a knock-on effect of, for example, cabin crew thinking about how often they should show duty-free items on routes so profits for JAL as company revenue would be increased. Detailed accounting is now presented to all departments making all staff members aware of profit and loss.

Third, Mr Inamori introduced a daily account management regime by department and section with accounts being submitted the next day. The data were produced in great detail so that the company understood revenue and expenditure according to each flight on a daily basis. He also assigned persons responsible for each flight route making them become specialists for particular routes so they would understand costs for employees, maintenance and airport use. JAL also reduced the number of fleets and employees to cut costs and return it to profit.

Mr Inamori did all this without taking any salary out of an obligation to assist his country. He was very careful to practice what he preached adding the social values of trust and confidence to a company that was bankrupt in many different ways. Therefore social invention coupled with trust and confidence can add enormous value to the prospects of companies.[9]

Unfortunately, the reforms that Mr Inamori was able to institute at JAL have found intense resistance in almost all other areas of the Japanese economy because of a rigid and intransigent government bureaucracy entrenched in the ministries. Some of the most important decisions in Japan that would facilitate innovative businesses are slowed or even seriously delayed by government bureaucracy. According to recent World Bank data, to start a business in Japan it takes 23 days compared to 13, 6 and 7 respectively for the UK, the US and South Korea. Some economists argue that Japan could move its economy out of the doldrums by embracing competition through joining a proposed pan-Pacific free trade group known as the Trans-Pacific Partnership. However, such competition would mean there would be winners and losers in Japanese business according to competence and profitability, which would be strongly resisted by ministerial bureaucracies that often, in my estimation, seek to control public funds under the guise of social equality behind the scenes.

Western and Asian linkages

Another perspective that is needed to understand the global harmonisation of value is one that addresses the linkages between IP, innovation, competition and economics within the Asian context, especially so when IPR are linked to innovation, which underpins competition. One such complexity is that modern competition law enforcement is based on both short-term efficiency and short-term price competition. Markets that are defined for competition law purposes based on price competition do not in all likelihood reflect the realities of competition in developed or developing societies. This is especially the case, in my estimation, in that the United States is viewed as being the main creator of not only modern IPR laws but also competition laws. The US economic model is known for its short-term outlook in relation to competition, its tendency towards litigation and success in innovation.

Such a short-term approach conflicts with the East Asian and Southeast Asian economic model of competition in that it is based on family and long-term goals. Competition and innovation is often suppressed to keep the family business intact because it supports the ancestors. The attempts by East Asian courts, for example, to avoid litigation and competition may be seen in the equal awards for patent infringement given in the Apple vs. Samsung cases brought to court there mentioned previously. This has been in contradistinction to the biggest infringement case in legal history also previously mentioned between Apple and Samsung in Silicon Valley in which Apple was awarded billions of dollars in compensation from Samsung. Therefore when trying to assess value based on innovation in both tangible and intangible assets it is sometimes difficult to balance global harmonisation between a US legal-economic model of IPR, competition and innovation and often the opposite definitions and behaviour of this same complex mix of disciplines in Asia.

Yet, Asia itself holds a broad spectrum of IPR, tangible assets, valuation, innovation and competition in this wide array of countries and cultures. Australia, for example, follows the Western model much more closely and there is variety as well in Hong Kong, Brunei, Singapore and Malaysia, which tend towards English common law while Southeast Asian including Indo-Chinese countries still follow some French law, and Japan, although moving towards US laws, is still heavily influenced by its initial choice of German technocratic law and has moved more towards US legal definitions of these areas.[10] Therefore, in this book we attempt to offer an analysis to further understanding of the linkages between innovation, valuation, intangible and tangible assets to further not only seeing the many perspectives from an interdisciplinary viewpoint, which explains valuation, but also with a view towards increasing global harmonisation. This is reflected in the wide areas of valuation we are addressing including value from the R&D stage, innovation, IPR, social innovation and maritime value. Our empirical evidence stems not just from Western models but Asian and elsewhere around the world.

Rule of law

In this book we also address the much required interdisciplinary approach to IPR, which a legal-economic approach brings to the subject. Douglas Ginsberg and Eric Fraser[11] argue an essential point that predictability and certainty are crucial to a rule of law regime. They note that economic analysis and evidence facilitates such values in allowing decision-makers to apply a coherent system to each case and private parties to better predict outcomes thereby avoiding litigation if possible. They point out, however, that this does not necessarily mean that economic analysis should indicate how a case will be decided but that it offers an added dimension of understanding of each individual case. As economic analysis in the US becomes a much more fixed feature in legal decision-making such as in competition law, they note that the law must never be made uncertain or inconsistent by the emergence of new economic theories. Rather, once economic theories are accepted generally and proved scientifically through empirical evidence, it is the right time to incorporate such economic analysis into legal decision-making to retain the stability of the rule of law. It is rule of law based on sound legal economic analysis that allows for a fair and proportionate assessment of cases linked to IPR, competition law, issues of innovation and ultimately value creation.[12]

Steve Allum's Chapter 6 on residual value in relation to the maritime sector also shows how very dependent the open seas are on the rule of law, especially internationally. The current Japanese Prime Minister Shinzo Abe recalled Margaret Thatcher's words from the 1982 Falklands War where she noted that Britain was defending the fundamental principle of international law in the dispute that should prevail over the unnecessary use of force. Prime Minister Abe stated in the Japanese Parliament 27 February 2013 in relation to the ongoing Senkaku Islands dispute (also claimed by China as the Diaoyu Islands): '[Now,] . . . [t]he rule of law at sea. I want to appeal to international society that in modern times changes to the status quo by the use of force will justify nothing.' If there was no rule of law in the international maritime context any nation could illegally grab any island or claim any ship proceeding through what a nation could argue was their territorial waters through which no one could pass, destroying all the value created by sea-borne trade.

It must be remembered throughout this book that value cannot be created or sustained in a society without the rule of law being the bedrock of the economy, society and business innovation/opportunity. The rule of law creates a stable society and economy in which innovative business can flourish thereby creating value. This is also linked to a democratic, participatory society in which people are given the freedom to create value through innovation and are not channelled into a constrained box that fits only the needs of a dictator, despot or a ritualised straightjacket. However, unbridled self-interest also destroys genuine creativity, innovation and value in that people will not create value unless it fits their narrow self-interest or through the encouragement of envy the mediocre are lauded in their attempts to damage and destroy genuinely talented people to boost their own egos or support delusions of competence. This is why talent must be encouraged and nurtured in every society to create value based on innovation that stems from true creativity.

Talent, value and innovation

The encouragement of talented individuals within a global context is the main facet of the aspect of labour that brings creative innovative individuals together. The global harmonisation of value may be seen within this context in that today there is a tendency for those who are talented to be involved in innovative work on a global scale. This may occur through global teleconferencing, working on a project-by-project visiting basis to companies and in sourcing[13] Such a process as insourcing strengthens global ties between the innovators and talent on a global scale. This means that should any company have a global requirement for assistance with a particular project that requires talented innovative people it is possible for such people to move from project to project around the world contributing their expertise and learning from each other and taking these experiences to new projects. Some of the areas that such groups of talented individuals can add value to may be a new product or service or a company that is inundated with work and requires solutions that assist with making the product or service even more valuable through creative and innovative input from experienced and talented individuals. The more the world opens up through modern communications such as the internet so too will the ability of talented individuals to further global harmonisation and the creation of value through products and services by educating those active in global business. This does not mean just large corporations but also small and medium enterprises (SMEs), which are often the innovators of business in having a concentration of talented individuals who cannot work within the constraints of overwhelmingly large institutions, or increasingly mothers who start small businesses based on their work experience before they decided to stay at home with their children. These women often become entrepreneurs who make substantive contributions to their local and national economies.

Innovation and value, however, does not just have to be furthered by talented individuals alone. It can be pursued by innovative organisations as well. Tim Jones, author of Chapter 2 in this book, has been working with major organisations across the innovation and growth area for over 20 years. He has led a number of projects such as Shell's Technology Futures programmes and has supported many large companies in building innovation capabilities. As leader of the Innovation Leaders analysis, Programme Director of the Future Agenda global openforesight project and co-founder of the Growth Agenda, he assists organisations globally in exploiting new opportunities to create value in products and services.

In his co-authored book *Growth Champions*[14] he stresses that the underlying Innovation Leaders analysis clearly demonstrates that innovative companies outperform their peers in terms of share price growth. He notes that over the years many who have worked in the innovation community have supported such notions as 'it is only through the introduction of successful new products and processes that companies and nations can improve their competitive position' and that 'innovation is increasingly seen as a powerful way of securing competitive advantage' or that 'innovation is the lifeblood of any large organisation'. Whereas others may support growth via acquisition or a focus on simply optimising current channels as optimal ways to drive value, it is a fundamental belief that better, more effective innovation drives improved organic growth and that, in the vast majority of industries, this leads to enhanced company performance by which is usually meant growth in company value. While a number of studies is generally supportive of this thesis, to date few have both identified the world's best innovators across multiple sectors and mapped their individual market performance to reflect tangible financial value through market capitalisation. After a decade of full economic cycles of boom and bust, and particularly in the light of current financial pressures, with the data to hand it seemed to Tim Jones that it was the right time to undertake such a study in the form of the Innovation Leaders analysis of the most effective innovators across 25 sectors for the last decade.

Initial assessments showed that, as a group of companies, average growth in share prices since 2002 was over 14 per cent per annum. This compares very favourably to average annual returns for the FTSE 100, NASDAQ and Standard and Poor (S&P) 500 indexes that respectively saw average growth over the same period of 2 per cent, 6 per cent and 3 per cent. This presents a significant opportunity not only for supporting the internal business case of innovation professionals within their organisations but also the global investment community from individual investors to multibillion dollar hedge funds. For the study he used two separate annual perspectives to assess the value creation of innovative companies. First, the Innovation Leaders analysis that is driven by detailed assessment of sectorspecific rations of innovation output/input and second, the BCG/*Businessweek* 'Most Innovative Companies' ranking, which is informed more by the opinion of the CEO interviews. While one can argue the relative pros and cons of both approaches, they each provide a consistent assessment of the world's best innovators,

14 *Ruth Taplin*

albeit seen through different lenses. As such, both have merits as inputs for company selection in order to demonstrate the true value of innovation. The aim was to build solid financial models that would replicate how a real fund would invest. To do this, he made three core assumptions. First, any portfolio would comprise of initially equal value investments in all companies that would be held for a period of time and then rebalanced so as to reinvest profits and limit exposure to any one high or low performing stock or sector. Second, the 'hold period' for all investments needed to provide time for innovation activity to have material effect on company performance, most likely two to three years as this more than likely covers average 'time to market' for innovation across most sectors. While third, he could choose which sectors to invest in and which to avoid as this could be seen as being retrospectively selective. Even though some industries' innovation activity has greater impact on company stock performance than others he had to maintain a diversified portfolio based on all the companies identified in the two assessments. Detailed models have now been created that show the performance of investment funds based on investing in the 25 most innovative companies, each innovative companies each year and holding these stocks two years before rebalancing the portfolio and then reinvesting all capital and profits.

Using the public data available two funds were modelled, one based on the decade of the Innovation Leaders analysis, which ran from April 2002 to April 2012, and the other based on the five years of BCG/*Businessweek* analysis, which ran from April 2006 (see Figure 1.1).

The results from the modelling are conclusive in that innovation does indeed pay. Both an Innovation Leaders Fund and a BCG/*Businessweek* Fund would have demonstrated above average growth. As Figure 1.2 shows, between April 2002

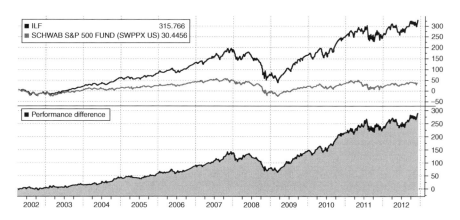

Figure 1.1 A back-test of the Innovation Leaders Fund against S&P 500 shows a clear outperformance over ten years (2002–12).[15]

Source: www.innovationleaders.org. Copyright 2012 Bloomberg Finance L.P.

Note: Compound Annual Growth Rate: 14.5 per cent, Std Dev: 19.7 per cent, Alpha: 12.1 per cent, Beta: 0.7 per cent.

Overview and introduction 15

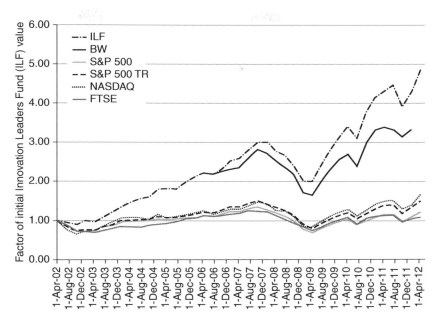

Figure 1.2 Although the Innovation Leaders Fund outperforms the BCG/*Businessweek* Fund, both provided better returns than the major cross-industry indexes over ten years (2002–12).[16]

Source: www.innovationleaders.org. Original source with permission http://magazine.ispim.org/2012/11/growth-champions/#sthash.6DLq7pgh.dpuf.

and 2012, while the FTSE100 overall rose by just 9 per cent, the S&P 500 by 23 per cent and the NASDAQ by 66 per cent, the value of the portfolio of companies in the Innovation Leaders Fund would have grown by over 300 per cent.

Equally in the six years since April 2006, an BCG/*Businessweek* Fund would have grown by 49 per cent at a time when the three reference indexes rose by between 0 per cent and 30 per cent (FTSE 100, 0 per cent, S&P 500 and NASDAQ 30 per cent). Although the Innovations Leaders Fund outperforms the BCG/*Businessweek* Fund, both provide better returns than the major cross-industry indexes against which most stock performances are compared.

Looking in more detail at the Innovation Leaders Fund analysis, he has also modelled returns against comparable market leading indices that many fund managers see as the definitive benchmarks. Over the past ten years, an Innovation Leaders Fund would have outperformed the best of these by more than 30 per cent. What this indicates is clear: during a decade that has included both overall market growth and major recession, a fund that invested in companies identified as the most innovative would have delivered significant returns; US$1 million invested in an Innovation Leaders Fund in April 2002 would have been worth US$3.2 million ten years later. When compared to both leading global indices and some of the better performing comparable funds, this is not only of great interest to the investment communities but it also underlies what those in the innovation arena have believed for many years. That is, in an increasingly competitive and globalised world where many capabilities are now considered commodities and are often outsourced, a clear relationship between internal innovation and stock price impact is evident. Across a myriad of different sectors sustained and successful innovation performance is matched to sustained growth in company value.[17]

Consumer invention

Mobile applications

Another aspect of who creates value from both tangible and intangible services and product production is that linked to newly emerging trends in the mobile applications market that encourage the consumer to be part of the creative process, even being able to obtain patents and copyright. Valeria Corna in Chapter 7 charts this course of increasing consumer invention to create mobile applications that make iPhones and tablets of greater relevance to themselves. She charts the emergence and evolution of consumer co-creation showing how it has shaped the processes of innovation over the last decade at many different levels drawing on many companies as examples of this process.

She argues that most co-creation and crowd-sourcing initiatives do not allow the consumers to retain the IP that they generate, showing how do-it-yourself trends with greater technology-friendly education and simplification are allowing consumers to become both innovators and entrepreneurs.

This trend is most readily seen in the role consumers play in mobile application creation, which has changed in the last six to seven years. In fact, consumers' increased involvement in application innovation has contributed, according to Corna, to the development of some of the most successful and innovative applications of recent years. However, with the evolution of technology as occurred in the past with blogs, the boundaries between consumers, innovators and entrepreneurs are melding and consumers will have a chance to capitalise on the IP they are generating.

In the past few years the mobile application market has burgeoned, with downloading and using applications being an integral part of a consumer's daily life. Increased customisation, consumer co-creation and crowd-sourcing are major trends that have affected many industries over recent years. In this manner consumers have become an integral part of a business' value chain.

When the mobile application market emerged, consumers played their traditional value chain role by not being involved in the application creation or innovation process, they were acting mainly as application downloaders and users. Despite this lack of involvement on the consumer side, the demand for applications was high and the market booming. The first applications to be launched addressed some of the consumers' most basic mobile needs such as accessing train times, reading books, using social networks, all while on the move. Smartphone owners, eager to make the most of their latest technology, became heavy users and the first billion application downloads were not far off.

Corna notes that to leverage market opportunities and address latent consumer needs, application development companies and individual developers are now beginning to recognise the importance of involving consumers in the application creation process.

In the simplest of cases, consumers are involved in an 'indirect way', meaning that they are not contributing to application innovation, but their needs and behaviours are considered key inputs in such processes.

Multiples are examples of innovative applications that have been able to succeed thanks to their ability to address user needs that no one else had been able to address before. These applications such as Flipboard and Hailo will be covered in Chapter 7. The latter Hailo overlaps with the chapter on social innovation as the mobile application is used not just for ease of payment and reducing waiting time but is a safer way to order a taxi, especially after hours, thus creating social value.

Applications created through a more direct involvement of consumers in the process are also emerging. Consumers can now share their ideas through communities such as IdeasProject, which helps application ideas to become a reality. Founded on co-creation through open innovation, the IdeasProject online community has allowed applications such as Blood Sprint and mGraffiti to come to life. Consumers can also become application investors and funders with success potential through websites such as AppStori, also known as the 'kickstarter of mobile apps'. All can become involved in benign, innovative business activity.

Finally, this has led to an overall democratisation of application developments, meaning that human social development no longer has to lag behind technology, which was one of the disasters of the twentieth century. Mobile applications can hopefully bring people closer together and have beneficial social outcomes, unlike the last century in which atrocities, war and hatred could be hidden with disastrous consequences for humanity because there was no instant communication backed up by pictorial evidence and instant messaging. With people being involved in invention and so many in contact with each other in a very short space of time it has the potential power to stop deceitful dictators and those with harmful intentions to certain groups of people and society.

It is essential for the future of innovation and entrepreneurship that young people become involved in the creative process. Too many schools rote teach or simply prepare children for examination targets set by the political agenda of governments often bankrupt of ideas. It hardly seems surprising that top entrepreneurs such as those who started Google or Amazon attended Montessori schools where thinking is at a premium. Britain, for example, is in dire need of such a thinking approach. Schools need to be more along the lines of Montessori but that seems a long way off. It seems the best way to teach children to think is through their family. Parents and extended family continue to be the main influence on children. There should be courses developed for both parents and children that involve them both in starting a business and innovating. This is not as strange as it may seem. A boy aged seven named Henry Patterson, with the support of his parents, started his first enterprise by selling bags of manure. He then went on to set up his own e-bay shop selling items he bought from charity shops and netted £150.00.

Now Henry has started a children's online sweet shop, which had 100 orders for sweets within the first week. He created his own logo for his business, markets his products, uses spreadsheets and gives out his own business cards. His mother Rebecca operates an online confectionery store and Henry has entered into partnership with her. His mother set up her Sherbetpip.co.uk site as a part of a programme with Bedfordshire County Council, which demonstrates to young people how easy it can be to start an innovative small business. Henry put his earnings into his bank account and uses it to develop his businesses further.[18]

Social innovation

The Bedfordshire County Council innovation with young Henry and his mother is a prime example of how lateral thinking can lead to innovative practices and subsequently creates value. In Chapter 3 Neil Reeder notes that innovations in social relationships can create real value and this can be seen in healthcare. He argues, however, that many would downplay the ability of social innovation to promote health. He quotes a practitioner who believes that the National Health Service is 'medicalised' with the greatest influence in service provision deriving from clinicians, whose training is based upon establishing a diagnosis and prescribing appropriate remedies, which in the majority of cases are in the form of medications.

Reeder notes that using a meta-analysis of the impact on health of social relationships has found that having high instead of low levels of social interaction over a seven-year time period decreases the risk of dying by some 50 per cent, which is in effect the equivalent to giving up smoking, and worse than excessive alcohol consumption. He concludes further that the analysis suggests close links between a person's decision to stay a smoker and the choices of family and friends. In fact, one study estimates that if a spouse stops smoking, it decreases their partner's chances of smoking by 67 per cent, while if a friend ceases smoking, this decreases the odds by 36 per cent, making a healthy case for the value social innovation can add, in this case concentrating on the powerful healing potential of valuable and genuine social interaction and support rather than dispensing just pills.

In an article by Marcin Czech and Pawel Kawalec, both medical doctors from Poland, they argue that diabetes mellitus type 2, which is not inherited as in type 1, is one of the most significant clinical problems globally affecting more than 346 million people and accounting for millions of deaths. Over half of sufferers are women. The social impact of this disease is great, causing a decreased quality of life, lost productivity and serious complications such as blindness, diabetic foot, neuropathy and arteriosclerosis of the coronary and renal arteries. They note that according to data from the World Bank diabetes holds second position as an economic burden to society, costing 5–10 per cent of the worldwide health care budget.[19]

Big Data

In Chapter 8 David Rankin and Adrian Fry of KAE address the thorny question of Big Data, which many people believe threatens to engulf our lives. The University of Cambridge's Psychometrics Centre has recently published (with other researchers funded by Microsoft) a study entitled 'Private traits and attributes are predictable from digital records of human behaviour'. It is based on the profiles of 58,000 users of American Facebook. The results are quite alarming in that the algorithms used by Facebook can pick up on an enormous amount of information concerning users' personal preferences including those most private to an individual.

What is potentially worrying is that by ticking likes and dislikes and offering one's thoughts on Facebook it is suggested by the authors of this study that algorithms employed by Facebook can make very precise predictions about an individual with 95 per cent accuracy in predicting ethnicity, 88 per cent in predicting male sexual orientation, with 80 per cent accuracy political affiliations and religious beliefs and even 62–75 per cent accurate in predicting emotional stability and personality types. Such detailed information is safe in benign hands but it can also be used for corporate manipulation of consumers who could unthinkingly be led because of their prejudices or emotional problems to buy certain products or follow particular political ideologies in the interests of a particular industry or governmental direction. Such uses can range from Tesco using its Club Card members' shopping histories to target its online advertising. In these times of economic depression/recession payday loan companies, which can charge the vulnerable and the low paid more than thousands of per cent annual interest rates on small loans, can shackle those taking out such loans to years of paying back interest that they cannot afford, often make their credit judgements based on data taken from social networking sites.[20]

David Rankin and Adrian Fry, who are marketers, argue in their chapter that Big Data, as a concept, is not readily understood by the consumer and look at some positive ways it can be used for the idea of a big society, creating socially useful value as well as value for both businesses and the consumer supporting greater consumer involvement rather than turning consumers into manipulated tools of industry.

Energy, value and global tax

In Chapter 5 Victor Bartenev offers the unique concept of dynamic added value taxation (DAVT), which globalises all important tax revenues through the regions of the world by taking the value of actual energy expended on products and turning it into a simple tax that has increased resistance to 'grey' financial schemes. DAVT introduction into regional economies promotes a global DAVT, instead of complicated and incompatible domestic tax systems that we see unbalancing economies in Europe such as Greece, Spain, Portugal and Cyprus during the current economic crises in which a reliable source of tax across the Eurozone countries is absent.

20 *Ruth Taplin*

The global DAVT would facilitate a more balanced distribution of the world GDP value in order to improve global socio-economic stability.

Innovation and crises

Chapter 9 by Alojzy Z. Nowak and Bernard Arogyaswamy argues that innovation is the only way to create value to overcome the current economic crises but innovation and value will vary according to cultural specificities in different regions in the world. We must not forget that although we live in a globalised world it is a world made up of different cultures thousands of years in the making that not only creates its own innovation practices but also value. This fact means that global harmonisation will never be a complete process but will occur on certain levels and in relation to particular processes that are essential for value creation but in the form of a dichotomy whereby global harmonisation of value will proceed with a limit on its movement because of cultural practices in each country and region.

Notes

1 Ruth Taplin (ed.), *Valuing Intellectual Property in Japan, Britain and the United States*, London: Routledge, 2004.
2 Michael Findlay, *The Value of Art: Money, Power, Beauty*, Munich: Prestel Publishing, 2012.
3 BBC News Technology 'Bankrupt Kodak sells off patents to investors for $525m', 26 December 2012.
4 See Ruth Taplin, 'Patents – an East Asian perspective', a Barclays networking event for the patent sector that took place at Barclays on Thursday 13 September 2012.
5 See, for fuller details, Ruth Taplin, *Intellectual Property and the New Global Japanese Economy*, London: Routledge, 2009.
6 14/01/2013 at uk.news.yahoo.com and Sky News.
7 See R. Ian McEwin, 'Editor's introduction', *Intellectual Property: Competition Law and Economics in Asia*, Oxford: Hart Publishing, 2011, p. 12.
8 See Ruth Taplin, *Decision-Making in Japan: A Study of Corporate Japanese Decision-making and its Relevance to Western Companies*, London: The Japan Library, 1995 (Reprinted Routledge, 2003).
9 JAL has a department for awareness-raising (http://alwaystaro.seesaa.net/article/183852784.html). 'Detailed accounting is now presented to all departments, which made us aware of profit and loss' (cabin crew) (http://diamond.jp/articles/-/19345?page=4). Sources for general translation (http://senkensoi.net/opinion/2012/02/06436). Inamori's interview (English) (http://blogs.wsj.com/japanrealtime/2012/07/30/mikoshi-management-how-kazuo-inamori-lifted-japan-airlines/). English (http://www.theaustralian.com.au/business/aviation/japan-airlines-ipo-hallmark-of-ceo-inamoris-turnaround-program/story-e6frg95x-1226442375361; http://www.bbc.co.uk/news/business-20293487).Japanese(http://goethe.nikkei.co.jp/serialization/takigawa/110630/01.html; http://diamond.jp/articles/-/19343).
10 See Ruth Taplin, *Decision making in Japan*, London: Japan Library, 1995 (Reprinted Routledge, 2003).
11 Douglas Ginsberg and Eric Fraser, 'The role of economic analysis in competition law', in R. Ian McEwin (ed.) *Intellectual Property: Competition Law and Economics in Asia*, Oxford: Hart Publishing, 2011, pp. 35–52.
12 Ibid.

13 See Cint Kortman chapter, 'Insourcing in the finance industry', in Ruth Taplin (ed.) *Outsourcing and Human Resource Management*, London: Routledge, 2007, pp. 138–53 for definition and examples of insourcing as a new, innovative way of working.
14 Tim Jones, Dave McCormick and Caroline Dewing (eds) *Growth Champions*, Hoboken, NJ: Wiley, 2012. (This book was authored by 19 contributors.)
15 Figure 1.1 with permission from innovationleaders.org.
16 Figure 1.2 with permission from innovationleaders.org.
17 Taken from the International Society for Professional Innovation Management (www.ispim.org), a professional organisation. Parts of this article were taken with permission from Tim Jones from http://magazine.ispim.org/2012/11/growth-champions/.
18 See http://uk.finance.yahoo.com/news/nine-year-old-entrepreneur-opens-third-business-125532959.html.
19 See Marcin Czech and Pawel Kawalec, 'Literature concerning Diabetes costs in Central and Eastern Europe – a systematic review and comparison to Western Europe' in *Interdisciplinary Journal of Economics and Business Law*, 2, 1 (2012) pp. 28–50.
20 'Definitely do not like: the downside to Big Data and social networking', Martin Webster, Telecom TV One, 14 March 2013.

2 Future of innovation and intellectual property

Tim Jones

Introduction

The realm of intellectual property (IP) covers more than just innovation and extends into many areas of art, culture and commerce. Equally the breadth of innovation is increasingly moving beyond the established arenas of product and technology development where IP has traditionally had a major role to play. Today we can see shifts taking place in areas such as business model innovation, open collaboration and social- and community-based innovation where, for many, the role of IP has become increasingly stretched and even marginalized. Equally, with ever-growing interest in patent protection of such areas as business methods, software-enabled experiences and plant biology, the boundaries of what is being covered, or not, by IP protection, at least in some regions, are also being pushed. If we are to be successful in innovating in the years ahead, we need to understand how changes in the future may impact, and be impacted by, shifts in IP.

This chapter takes a look at some of the major shifts taking place in the crossover between innovation and IP today and draws on multiple discussions with leading experts and companies about the future to see what issues may be on the horizon. It seeks to identify some of the macro drivers of change that may impact how IP supports and impacts innovation at a global level, or not, and also highlights a number of more regional or sector-specific perspectives that may well be signals of wider bottom-up change in the next decade or so. The primary source for many of the insights used is the Future Agenda programme that, as the world's largest open foresight project, is in itself changing perceptions of what many companies consider to be confidential knowledge and what can be shared. The chapter is written very much from the perspective of an innovation leader seeking to create the most value and deliver the greatest impact from new ideas, even if that means changing some of our existing assumptions. As such, some of the views may challenge current opinions within the IP community, but hopefully many will also support some of the shifts being discussed and debated.

Looking forward

It is important to first consider some experiences of looking ahead as there are many misconceptions and alternative perspectives of foresight that often cause confusion. If we are to look ahead over the usual horizon and seek to see emerging issues, foremost we have to be comfortable with uncertainty. While short-term shifts around consumer insight and even medium-term trends a few years out are often relatively predictable, longer-term foresight is, by its very nature, less certain. Often the short-term shifts can be seen as extrapolations of today, be that a faster, cheaper, bigger, smaller, more integrated or more fragmented version of what we can see right now. Most long-term views are open to greater potential change, but also, when talking to different sources of expertise and foresight, there is a lot of noise in the system: one hundred people may have tens of different views of how a particular issue may evolve and so knowing who to believe and who to potentially ignore is always a challenge.

Companies including Shell, IBM, Siemens, Microsoft and Procter & Gamble and governments in places such as South Korea and Singapore are all well regarded leaders in the areas of foresight, scenarios and futures thinking. When these organizations look forward, they do so by considering several different levels of confidence in what they see. While they all agree on a certain set of known global changes such as increasing population growth, resource constraints and universal connectivity, there is a wide range of unknown shifts around which there is not 100 per cent alignment. Separating the 'known' from the 'unknown' is therefore critical.

One approach is to look at what is predictable or certain against what it uncertain. This view is key as very little about the future can actually be predicted – at best it can be anticipated. As such the predictable certainties such as increasing population growth, resource constraints and universal connectivity are few in number: Shell sees 'three hard truths' while others see up to four, or maybe five, certainties.

Another, less binary, view is to separate different perspectives of the grey of 'what might happen' into different groups. Most commonly organizations seek to categorize shifts into what is plausible, what is possible and what is probable: while a few things are implausible for reasons such as breaking of natural laws, most future events are to some degree plausible and hence this is the widest net. In terms of the other two, people tend to think of possible events as those that could happen, and probable events that most likely will happen.

At the same time, some organizations use combinations of probable and possible events to create alternative scenarios for the future. For instance, as it looks at the future of energy supply and the response to climate change, Shell presently sees two potential scenarios in play for the next 20 or so years. One, called 'blueprint', is based on countries and companies around the world recognizing the challenge ahead and getting together sooner rather than later to agree how to collaborate and collectively change direction. The other, termed 'scramble', paints a bleaker picture of a world where everyone is initially out for themselves securing as much future energy supplies as possible, irrespective of whether they are fossil based or cleaner alternative fuels. Both of the scenarios are plausible futures and so we have to plan for both. We may prefer the idea of 'blueprint' instead of 'scramble' and may well seek to advocate that the world heads that way. However, we cannot control the way others move and so, in order to be confident about being prepared for the future, we have to build plans of how best to live and operate under both extremes.

As we move ahead to look at the potential changes in the future of innovation and IP, we will use these categorizations to help us make sense of what may happen, not to prescribe a specific percentage chance of change, but more to separate out the higher probability events from the lower probability ones. In other words, we will seek to see what may be the 'strong bets' for the future of IP, and what may be the 'wild cards' – the less likely, but potentially equally as significant changes – sometimes also referred to as 'black swan events' after the theory developed by Nassim Nicholas Taleb and shared in his book published in 2007.[1]

The link between foresight and innovation

Innovation is by its very nature about creating something new, and ideally unique and of value to someone: one common definition is that innovation is 'the successful exploitation of new ideas' – this is widely embraced because it clearly spells out and connects both the creation of economic value (successful exploitation) with the creation of something novel (new ideas).

Within this overall ambition, those in the innovation community tend to talk about incremental innovation and radical, break-through or even disruptive innovation. Incremental innovation is by its nature all about small changes while the others are about potentially big change. Some characterize short-term innovation as incremental and imply that longer-term innovation is therefore radical. This is an error: long-term innovation can also be incremental – it just may take a while to get traction and scale for wide impact. In reality well over 95 per cent of the innovations that make it into the marketplace are incremental changes and only a few, such as the iPad, Teflon, hybrid engines and maybe Twitter can really be considered radical. From an IP perspective radical innovation is often the most attractive but a good majority of incremental innovation also includes and relies upon creative shifts that may well merit patent, copyright or design protection.

Irrespective of whether the eventual innovation may be incremental or radical in nature, longer-term innovation is influenced, stimulated and enhanced by good foresight: being better informed about the future helps us to better focus innovation activity and hence see how and where we can best create new value generating platforms and drive the economic growth that is still largely the primary ambition for most companies and governments. Seeing what challenges we face in the future and hence understanding more clearly what new opportunities for innovation may be emerging onto the radar is an important factor in thinking ahead of the masses and so more organizations are now seeking to better integrate their foresight and longer-term innovation activities. As they do this, many are focused on new technologies, emerging demographic shifts, societal changes and other economic and political developments that may impact the scale, shape and nature of the innovation opportunity.

On top of this, as an ever more globalized and competitive world seeks to be first to exploit new opportunities, protecting the innovations in the most appropri-

Future of innovation and intellectual property 25

ate way is clearly still a priority. However, as there is a number of possible and probable shifts on the horizon that could impact how ideas are created, shared and exploited, the corresponding changes in the options for generating and making best use of any IP is a growing concern. For the vast majority of companies, innovation is fundamentally about making money from new ideas. As such creating, capturing, securing and trading the associated value are pivotal. The priority for many continues to be using IP as a primary mechanism for this, just as it has been in the past. However, for some, the nature of the value creation, sharing, protection and realization balance is on the move and so seeing new options that can link to the innovations that maybe in the pipeline is critical. Innovation is how we can change the future, but is also how many organizations create value: if we are to be successful in innovating in the years ahead, we need to understand how changes in the future may impact, and be impacted by, shifts in IP.

Looking back

Within the arena of IP and its relationship with innovation we can clearly see several issues changing – both as a reflection of innovation, as a stimulus and as a means to capture and exchange value. We will detail these shortly. However, before looking forward to see what may be on the radar, it is good to first take a peek in the rear-view mirror and review some of the recent changes in and around the innovation space that have impacted on the relationship with and the role of IP.

Looking back 10 years or so, some of the big topics on the IP/innovation agenda were new strategies and issues such as the resurgence of patent pools, the emergence of IP development companies, and new financial strategies such as asset-backed securitization:[2]

- Although a long-standing approach starting in the early days of the automotive and sewing machine industries, patent pools had been gaining momentum in the communications and consumer electronics space as the de facto approach for rapid standard sharing. Whether discussing BlueRay DVDs, Bluetooth, MPEG video compression or 3G mobile, companies were increasingly seeing the benefits of sharing and licensing collective know-how in order to accelerate the adoption of new global technology platforms.
- Focusing on the generation of revenues from IP that one company develops or manages but others take to market, a number of firms were created as IP development companies: BTG, The Generics Group, Accentus, Isis Innovation and Scipher were just some of the UK-based independent organizations that were created to specifically manage the exploitation of IP – either as a spin-out from a parent group or university or as a standalone entity operating within a specific industry.
- Led by changes in the music industry, new income streams from royalties were being constructed using asset-backed securitization allowing companies and individuals to gain income today against future value creation. David

Bowie was one of the first to benefit as $55m worth of 15-year bonds were backed by the royalties from the publication and recording rights to over 300 of his songs. Others followed suit and many were also looking at how this approach could change the approach to financing technology start-ups.

A decade on, patent pools continue to play a growing role in the innovation arena and IP development companies are still with us although they are rather niche; asset-backed securitization however has largely disappeared as a financial strategy.

Case study: ARM Holdings PLC

One particular development of note in the crossover of patent pools, standards and IP companies has been the success of ARM: after successful technology licensing activities by the likes of manufacturers such as Ericsson, IBM and Qualcomm, we have seen the successful emergence of several IP revenue-only business models in the information communication technology arena. The most significant of these has been Cambridge-based ARM that has used its IP portfolio on the basis of creating a completely different business model in the smartphone and tablet markets and is now also broadening into the wider personal computer (PC) arena.

Every iPhone runs on an ARM-designed chip. In fact 95 per cent of all smartphones, most tablet PCs, including the iPad, Samsung's Galaxy and Motorola's Xoom, and over 10 per cent of laptops globally use ARM chips because they are faster and use less energy than many of the competing designs from the likes of Intel and AMD. Tracing its history back to the 1980s, the seed that became ARM was the first ARM (Acorn RISC Machine) chip developed by the research and development (R&D) team at Acorn Computers, previously famous for creating the BBC Microcomputer. In 1990 ARM Ltd was spun out of Acorn and, with backing from Apple and VLSI technology, created as an IP licensing company. Twenty years later with revenues of more than £450 million and operating margins of 45 per cent, over 740 licenses for ARM design chips had been granted to a host of major manufacturers. The company is now the world's leading semiconductor IP supplier with its products at the heart of an increasing array of digital products from phone and laptops to cameras, digital TVs and even washing machines.

What is particularly interesting about ARM, and of great concern for its competitors, is that the company doesn't actually manufacture anything. It has no factories, relatively few employees, and yet it leads the semiconductor world in developing the latest technology platforms for a growing majority of consumer electronics products. ARM makes its money by conducting leading-edge R&D from its headquarters in Cambridge and then licenses the designs that emanate from this to over 300 companies around the world.

Instead of ARM bearing the cost of manufacturing, a network of partners of the world's leading semiconductor manufacturers does that. By designing once and licensing many times an industry's R&D cost is spread over a whole sector. In a sector where technology licensing has been an interesting revenue contributor for several companies for a number of years, ARM has made it the business model. With a pipeline of innovative new products coming to market, 2012 revenue growth was over again over 15 per cent, while profits rose by over 20 per cent.

As ARM's partners are the world's largest semiconductor manufacturers, their regular royalty payments have become a highly reliable cash flow and, given the broad base of partners and end-markets, ARM has diluted dependency, and is not overly reliant on any one company or consumer product for future profits and cash. The successful growth of ARM is built upon its ability to use its IP to choreograph its technology-sharing communities and partnerships supported by its focus on design rather than production. This success has established ARM as an important partner for many of the big players in the consumer products space and given it the base to continue to develop technology solutions and deliver further growth.[3]

Open innovation

Although issues such as patent pools, IP development companies and asset-backed securitization were in 2002 seen as potentially major shifts that could have significant impact, in the following ten years or so other external catalytic forces have evidently had influence. Some of these were foreseeable but the levels of impact were not. Two stand out. The first of these, the rise of open innovation, was certainly not on many organizations' radars a decade ago.

For many in the innovation world, 2003 was when the game changed with the publication of Henry Chesbrough's *Harvard Business Review* article[4] and subsequent book[5] named after a term he coined: 'open innovation'. The subsequent widespread embracing of the 'open innovation' philosophy, where ideas flow into the organization from an ever-increasing ecosystem of partners, universities, consultants, customers and entrepreneurs has had significant impact. It has rapidly become a mantra for many in the corporate innovation space and has raised the issue of IP trading out of R&D and into the boardroom. Over the past few years, pretty much every major organization has sought to have an 'open innovation' programme. However, although many now have such capabilities in place, according to Henry Chesbrough only around 10 per cent are yet to create additional value from this route – largely due to cultural rather than process reasons.

In firms such as P&G, which has staked a huge bet on the open innovation philosophy with its Connect + Develop approach, this has already meant a shift to engaging a wider, deeper supply base of innovation than was traditional with just internal marketing, approved agencies and R&D as the focus. In a similar vein,

Novartis has relocated its R&D headquarters from Switzerland to Massachusetts and is now well plumbed into the local biotech system as a source of new candidate molecules; and the likes of Microsoft, IBM and Intel have all set up research labs in varied locations for specific reasons – for instance Beijing to access the local talent, especially around the field of speech recognition. As we shall discuss in more detail later, these companies are, in their different ways, all demonstrating the ability to unbundle organizational capabilities from one part of the business and align them with a wider external ecosystem. Ideas and the associated IP are being increasingly traded between companies and across sectors so that organizations can create the maximum value from the IP assets that they, or their partners, either own or have built. Open innovation has encouraged the heart of many an organization's future growth to become a network.

For the companies such as P&G, DSM and Cisco that have successfully aligned process, strategy and culture around sourcing ideas from outside the organization, the open innovation approach has provided evident benefits. The R&D ecosystem has been expended well outside the corporate boundaries, a wider selection of candidate concepts have become available to new product development teams, associated development risk has been reduced and overall return on investment for innovation has in turn been increased. However for others that have not appropriately aligned process, strategy and culture and have often seen open innovation as a quick alternative for getting ideas from outside the firm instead of building internal capability, this is proving to be a difficult route. The views that open innovation is a quick fix for a poor portfolio, that it is a substitute as opposed to a complement for effective internal innovation capability, and that is less costly than internal innovation are all common misunderstandings in several companies that have failed to make a success of an open innovation strategy.

The HBR coverage of P&G's Connect + Develop approach in 2002 and 2006[6] resulted in hordes of other companies jumping on the open innovation bandwagon but many without fully understanding the implications. A key one of these is excellence in IP management: since open innovation is fundamentally all about trading of IP, the winners have been the ones that have not only identified the most promising external opportunities but have also executed the associated IP licensing and transfer agreements to the greatest effect. Effective IP management capability is often lacking in the companies that have failed to make the most out of adopting an open innovation strategy. However, with the momentum that has already built up and the high-profile successes that are covered in the innovation media, there is no doubt that open innovation will continue to play a significant role in many a corporate growth strategy in the years ahead.

Open source vs. open innovation

One important point to highlight in passing is that in recent years many organizations have made some basic errors in confusing two similarly named but distinctly different concepts – open innovation and open source. Whereas open innovation is largely a mechanism for trading the IP associated with ideas and innovation, open source is means by which ideas are shared and innovation is created largely outside IP. The early success of Linux, followed by Wikipedia and the whole creative commons movement, has been pivotal in building up momentum of the open source community. Starting with Netscape's release of the source code for Navigator in 1998, the software environment has been at the fore of the open source movement. Whether we consider apps such as Blender, WordPress and Mozilla Firefox, operating systems such as Android and Linux or server software including Apache and MediaWiki, open source has had and is continuing to have a significant role in the development and sharing of new software. The only common element between open source and open innovation is focused around the principle of sharing and cooperation between parties. However, in terms of how value is created and shared there is a significant chasm between the two approaches. The fundamental principle of the open source approach is that either no one owns the IP, or that if they do, they grant everyone else royalty free licences for its use, development and wider application. As Wikipedia itself puts it:[7] 'open source refers to a program in which the source code is available to the general public for use and/or modification from its original design free of charge.'

Business method patents

Alongside the open innovation movement there has been another change in the world of innovation and IP that has captured the mainstream imagination with dramatic effect. Potentially this one could have been anticipated as a possible shift but certainly not predicted as a certainty. In fact other developments may well have been top of the potential impact list: if asked what would be the biggest change to the innovation and IP landscape by 2012, many commentators ten years ago may well have chosen the movement by some biotech, pharmaceutical and chemicals companies such as Monsanto in seeking to patent plants. Throughout the decade there have indeed been numerous attempts by biotech companies to gain IP protection on what others would see as nature. Especially in the area of personalized medicine lobby groups such as the Biotechnology Industry Organization have argued that patents have long covered clever applications of natural laws. However in May 2012, in a ruling of *Mayo v. Prometheus*, the US Supreme Court threw out two key patents that were seeking to protect natural laws on the basis that they would stifle innovation and in doing so sent many a biotech company's patent attorneys into a spin. What some had seen as a highly probable move in the field of innovation and IP at the start of the decade had been unequivocally halted.[8]

In actuality however, an issue that was on several experts' radars as being potentially big, and has proved to be so, is that of business method patents. Back in 2000, the high-profile court cases over Amazon's patent on its one-click shopping process and Priceline's patent on its reverse auctions had propelled the notion of patenting business methods into the limelight. Although not a new issue, in an information economy, in which entire business models can be embedded in digital code, attempts to use business method patents as competitive weapons have been seen to be significant.[9] One important factor around this has been the different stances taken by the EU and the US on the matter. Under the European Patent Convention, 'Schemes, rules and methods for doing business' are not regarded as being inventions and are hence not patentable. However, there is no exclusion for methods of doing business under US patent law: patent applications for methods of doing business are examined using the same standards as any other invention.[10] Although the United States Patent and Trademark Office (USPTO) allegedly typically rejects ten times as many business method patent applications as it does applications for protection of more conventional technology and product inventions, over the decade many companies have sought to go down this route. Two of the most successful have been Amazon and Google.

Case study: Amazon and Google

Two internet-enabled, US-based companies have gained most from changes in IP strategy over the past decade and show how things are currently shifting. These are Amazon and Google – each of which are masters of using data and its analysis to fundamentally change a host of sectors – not just retailing and advertising where each respectively generate the majority of their revenues. Over the past decade, the level and use of IP, and particularly business method patents in both of these two organizations, has changed significantly.

Amazon and Google are two of the largest and most successful companies in the consumer internet space. Both have helped construct and reshape the industry, delivering new services and capabilities that improve the way consumers engage with information, with companies and with each other. Both have created new categories while disrupting others, support thousands of other businesses and extract value from mind-boggling amounts of user data. Both are still led by their brilliant, billionaire founders, who it turns out all attended Montessori schools in their youth – a system that strongly encourages students to think for themselves, rather than accept the status quo. And both companies have seen extraordinary and consistent, mostly organic, growth over the past decade in revenues and user metrics. Yet these two companies have taken very different routes to success, and have markedly different approaches towards innovation and growth.[11]

Google is obsessed with solving hard problems around information access and management. It built a search engine for the web that was markedly better than anything available at the time, bringing order to the chaos of the Web. It taught people that mess was OK, as long as Google was on your side. Users flocked to the site, and Google monetized them by reshaping the advertising world, providing a business model for a whole generation of new companies. The users, and the petabytes of data they trail in their wake, are in many ways commodities to Google – sources of input into a relentlessly analytical machine. Nuances of human life, emotion and meaning are expressed, captured, digitized and monetized.

Amazon takes a different approach. It uses data as an input to get closer to its self-imposed goal of being a user-centric company. Top down, rather than bottom up, Amazon more closely resembles a 'traditional company' than the more decentralized Google. It moves more deliberately and has executed its strategy with remarkable consistency since alighting on the opportunity of internet commerce. It had no prima facie reason to own the segment, but through a tight focus and years of investment in infrastructure has now built up a remarkable position. Although retailing is Amazon's day job, its real business is customer satisfaction.

As each company has taken a different route to their leadership position, so each faces unique challenges to continued growth. What is clear, as we look at each of these in more detail below, is that they have already had a very profound impact, and it's likely their next steps will continue to shape the business landscape in the years to come.

Amazon

In Amazon's world, online retail businesses tend to have high fixed costs and low marginal costs. They involve significant investment in order to build websites, establish warehouses, implement and manage logistics systems and design product recommendation algorithms, and thus require a large user base over which to spread the costs. This created a need for growth and long-term thinking that pervades the company. Starting out Amazon struggled to match the buying power of large book retailers such as Barnes and Noble, and instead harnessed the efficiencies of the internet – avoiding staff costs and high-rent real estate charges for stores. As it has grown it has been able to apply increased price pressure on suppliers to generate discounts.

As the company moved beyond books it found itself squaring off against the king of retail, Walmart, resulting in price wars, both offering deeply discounted mass-market titles.

One of the most contentious tools in Amazon's armory used to keep prices low is its ability to avoid levying sales tax in US states where it doesn't have a physical presence. The idea is that consumers self-report tax for out-of-state purchases with their annual returns, though in practice few people do. Recent legislation in California has brought this simmering debate to a head, with many state legislatures and bricks-and-mortar stores waging battle to remove this advantage. The *Economist* described the showdown as 'more complicated than the Boston tea party, but potentially as colourful'.[12] With warehouses, distributors, design centres and affiliates all over the US, battle is waging over what constitute a physical presence with Amazon choosing to site key facilities in low-tax states.

Whatever the outcome, Amazon has already benefitted for many years and used this advantage to help build its infrastructure and cement its brand values in consumers' minds. The 2012 focus in the UK on the tax practices of Amazon, Google and Starbucks further highlighted how the nominal location of where business activity and especially IP occurs opens the doors to even wider minimalization of global tax exposures.

From the start Amazon has been able to avoid the physical limitations of shop shelf space and has operated a network of suppliers working as virtual storerooms. This model has been expanded with Fulfillment By Amazon, which allows third parties to advertise their inventory with Amazon, and utilize the same infrastructure such as customer service and shipping. On top of this Amazon's pioneering use of customer reviews and recommendation algorithms has made navigation and selection considerably easier than in a physical store. As a result 30 per cent of the products now sold on the Amazon website are from third parties.

Amazon also recognized that one of its biggest weaknesses was the perceived lack of customer service in online commerce. By making this its primary objective, the company has successfully turned this potential weakness into a strength. It has proved itself a growth champion due to the size and scale of its growth, the clarity of its vision and its ability to reinvent itself. Amazon now accounts for a third of US ecommerce and is growing twice as fast as online commerce in general. It has also been growing fast internationally: almost half its revenues now come from international sales.

While moving first from books to music and then to other online retailing activities such as cosmetics, clothing and cars can be all considered incremental innovation, the Amazon Web Services (AWS) and the Kindle are entirely different industries – enterprise services and consumer technology hardware respectively. Traditional retailers, booksellers in particular, were disrupted by Amazon's online efficiencies; it seems that likely that this retail engine will also disrupt other outlets.

AWS and Kindle are expected by analysts to meaningfully contribute to bottom line results – no easy feat when just delivering 10 per cent growth rate requires additional revenues of over $4bn annually. A steadfast focus on customer-centricity, coupled with an operational approach that is resilient, yet adaptable, has proved to be a successful recipe for Amazon.

Google

With its launch in 1998, Google changed the face of the internet. Instead of jumbled portal pages brimming with human-derived categories, Google provided a new way in to the web – a blank page with a simple search box.

Search was no longer an appendage to a portal; it *was* the portal. Cognitive overload was relieved with Zen-like simplicity, and the web pages it offered up seemed almost magically accurate. For many this represented the first step of a journey in which Google was to become increasingly central to their lives. In May 2011, Google reached a milestone, becoming the first company in history to have over a billion visitors to its sites in a month.[13] Google has had a remarkable propensity for solving users' problems, and a unique business approach that can offer inspiration for many looking to grow and monetize an online service business.

The Google mission is to 'organize the world's information and make it universally accessible and useful'[14] and that requires overcoming three challenges.

1. First, finding information. Although content on the web is growing at an exponential clip, some estimates suggest that only 20 per cent of information in the world is currently online, the rest is in books, company filing cabinets, on TV and so on. Indexing the web's billions of pages is a relatively trivial matter compared with finding information not on the web today, and Google is leading the charge. This ambition has driven the acquisition of YouTube in order to access video content and the Google Books project, which began scanning libraries around the world.
2. The second challenge is to make this information accessible over multiple channels. The first two billion people who went online did so primarily via fixed wires and a personal computer; however the next two billion, most of who will be in today's developing countries, will connect via their mobile device. This explains the importance of the company's Android mobile operating system, and the acquisition of Motorola Mobility.
3. Third, Google wants to make information 'useful'. This means going beyond the simple keyword search query to discover what the user actually means. As former CIO Douglas Merrill put it, 'Our goal is to have the result be not what you asked for, but what you *should* have asked for.'[15]

Google is a data-driven technology company, whose core competences are technical rather than service orientated. A number of these are unique to Google, hard to replicate and have a major impact on improving the quality of the end-user experience.

Google's major breakthrough was its Page Rank algorithm that created meaning from links between websites. Now in addition to Page Rank, Google's search engine uses around 200 factors that determine the relevance of results. These include search terms, synonyms and website quality. Massive quantities of user data and query logs allow Google to intelligently guess what was meant by a certain request, and improve the experience with spelling correction, or more recently Google Instant – where results are displayed in real time as the user types the letters of their query.

As a result of its search capabilities Google has created new platforms for innovation. Not only does it extract meaning from data, it also gives it commercial value. The ability to create value out of search – not only for itself but for other organizations prepared to pay for the benefits that this provides – puts it on the frontline of innovation in the online world. The company now sits at the centre of an ecosystem, which means that it has visibility of a large amount of data generated by its products such as Google Ad Words, which allows companies to bid for keywords and appear next to relevant search results, and Ad Sense, the service that allows online publishers to earn revenue by displaying relevant ads on a wide variety of content. Content creators can now get meaningfully paid for the work they are doing.

Google's approach to innovation can be thought of as two separate processes – 'left brain' and 'right brain' – that balance each other out. It starts with an anarchic and unfocused celebration of creativity and individuality, which the founders ascribe in part to their education in the famously creative Montessori school system. This meets a highly analytical, data-driven process that reviews the portfolio, culls losers and doubles down on winning ideas.

An article in the *Wall Street Journal* suggested, only half joking, the existence of a 'Montessori Mafia' – due to the large number of some of creative and successful graduates such as Amazon founder Jeff Bezos and Wikipedia inventor Jimmy Wales.[16] Google founders Page and Brin readily credit their schooling: 'We both went to Montessori school, and I think it was part of that training of not following rules and orders, and being self-motivated, questioning what's going on in the world, doing things a little bit differently.' There's a sense of irreverence and fun at Google that is most palpable in a visit to the Mountain View headquarters; open meeting areas, free food, bright colours and games adorn the offices, and a dinosaur skeleton greets visitors outside – a daily reminder of the desire not to follow the herd, and become extinct.

The other side of the Google brain is more systematic. Executive chairman Eric Schmidt says Google aims to be a 'systematic innovator at scale'. By this he means, 'can systemize the approach – we can actually get our groups to innovate. We don't necessarily know this month which one [will succeed]. But we know it's portfolio theory. We have enough groups that a few [innovations] will pop up.'[17]

Google's innovation approach has allowed it to maintain a sense of freedom and autonomy for its employees as it has scaled to a head count of over 20,000. However, this is business creativity as an extreme sport, and not necessarily appropriate for the many companies that need more structured hierarchies, don't have such a flexible business model or have less access to data.

Key insights and IP implications

While Amazon innovates in a more traditional way, with incremental and major initiatives being driven largely by the corner office, Google's approach is flatter, less hierarchical. Its innovation model is more like a seesaw, balancing individuals' zest for freedom to experiment with an actuary's zeal for the numbers. Both approaches have delivered breakthrough results and changed their industries to benefit consumers and their business partners.

Amazon's approach requires a particular confidence to understand the mind of the customer, and place large bets – such as in the infrastructure build out – that become the basis for future growth. This confidence is evidenced by the focus and clarity of mission, and the way that a new skill set can be protected and developed if it comes with top-down blessing. It's easy to imagine there were plenty of book lovers at Amazon, though less likely that people pushing mobile e-readers would have got much attention without support from the top.

Google's more disparate approach risks shareholders' ire, as it can appear unfocused. Its democratic philosophy may limit new ideas to those the company is already good at, and its employees like to do. Also its approach favours new services that can instantly garner online customer data, which may not be realistic in many sectors. A bundled device and service such as Amazon's Kindle is expensive and slow to produce, requires involved outsourcing contracts, and needs a marketing campaign targeting to a more traditional, slow to adopt demographic. This is not the stuff of 20 per cent time, but of daily CEO involvement and sponsorship.

Despite their relative youth, both Amazon and Google function as 'grown up' companies, and youthful exuberance is no longer acceptable to the public as an excuse when things go wrong. Amazon fights hard – and some would say dirty, such as in the ugly spat over sales tax – but it has done a good job at conveying the impression that it is doing so on behalf of its customers. Google's errors by contrast often result in harsher backlash from a media and public in awe of its prowess but still not entirely sure about its motives.

So while both companies offer differing approaches to competing and winning in the online space, together they offer a rich source of learning that can be applied across a variety of industries. In a world that is awash with data, the companies that find new ways to make sense of data, create greater insights into stakeholder needs and develop compelling reasons for others to trust them will be well positioned for growth.

As shown in Table 2.1 and Figure 2.1 below, over the past few years there has been a correspondingly significant rise in patent activity by both Amazon and Google with, on average, a doubling of the number patents being granted year-on-year for the past five years.

Table 2.1 US patents granted

Year	Amazon	Google
2001	0	0
2002	1	0
2003	0	4
2004	0	3
2005	0	7
2006	4	22
2007	7	35
2008	26	60
2009	56	147
2010	122	282
2011	182	427
2012	290	1,170

Source: USPTO/Innovation Leaders Analysis (innovationleaders.org).

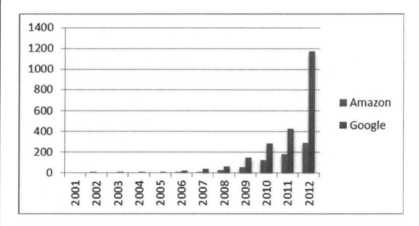

Figure 2.1 US patents granted.
Source: USPTO/Innovation Leaders Analysis (innovationleaders.org).

Looking in more detail at the US patents that are being granted to these two companies, many refer to content management, routing architecture, dynamic pricing, visualization of data, methods and systems, mining data and object query. While there is an increasing number of more conventional product and technology patents, especially in the Google portfolio, for things such as digital cameras, radio frequency identification networks, keyboard interfaces and battery management, the vast majority of the IP being generated by these two companies can be seen to be business method patents.

As Amazon and Google have both used their business models to drive sector-leading growth over the past decade, this core strengthening of their

> respective IP positions through the leverage of business method patents has been a core weapon in the corporate armoury. Not only has it enabled the two companies to build arguably near dominant positions in the markets they choose to operate in and simultaneously use the associated IP to minimize business costs and maximize profits in tax efficient locations, but it has also very much brought the whole business method patents into the wider corporate mainstream.

Open foresight and the Future Agenda programme

Today, as we look forward, we can see new changes creating a potentially new potential IP playing field. So how do some see the world in and around innovation and IP changing over the next decade? Reviewing varied opinions, what is clear is that, just as occurred ten years ago, there are many potential issues on the radar – some of which will undoubtedly have greater impact in the future than others. Some of the changes that people, governments and companies see may be more probable than others. Some may be like business method patents and patent pools and have higher impact than others. Some approaches and changes will be driven into the mainstream by individual companies taking a lead, just as ARM, Amazon and Google have done in the past decade, while others will stay on the margins.

As discussed earlier, looking forward is never easy and, as we seek to separate the known and the unknown, separate certain change from uncertain change and then categorize this into what is plausible, possible and probable, there are many sources of opinion to sound out – some of which will be more credible than others. Building on the successful foresight activities of the likes of Shell, IBM, P&G and co., more companies are now seeking to look ahead. They want to gain insights on and around potential changes over the horizon so that, in an increasingly connected but shifting world, they can better understand the options ahead.

Traditionally organizations have undertaken foresight activities either alone or in partnership with agencies and sought to keep the views private. With the exception of Shell and IBM, few companies have shared their perspectives on the future, preferring to keep their views confidential. The reality is that for many it is what you do with insight and foresight to inform strategy that is confidential. What you or others think may, or may not, happen is opinion. In this increasingly data-driven world, some have suggested that it would be better for all if we all had access to what each other think may happen in the future and so that we can use this to create a richer, deeper and more informed view. This can then be put through the appropriate filter to reveal specific opportunities and risks for individual companies or industries.

Given this proposal, and building upon the open innovation movement, the concept of 'open foresight' was developed. The premise was that if many different organizations around the world could share, in a suitable manner, what they all think about the key changes for the next decade; we could create a single, well-informed source of foresight for all. In 2009, with the support of Vodafone Group, the Future Agenda programme was launched to act as a mechanism to achieve this objective.

Looking initially at 16 different topics, experts in the respective fields from around the world were invited to propose their own views of everything from the future of cities, energy, food, health, money and transport to the future of authenticity, data, identity and migration. These starting points – initial perspectives on the world in 2020 – were then used to stimulate debate online and in workshops. Throughout 2010, 50 events in 25 countries brought together over 2,500 people from 1,500 organizations to challenge, enhance and rebuild these initial perspectives and so provide a collective body of work into being one of the major sources of change for the next decade. The results of all these discussions were synthesized into a single detailed collation of 52 major shifts for the world in 2020 and shared online, via books and varied social media platforms. Since the launch of the results from the first Future Agenda programme in December 2010, thousands have downloaded the content and hundreds of organizations have used the insights to inform strategy, stimulate thinking and identify new innovation opportunities.[18]

The Future Agenda programme has enabled thousands of people to share their insights and overcome prejudices about what is secret and what is open: today many organizations have changed their perspective on what about their views of the future is confidential and what can be made available for others to use and comment upon. The principle of open foresight is gaining momentum and in its own way encouraging people and organizations to more freely share their knowledge so that all gain better insights.

Within the Future Agenda programme there were many discussions that relate to innovation and IP. From debates on the future of work, the future of data and the future of authenticity there were specific comments about the changing role of IP around the world. In addition, in workshops on topics such as privacy, wealth, health and food, other related views were added into the mix.

Seven shifts for the future of innovation and IP

So, from the numerous discussions that took place with all the different companies in the varied Future Agenda workshops around the world, what was most relevant to the future of IP and innovation? What are the core underlying drivers of change and what may be some of the key implications and for whom? In addition, was there anything that everyone was nearly 100 per cent certain about or was it more a case of people suggesting potential options for the future? If the latter, then which were seen to be more probable than possible and in what context? Below we share and discuss seven potential shifts:

1   differentiated knowledge;
2   the end of IP;
3   failed drugs;
4   business model open innovation;

5   Corporate Lego;
6   projects worth working for; and
7   big collaboration.

None of these were seen as 100 per cent certainties, but they were all viewed as plausible and probable shifts. In multiple discussions with different communities and informed experts in varied fields, these seven potential changes were viewed as credible changes that could have potentially significant impact on IP in the next decade or so.

Differentiated knowledge

> As information is shared globally and insight is commoditized, the best returns go to those who can produce non-standard, differentiated knowledge.

In his books *The World is Flat*[19] and *Hot, Flat and Crowded*[20] Thomas Friedman, *New York Times* columnist and three-time Pulitzer Prize winner, shared how the flattened world of the past decade has been driven by quicker and easier knowledge access and sharing. Through his multiple examples from India and China, in particular, he highlighted how the alignment of increasing globalization, high-speed internet connections and new business models all helped the likes of Infosys, Wipro and Tata to become knowledge engines. Outsourcing of call-centres to lower cost economies merged with offshoring of key data-intensive tasks to a similar group of countries, and know-how was steadily transferred from the 'developed' to the 'developing' world.

As Harvard's Clayton Christensen, author of numerous books on disruptive innovation,[21] has also highlighted through his stories about the changes in the PC industry, outsourcing drives knowledge sharing and a transfer of value creation. He focused on the way in which US computer companies such as HP, Compaq and Dell shifted parts manufacture, then assembly and then, finally, design to China and Taiwan. As a result, the likes of Acer, Lenovo and HTC have been able to build up their expertise to a point where they themselves have become the incumbent competition and the world's leading brands: know-how transfer has enabled new competitors to emerge to rival and supersede the US-based leaders, which in principle still own the original IP but increasingly gain little of the value.

Today, the fast-growth economies are no longer fast-followers but have become global centres of excellence in their own right. Microsoft's lab in Beijing is one of its most advanced in the world; China's Lenovo is the world's leading PC brand; in Bangalore Infosys designs engines for GM and wings for Airbus; and much of the pharmaceutical industry is steadily shifting capability to China and India. Meanwhile, the old economies are finding it more and more difficult to keep pace. New knowledge creation has therefore been the common focus for many and the idea of building knowledge economies has been in the policy reactions of many countries that have seen their value-creating manufacturing capabilities disappear.

At the same time, to build new knowledge, some universities around the world have been increasing their status as knowledge hubs. But, just as many institutions have been trying to create exclusive content, leaders such as MIT, for instance, have put all their course materials online free of charge through the OpenCourseWare platform. So, how can others unable to provide such magnets for talent compete?

The future challenge here is that for any knowledge economy to really work, it is a matter of both scale and differentiation. Chris Meyer has argued the case that, 'as the half-life of knowledge continues to shrink, 2020 will see greater commoditization of knowledge'.[22] He sees that, over the next decade, 'the industrialization of information work is certain, and will affect pretty much every business'. Add into the mix a massive imbalance between the US and China in terms of graduates and the US and India in terms of engineers and it is easy to see why some envisage a one-way shift clearly taking place: a notable example of this move is in China, where over 50 per cent of Tsinghua University's graduates go on to do doctoral research and Tsinghua now provides more PhD students in the US than any other institution including MIT, Yale and Stanford. While some question the quality and creativity of Chinese graduates, others argue that the sheer volumes will probably deliver significant impact.

However, there is an alternative view – that of creating differentiated commoditized knowledge. Gary Hamel has commented that 'in a world of commoditized knowledge, the returns go to the companies who can produce non-standard knowledge'. Apple, fiercely protective of its IP, is often given as a company whose sales and margins are a reflection of its unique knowledge and know-how. While at a company level, the story is less strong than at a national level, this view suggests that at a large/global scale, the competition is on to be the differentiated source of insight. At a national economy scale, where one cannot have everyone producing non-standard knowledge, the challenge is more about speed and efficiency of knowledge development and sharing at a broader scale.

Another development adds complexity to the argument. Companies such as San Francisco-based Maven Research are scaling up and positioning themselves as intermediaries for sharing of expertise – namely, differentiated commoditized knowledge:

> Maven is the Global Knowledge Marketplace. We connect knowledge seekers with knowledgeable individuals for the rapid exchange of expertise, perspective, and opinion. Our Members ('Mavens') include individuals from all professional backgrounds, geographies, and functional roles. Mavens are paid to participate in short telephone consultations and custom surveys conducted by other professionals who seek to learn from their knowledge.[23]

So, here is a development that is further seeking to commoditize knowledge by connecting individuals within companies, academia, governments – in fact, anyone with insight – to people and organizations prepared to pay for that insight. It is early days for Maven but, in principle, this is a disruption to the knowledge-based consulting and research sectors that erodes differentiation. What are the implications for the future as more programmes such as Maven ramp up and begin to have a major impact, especially in fast-developing knowledge economies? Probably faster migration up the scale from novice to expert, and possibly further erosion of developing countries' lead in key areas as the channels for personally profitable dissemination of know-how override the economically significant retention and development of non-standard knowledge.

With the evident rebalancing of economic power from West to East – and, with it, associated expertise – it is clear that, to 2020 and beyond, the knowledge creators may be a significantly different set than they were in the twentieth century. Those, be they individuals, companies or countries, that rise above the mêlée will, in their own ways, have worked out not only how to create non-standard knowledge that others value, but they will have also been able to sustain this so that it continues to be differentiated. They may well have moved beyond the IP frameworks designed to protect ideas to operate in a truly open network of constant and fluid information exchange where IP is not the essential tradable asset. An increasing selection of commentators is predicting that commoditized knowledge may even slow down traditional innovation and the formal creation of IP. In January 2013 the *Economist* went as far as to argue that our global innovation activity may well have peaked.[24] The winners in 2020 may well be those that manage the delicate balance of new knowledge creation and global sharing in a way in which, even if there is less formal protection available for IP, the value of the key know-how is in itself more recognized.

The end of IP

> Following change in the music industry, technologies such as 3D printing are decoupling the production of content from the original creator and, in doing so, IP is becoming irrelevant.

Although the end of IP has been on the cards in some sectors for several years, it has now become a more widespread concern. Just as new business models have challenged copyright in the music and education industries, many see that global regulation will fail to keep up with digital collaborative platforms for innovation and production. With the growth of the creative commons and open source movements mentioned previously, core components of corporate and institutional knowledge will increasingly be shared without restriction and, in the eyes of some, result in weaker patents and the further decline of copyright. As one expert has asked

> If IT has reduced the marginal cost of IP to essentially zero, how will incentives for creative work change to recognize these two powerful economic shifts? Will the open innovation movement evolve to a point where know-how and capability rather than pure IP in the traditional sense is the currency? If so, how will organizations monetize collaboration?
>
> (Future Agenda workshop comment)

MIT professor Eric von Hippel, for one, has suggested that a major shift is taking place:[25]

> If Alice gives Bob a material object, Alice no longer has the object. But if Alice gives Bob an idea, Alice still retains the idea. Information – unlike matter and energy – is not conserved. That is why, when teenagers swap music files, they do not instinctively feel that it is theft. Consequently there is – in reality – no copyright in recorded music any more; every seventeen-year-old has twenty gigabytes of illegal MP3s on their hard drive, and film and video will soon go the same way.
>
> The whole concept of intellectual property is only stable when copying is difficult and legal penalties mean significant losses for those who would copy. Make copying easy and undetectable (as computers have for music) and the very idea of intellectual property starts to fade.
>
> But creativity doesn't fade with it. There is now an outpouring of music all over the whole world unmatched since that in late eighteenth century Vienna. This is happening because the same technology that is eliminating music copyright allows anyone to make music and to try to find an audience for it. Most musicians don't compose because they have rationally calculated that it is a good way to get rich, they compose because they are driven by an inner compulsion.
>
> So copyright is sublimating away under the twin fires of ease-of-copying and people's desire to give their creations away rather than have them remain obscure. But what of patents? Copying an iPod is not nearly as easy as copying tunes into it.

Emerging from the world of rapid prototyping, the much-discussed technology of 3D printing is now building up steady momentum. Like others, von Hippel makes a specific point about the role that this fast-evolving technology will have in ceding control of production to the masses:

> 3D printing will completely replace vast swathes of conventional manufacturing processes as it becomes less costly. And what will really drive the cost through the floor is 3D printers that print 3D printers. Conventional manufacturing produces goods in an arithmetic progression. But a self-copying 3D printer produces goods – and itself – in a geometric progression. And, no matter how slow it is, any geometric progression overtakes every arithmetic progression, no matter how fast, eventually.
>
> The self-copying 3D printer will be something cheap enough for individuals to own and be something they can copy for their friends. When everyone can print almost any device or machine the same will happen to the idea of patents as has happened to music copyright.
>
> Self-copying 3D printers will make it an order of magnitude cheaper again, and will finally kill the idea of intellectual property. But – just as with computers and music – they will also expand creativity, because people don't create things just to make money; the real reason they create things is to get noticed by other people with whom they want to have children.

3D printing has in the recent past been largely constrained to university demonstrators and the replication of battlefield spare parts for the military where the cost of production outweighs the burden of maintaining extensive supply chains. However with commercial applications now migrating from aerospace into consumer electronics and companies such as MakerBot offering reasonably priced desktop product, some see that a wider impact on the mainstream is not far away. Chris Anderson, former *Economist* correspondent, editor of *Wired* and author of *The Long Tail* and *Makers* sees that 2012 was the year of scaling of 3D printing: 'It's what happens when DIY meets Web 2.0.'[26] Others such as the *FT*'s Peter Marsh also see that it is going to be pivotal in the next industrial revolution. Alongside other emerging digital replication technologies, just as MP3 did in the past, 3D printing opens the door for easy and unrestricted copying and use of ideas that cannot readily be tracked for royalty or similar payment. As such the core IP itself becomes increasingly irrelevant. This raise questions about value protection but some see that we may well be entering a period where such competences as speed of delivery and global reach may trump innovation capacity.

Failed drugs

> With pressure on big pharma to deliver more effective R&D, the IP associated with drugs that fail in clinical trials is being more openly shared for others to find beneficial applications.

Of all industries convinced that IP will continue to play a major role in the future, it is the pharmaceutical sector that was most forthright in the view that patents will remain the currency of innovation in the years ahead: patents are both the core output of innovation and R&D in the pharmaceutical sector and a basis upon which many companies are valued. However, with the average drug development looking to be soon costing nearly $1bn, increasing focus has been turning to making more of the lost value associated with the drugs that don't make it all the way through to market, especially those failing in late clinical trials.

The traditional perspective has been that drugs are developed to target specific therapies and tested in clinical trials against these. Given the complexity and cost of clinical trials, if a drug fails to deliver the desired benefits or has unacceptable side effects, standard practice has been to shelve development. While there are notable examples such as Viagra where a drug has been found to have alternative benefits, in the main when a drug fails to deliver against target performance, even if it is a near miss, development is stopped and all associated IP is locked away – and accounted for largely as lost value.

Some of the companies we talked to have been seeking to unlock some of this lost value by looking at how they can share some of these near misses with others by releasing the associated IP to either academic researchers, non-governmental organizations (NGOs) or even other companies. By handing over a near miss failure to another organization, a different therapeutic target may be found where the developed drug could have some benefit and so all of the R&D investment is not lost. The challenge, however, is whether the associated IP is simply given away in the hope that society will benefit from any successes via an open platform, or whether some revenue-sharing deal structure can become the norm where the initial pharmaceutical company would gain some upside from any future success. This is a contentious strategic issue for many in the sector but one that, from an external affairs perspective as well as from a desire by scientists for all their work to have some good, can be seen as a possible route forward.

There will undoubtedly be many hurdles to cross, not just in terms of how IP is best shared and the business constraints and implications that are wrapped around it. However, a good number of people inside and outside the sector feel that something has to be done about all the 'wasted' effort on near misses. The biggest obstacles seem to be in changing perspectives about the core business model for big pharma and its reliance on protecting via patents both the value in the drugs that are successes and those that have received high R&D investment but are not launched. If an approach can be developed that works, then in the same way as some, such as GSK, have now shifted their strategies on changing the price vs. cost of drugs in emerging markets, we may see a fundamental move in how IP is used as the vehicle to enable wider societal value creation.

The recent signals are that this in now in motion and gaining momentum:

- In May 2012, the National Institutes of Health's National Center for Advancing Translational Sciences launched a collaborative programme with leading pharmaceutical companies to find new uses for drugs that had failed to work in the indications for which they were being developed.
- In November 2012, the United Kingdom's Medical Research Council announced £7 million in funding for up to 15 research projects that will seek to find new uses for 22 AstraZeneca compounds that had been studied but shelved for a variety of reasons.
- And later in the same month, Roche's Translational Clinical Research Center revealed a new collaboration with the Broad Institute at MIT on a multi-year effort to find new uses for development-stage compounds that had failed to meet the goals of clinical trials in the indications for which they were being developed or had been shelved for strategic reasons.[27] Under the agreement the Broad Institute will use its screening technologies to work through the Roche Repurposing Compound Collection, a collection of more than 300 compounds intended for a wide variety of indications. Karen Lackey, head of medicinal chemistry at Roche, shared the view that 'by compiling these compounds into an annotated set and collaborating with the Broad Institute to put to use its technologies and disease expertise, we hope to discover ways to repurpose these compounds that will be beneficial for patients'.[28]

These varied approaches are expected to reveal unique targets for new drug discovery projects. Novel disease associations may be found that will lead to new clinical evaluations in which the compounds may have a higher probability of success. More widely shared IP could be the route through which the overall system becomes more effective, albeit with a change in the balance of power from today.

Business model open innovation

> Increasing sector-to-sector transfer of know-how independent of IP enables successful approaches to be adopted and adapted without value transfer between parties.

The growth of the open innovation movement over the past few years has led to an increasing focus on IP as a tradable commodity. In the context of organizations seeking to source new product ideas and technologies from outside, IP licensing or sales have been the mechanism by which the value is transferred. Equally the same is true for companies that have sought to generate revenues through releasing some of their ideas into the outside world, either as a single transaction with a single entity or as a pooled patent agreement such as Bluetooth.

Today there is growing focus on business model innovation as a core source of value creation 'beyond the product' and many organizations have set up dedicated teams to explore new options. Sometimes the focus is around changing revenue structures through the introduction of more personalized and dynamic pricing. Sometimes, as in the cases of Zipcar and mobile payments, it is about creating different revenue models. Either way, companies are increasingly looking to use the option of changing business models to enable them to create more value from delivering the same customer outcome but in a more effective way that better matches emerging needs and improves the experience. The challenge here is that in the vast majority of cases there may be know-how wrapped around the new way of product or service delivery but sometimes there is no formal IP to speak of. Although business method patents have been growing steadily in the US for the past decade and, as Amazon and Google have shown, some leaders are using them to great effect, for the majority of organizations how they do what they do and their underlying business models have either been kept as internal know-how, or shared openly without protection.

As business model innovation takes a more significant proportion of the typical corporate innovation portfolio, we shift from IP to know-how; the way this is shared and valued will move us beyond traditional views of IP transfer. Take, for example, an airport looking for ways of speeding up key capacity bottlenecks such as security screening. Recognizing that there may be a more effective way of organizing and managing queues to both accelerate the process and make the experience less tedious for the passenger, one airport operator turned to a global theme park organization for inspiration. For busy, successful attractions, such as theme parks, effective queue management is a core capability and one where some companies excel in delivering a memorable 30 minutes rather than stressful lost time. If the airport learns from the theme park, how is the associated know-how transfer both valued and rewarded? Given that a new approach to queue management for the airport is a new way of doing an activity already existing in another sector, the gain for the airport does not impact the theme park organization. The know-how is simply adopted and adapted but with no transfer or reimbursement of value. As similar cross-sector exchanges occur more widely as an integral part of the momentum building up around business model innovation, counter to the earlier examples of Google and Amazon seeking to protect everything they can, many other see that companies will be less concerned about any potential loss of IP value: successful approaches will simply increasingly quickly migrate from sector to sector.

Corporate Lego

> With more free agents and outsourcing, more functions within organizations are interchangeable and easily rebuilt around new value-creating units.

Organizations have already started to be more permeable and flexible. Increasing use of consultants, freelancers and other temporary staff has blurred the boundary between employee and contractor in many large companies. In addition, the outsourcing of such functions as IT, HR, finance and other so called 'back-office' jobs, often to different countries, has saved money but also increased the complexity of the organizational framework. While many companies today still see themselves as entities with employees in control of a wide range of value-creating and support activities, by the end of this decade more and more organizations will be networks.

'While there will be a permanent core to the business, it will become increasingly small and more of a direction-setting and delivery-choreographing entity' (Future Agenda workshop comment). Businesses of 2020 will have fewer people managers in charge of cohorts of workers and more project managers ensuring that the right activities are undertaken in the most effective manner irrespective of whether the project team is internal or external to the organization. Some examples of this shift are being collated in the world's business schools and associated organizations such as the Management Lab in California. What they are pointing to is a world where organizations are becoming increasingly unbundled and recombined around different tasks and issues. The ability of companies to manage a community, rather than employees with a clear reporting line, presents a challenge that will be difficult for many to deal with. Some business leaders are already learning how to play Corporate Lego. In fast-changing markets and technology areas, more and more companies will have to learn to plug and unplug capability from inside and outside the organization on a project-by-project basis.

The initial drivers for change in organizations are generally cost and efficiency. Pressure on costs, reach and access forced many firms to outsource or offshore many of their commoditized functions. Conversely, to date, most companies have generally kept their value adding, differentiating capabilities 'within the tent' – R&D, marketing and design have all been viewed as the key capabilities and so have been protected, nurtured and kept close to the strategic heart of the firm. However, as companies and brands are becoming increasingly more differentiated by the world-class expertise they can access to create and deliver their new products and services, some organizations are now obliged to plug and unplug the leading-edge capabilities to meet ever more challenging local and global needs.

One expert highlighted: 'Web 2.0 is teaching organisations about the power of collective work product, leading to Enterprise 2.0, an organisational form with porous boundaries, shared responsibilities, greater transparency, and fewer mandatory rules and practices' (Future Agenda workshop comment). Increasingly, decentralized corporations are fast becoming a combination of amalgams of a series of independent capabilities that share common processes, systems and cultural norms but are structured as separate business units or profit centres with independent management and customers. Rapid changes in technologies, markets and strategic priorities are increasingly resulting in the separation and reformation of corporate structures using these independent units as organizational building blocks.

With outsourced back-office functions, organizations can manage risk to delivery and support through contractual service-level agreements (SLAs) that set out exactly what needs to be done and to what standard. In the world where innovation, strategy and the best ideas sit outside the organization and are developed by a group of individuals who are attracted by the challenge and opportunity for addressing them, the way companies manage corporate risk necessitates a fundamental shift from the past. Where business model discussions mean that know-how is freely shared outside the constraints and protection of IP regulations, trust between colleagues and project teams becomes ever more important. As one Future Agenda workshop participant saw it: 'The ability of corporations to serve their customers is largely driven by access to and the use of data. Data integration is a growing challenge. The future will see more agile corporations, more decentralisation and new IT infrastructures.'

At the same time, more organizations are seeing a future in which their brand can no longer be managed. Old and new economy companies increasingly discuss how the ability to 'broadcast' your brand to customers and the outside world is being replaced by participation in networks: Rather than brand managers, organizations are progressively having internal reputation managers – value-protecting professionals that mix traditional PR and investor relations with proactive participation in pivotal social networks. What is more, these individuals increasingly sit outside the corporate entity and work as consultants. Moreover, as highlighted by the foresight on differentiated commoditized knowledge, 'with the growth of the creative commons and open source movements, core components of corporate and institutional knowledge will increasingly be shared without restriction' (Future Agenda workshop comment). In a world where Corporate Lego is the biggest game in town and companies continue to seek to grow globally through fast and more effective innovation, some pivotal business challenges for the next decade are already quite clear.

As the boundaries of the corporate entity become increasingly blurred and porous, ideas and know-how more easily flow in and out of the organization. Seeking to try and control the associated IP flow and ownership as networks of small firms, large companies and individuals increasingly unplug and re-plug capabilities is already seen as a barrier to more effective working. As such many see the advance of Corporate Lego as a catalyst for both the end of IP in some sectors and wider collective ownership of IP, and hence future value capture, in others.

Projects worth working for

> In a world where innovation talent is global, fluid and attracted by the challenge and the reputation more than the paycheck, the winners will be the organizations that provide the most interesting projects.

As Swedish academics Kjell Nordstrom and Jonas Ridderstrale forecast over a decade ago in their book *Funky Business*,[29] there is a fast developing future where most workers and most companies become increasingly average except for a few 'people worth employing' who are increasingly attracted to the 'organisations worth working for'. While this may have meant more power to the top employers over the past few years, today many see that the best people want only to work on the best projects and not for organizations per se: they want to collaborate with other leading-edge talent addressing a series of interesting, big and meaty challenges. As such, long-term relations with any single institution are increasingly irrelevant and so standard contracts and timescales are replaced by project-focused commitments. Above individuals increasingly managing portfolio careers, other core implications are less clear: organizational knowledge and more temporary groups where IP creation and transfer are more fluid and flexible.

Only around half the 120,000 people working at Microsoft's headquarters in Seattle are employees: the rest are freelancers, consultants or vendors there on a project-by-project basis. Indeed, over 30 per cent of the US population are already 'free agents' working either independently or as subcontractors. Within ten years, around half of the Western workforce is expected to be self-employed, increasingly working on a project-by-project basis. This fundamental change is providing a plethora of experts and consultants available as subcontracted resources to be pulled in and out of firms as needs demand. At the same time, how we work is changing. The project team members of tomorrow are increasingly people who have grown up in the connected world. As many of these 'digital natives' go mobile and become 'digital nomads', they will be looking to create value wherever, whenever, using whatever devices they like: in the 'always connected' world this becomes an accepted way of life for those who can contribute the most.

As such 'the heart of value creation for organisations will increasingly shift outside the traditional corporate boundaries to embrace people more interested in portfolio careers than company progression' (Future Agenda workshop comment). With organizational boundaries increasingly porous and less relevant, this places greater challenges for companies across the board, especially in managing risk. As globalization finally starts to make the innovation world a flatter one, connectivity to the key sources of innovation – anytime, anywhere, anyhow and

Future of innovation and intellectual property   49

any-who – is driving new perspectives about accessing and recruiting the leading talent. This presents both opportunities and challenges.

With rising innovation spending should companies build more internal innovation capabilities or should they look to better exploit others' investments? In particular, the shift from technology transfer to know-how transfer will raise key questions such as how will companies manage and value knowledge transfer as the limitations of IP systems become apparent? As firms release their proprietary hold on knowledge, how will sharing it be monetized? So, how should companies balance the need for gaining prowess in shifting to the new world of knowledge transfer ahead of their peers?

Most companies see that, to be the exemplar innovation company they aspire to be, they will need to manage globally dispersed networks of talent drawn from a plethora of individuals and companies, and manage these on a project-by-project basis. Attracting internal and external innovation talent is already recognized as a top priority for many US organizations struggling to find the right resource; when you fold in the future role of India and China, the global marketplace for the leading talent is becoming flatter: in 2012 outsourced R&D in India accounted for $20bn and programmes involving research is forecast to rise from 10 per cent today to 30 per cent by 2020; in China, the future shift is even greater. In 2012 China passed the US in new patent applications.[30] Again some can question the quality vs. quantity angle, but a growing trend is evident. By 2015 legacy cost issues will be irrelevant and by 2020 as much research will be taking place in China as in the US – the Chinese domestic market is so great that China is increasingly setting global standards[31] especially as, for example, Chinese companies such as Huawei become more influential in the international telecoms market.

These are some of catalysts for a shift towards truly 'flat world' innovation. The best future talent will be free to choose what projects they work on, for which companies they like. As free agents become the norm, the innovation expertise that companies need to bring into the fold will reside in a more fluid market. If you are going to attract the leading talent are you going to access global talent locally or are you going to rely on the network effect bringing the talent to you? And, in such context, how will you engage with the best on a basis of reputation?

Whichever approach organizations take to providing the most compelling projects and attracting the best talent to work on them, some increasingly see the need for a shift in expectations around the associated IP ownership. As we move from employees working under contracts to collective temporary teams of individuals with no legal affiliation other than to themselves, how we seek to capture, share and, if relevant, protect concepts will be significantly challenged.

Big collaboration

> Addressing future major challenges relies on deeper and wider collaboration between organizations with no lead company and IP value creation replaced by new recognition.

Many companies now see that over the next few decades we are facing a period of systemic stress: more people on the planet, increasingly constrained resources and 'a debt-ridden West with more power for the Rest' are all leading us to a world where we face challenges never before seen on the planet. Whether we are talking about insufficient food to feed an increasingly high-calorie intake, meat-eating population; the slow uptake of clean energy technologies that means we are more likely to need to adapt to climate change than mitigate it; a sick-care system in the West that cannot really be afforded; or not enough fresh water to meet demand from a growing and ever more economically active global population, we are having to consider big problems. To date governments have largely proven unable to regulate to avoid crisis and in the one example where global agreement occurred, that of ozone depletion, it took decades to bring all parties on board. As many view cities and companies taking over from governments in tackling the big challenges for the planet, some are also seeing that old-fashioned notions of ownership of solutions and the associated IP will have to be replaced by more open collaborative protocols and agreements.

The challenges outlined above are way beyond the capability of one industry or country, let alone one company, to address. They are highly complex, inter-related issues that all require a combination of proactive regulation, accelerated technology development, mass consumer behaviour change, financial subsidy and open access to solutions. They require big collaboration on a scale not yet experienced and success will necessitate a new way of cross-sector working that make previous major projects such as putting a man on the moon and mapping the human genome seem like small fry. These challenges are clear and present and have to be addressed.

An increasing proportion of those in major energy, food, healthcare and water companies, governments and NGOs who are already working on these issues increasingly recognize that IP cannot be a barrier. Ownership of the ideas that make a difference at a planetary level cannot be given to those individuals and organizations that may come up with the solutions. If tens or maybe hundreds of companies and research organizations are needed to collaborate on these types of challenge then the notion of IP as a driver of value attribution and creation has to be put to one side.

Evidently, this has not been done before, but given the impending and dramatic needs, many see that a new way of working together has to be found. Whether this comes from a corporate social responsibility agenda or a wider CEO leadership initiative is yet to become clear. But when it does occur, it may completely change the way we see mass-scale innovation. A new modus operandi could be created where big collaboration sets a different set of rules with new means of finance, new mechanisms of reward and new principle of legacy ownership. Whatever, it is clear that with the implicit sharing and co-creation of know-how that has to be involved, a model more like creative commons or open source will have to be adopted. For big collaboration to deliver the goods against the significant challenges that are now on the table, IP cannot be a barrier to mass cooperation or global roll out of solutions.

Conclusion

Each of these seven potential drivers of change could evidently individually have significant impact on the innovation landscape. Today, looking forward we do not know which ones will build momentum and which will fall by the wayside. However we do know that shifts such as those outlined above could dramatically challenge existing assumptions on IP and innovation. While several are arguably natural extensions of what some see already in momentum, others are more disruptive changes that may occur from left field.

As discussed previously, few changes are certain and can be fully predicated, but potential shifts can be anticipated. The individuals and companies that shared their perspectives clearly believe in the possibility of some of these seven changes. Right now few would place specific percentages or odds on them individually having widespread impact but many would be confident of some change.

From a personal perspective, I can see major shifts now building momentum across the innovation arena that will clearly grow over the next decade. The rise of business model innovation, the need to extract more value out of corporate R&D activities and the war for talent that results in more flexible working practices will all mean that the barriers created by traditional defensive IP policies will have to be changed. The direction is clear but the level of immediate change in not. Whether they are completely removed to create a fully open sharing of knowledge and ideas as advocated by some or are adapted to enable more fluid transfer of innovation is a point of debate for many in and around the innovation and IP arenas.

The big spenders in R&D will certainly want to try and protect their investments, as they have done in the past. However, for many new routes to value creation that lead to more proactive IP polices may well come into force: if you look at the companies that have made the most out of their innovation resources in terms of relative value creation rather than just those that have invested the most, you quite clearly see companies such as Samsung, VW and Reckitt Benckiser delivering more overall value creation that the like of Sony, GM and P&G. Innovation success today is increasingly less about who develops and owns a core product or technology and more about who is best at exploiting it: mandates such as 'steal with pride' are not unheard of in the corporate culture of fast-growing multinationals. As mentioned earlier, innovation is all about the 'successful exploitation of new ideas' and with more fluid movement of ideas and talent across the world, it is increasingly about gaining access to the right innovation from wherever it may be and whoever may have come up with it in the first place. As innovation as the core enabler of sustained organic growth continues to rise up the corporate agenda, many organizations may start to decouple the traditional grouping of R&D, invention and IP and seek to create new more flexible and more agile mechanisms for value creation.

These shifts may well mean that recorded IP and any associated value to the firm migrates from R&D and finance into the hands of strategy and business development. IP may cease to have explicit value for a company but become an implicit means of making the right things happen. We will undoubtedly see the emergence of new challenger companies that seek to use IP in a stronger manner and new way in the next decade – just as Amazon and Google have done in the last. Equally many of the systems and protocols already in place will evolve. For me, seeing on a daily basis the real need for us to deal with the major challenges across the health, food, energy and water arenas, I think that the big collaboration shift will force us to proactively come up with new approaches to reward and stimulate innovation. The days when scientists and chemists were financially rewarded on the number of patents they filed each year are clearly long gone in many organizations. The era of open innovation has changed the mindset for many towards growth and overall value creation for the whole company being the priority. Going forward, in a world of open business model innovation and Corporate Lego, if it is to have a significant role, perhaps IP is no longer going to be seen as an asset to be created, recorded and sold or licensed but rather may become a pivotal enabler of collaboration and wider value creation. The challenge however may be whether the global IP system can evolve quick enough to keep pace not only with the changes already taking place within the innovation arena, but also pre-empt those on the horizon. Informed, proactive but balanced anticipation will be key.

Notes

1. Taleb, N.N. (2007) *The Black Swan: The Impact of the Highly Improbable*, New York: Allen Lane.
2. Fitzsimmons, C. and Jones, T. (2002) *Managing Intellectual Property*, London: Capstone.
3. Coates, D. (2012) 'Rolls Royce and ARM – technology partnerships for growth', in Jones, T., McCormick, D. and Dewing, C. (eds) *Growth Champions: The Battle for Sustained Innovation Leadership*, London: John Wiley & Sons.
4. Chesbrough, H.W. and Teece, D.J. (2002) 'When is virtual virtuous?', *Harvard Business Review*, August [online] available: http://hbr.org/2002/08/when-is-virtual-virtuous/ar/1 (6 February 2013).
5. Chesbrough, H.W. (2003) *Open Innovation: The New Imperative for Creating and Profiting from Technology*, Boston: Harvard Business Review Press.
6. Huston, L. and Sakkab, N. (2006) 'Connect and develop: inside Procter & Gamble's new model for innovation', *Harvard Business Review*, vol. 84, March [online] available: http://hbr.org/2006/03/connect-and-develop-inside-procter-gambles-new-model-for-innovation/ar/1 (6 February 2013).
7. Wikipedia (2013) 'Open source' [online] available: http://en.wikipedia.org/wiki/Open_source (6 February 2013).
8. The *Economist* (2012) 'Prometheus unsound: America's Supreme Court wallops the biotech industry', The *Economist*, 4 March [online] available: http://www.economist.com/node/21551087 (6 February 2013).
9. Ovans, A. (2000) 'Can you patent your business model? A conversation with Q. Todd Dickinson', *Harvard Business Review*, July [online] available: http://hbr.org/2000/07/can-you-patent-your-business-model/ar/1 (6 February 2013).
10. Wikipedia (2013) 'Business method patent' [online] available: http://en.wikipedia.org/wiki/Business_method_patent (6 February 2013).
11. Johnston, S. (2012) 'Amazon and Google – expertly using data to get ever closer to customers', in Jones, T., McCormick, D. and Dewing, C. (eds) *Growth Champions: The Battle for Sustained Innovation Leadership*, London: John Wiley & Sons.

12 Http://www.economist.com/node/18988624 (27 June 2013).
13 Comscore Data Mine (2011) [online] available: http://www.comscoredatamine.com/2011/06/google-reaches-1-billion-global-visitors/ (6 February 2013).
14 Http://www.google.co.uk/about/ (27 June 2013).
15 Merrill, D. (2007) *Innovation at Google*, YouTube, 2 August [online] available: http://www.youtube.com/watch?v=2GtgSkmDnbQ (6 February 2013).
16 Sims, P. (2011) 'The Montessori Mafia', *Wall Street Journal*, 5 April [online] available: http://blogs.wsj.com/ideas-market/2011/04/05/the-montessori-mafia/ (6 February 2013).
17 Manyika, J. (2008) 'Google's view on the future of business: an interview with CEO Eric Schmidt', *McKinsey Quarterly*, September [online] available: https://www.mckinseyquarterly.com/Googles_view_on_the_future_of_business_An_interview_with_CEO_Eric_Schmidt_2229?pagenum=1 (6 February 2013).
18 Jones, T. and Dewing, C. (2010) *Future Agenda – The World in 2020*, Oxford: Infinite Ideas.
19 Friedman, T.L. (2005) *The World is Flat: A Brief History of the Twenty-First Century*, New York: Farrar, Straus and Giroux.
20 Friedman, T.L. (2008) *Hot, Flat, and Crowded: Why We Need a Green Revolution – and How It Can Renew America*, New York: Farrar, Straus and Giroux.
21 Christensen, C.M. (1997) *The Innovator's Dilemma: When New Technologies Cause Great Firms to Fail*, Boston: Harvard Business Review Press.
22 Jones, T. and Dewing, C. (eds) (2009) *Future Agenda: Initial Perspectives*, London: Vodafone Group plc.
23 Http://www.maven.co/maven-research (27 June 2013).
24 The *Economist* (2013) 'Has the ideas machine broken down?' The *Economist*, 12 January [online] available: http://www.economist.com/news/briefing/21569381-idea-innovation-and-new-technology-have-stopped-driving-growth-getting-increasing (6 February 2013).
25 Von Hippel, E. (2007) 'Intellectual property is dead' [online] available: http://reprap.org/wiki/EndOfIntellectualProperty (6 February 2013).
26 Anderson, C. (2012) *Makers: The New Industrial Revolution*, New York: Crown Business.
27 McBride, R. (2012) 'Roche, Broad band together to bring failed drugs back from the dead' [online] available: http://www.fiercebiotech.com/story/roche-broad-band-together-bring-failed-drugs-back-dead/2012-11-28 (6 February 2013).
28 Ibid.
29 Nordstrom, K.A. and Ridderstrale, J. (1998) *Funky Business: Talent Makes Capital Dance*, New York: Bookhouse Publishing.
30 The *Economist* (2012) 'Patent applications', The *Economist*, 15 December [online] available: http://www.economist.com/news/economic-and-financial-indicators/21568402-patent-applications?fsrc=scn/tw_ec/patent_applications (6 February 2013).
31 Ibid.

3 Creating value in health care through social innovation

Neil Reeder

Introduction

Social innovations are new ideas, institutions or ways of working to meet social needs, by harnessing and strengthening relationships between people. Social innovations tap into the many unused possibilities when people work or talk or play together.

The importance of social relationships

Many would downplay the ability of social innovation to promote health. As one practitioner has put it: 'The reality is that the National Health Service (NHS) is "medicalised" and the greatest influence in service provision comes from the clinicians, whose training is based upon establishing a diagnosis and prescribing appropriate remedies, which in most cases is medications.'[1]

Yet a meta-analysis of the impact on health of social relationships has found that having high instead of low levels of social interaction over a seven-year time period decreases the risk of dying by some 50 per cent – an effect equivalent to giving up smoking, and worse than excessive alcohol consumption.[2] Furthermore, analysis suggests close links between a person's decision to stay a smoker and the choices of family and friends – one study estimates that if a spouse drops smoking, it decreases their partner's chances of smoking by 67 per cent, while if a friend ceases smoking, this decreases the odds by 36 per cent.[3]

Deep problems to overcome

A lack of social relationships is a prominent feature of many countries. In the UK, around 5 per cent feel 'completely lonely' in their lives[4] and approximately 20 per cent have some level of psychological distress.[5] In the USA, a study of adults aged over 60 found that more than 40 per cent felt lonely, even though only 18 per cent lived alone.[6] In China, a study of adults over 60 living alone in Shanghai found over 30 per cent of participants reporting symptoms of a mild or above mild level of depression.[7]

A propensity for harmful behaviour is also of grave concern. The level of regular smokers in the UK is around 20 per cent of adults, even though one in two of them are likely to be killed by their habit.[8] Some 19 per cent of adults are smokers in the USA,[9] and the figure rises to 30 per cent in China.[10]

So the potential for major improvement is there, which raises the fundamental question – how can such improvement be grasped through use of social innovation?

Social innovation initiatives to improve health

Many answers have been tried – and many are needed. Some of the innovation is about changing the ways that people interact with health care services. This includes taking the chances for identifying root problems rather than symptoms, and so achieving deeper insights from the one-to-one discussions that take place. One approach trialled in the UK is changing the design of GPs' offices to include space for sofas, to improve the chances that the patient will relax and speak to the GP as a confidant.[11]

Some of this is about using support structures outside formal organisations. Homeshare International, for example, is a scheme running in Australia, Europe and the USA matching students in need of accommodation with older people who are living alone and can benefit from both company and help with household tasks.

It is also about making the most of professional resources. For instance, 'Best Doctors' is a programme active in a number of western countries. A patient explains their case to a nurse; records and tests are collected; and then a specialist chosen by peers as a 'best doctor' then provides a second opinion on diagnosis and recommended course of action.

Some of this is about recognising that oblique solutions to the problem are available from what can be very untraditional health care settings. The Comedy School in the London Borough of Camden, for example, works with schools, mental health organisations and the police. By learning how to stand up in front of strangers and make them laugh, participants obtain a greater ability to express themselves, engage with peers and integrate into society.

Another oblique route is taken by Pawprints, a scheme in Boston Children's Hospital, USA. Its aim is to support those feeling somewhat cut off from the outside world. In this scheme, a volunteer with a trained therapy dog goes in to visit children in hospital wards, and for five to ten minutes, a child can pet, play with or simply watch the dog.

Facilitators of value

Social innovation can take place within any of the four socio-economic sectors of society – whether public sector, private sector (which can potentially include social entrepreneurs or social enterprises), third sector (charities and non-profit organisations) or households and individuals.

From the examples cited above it can be seen that there are at least three different possibilities for creating value through social innovation:

- Organisations in the field of health care using innovation to improve health outcomes. For example, a public hospital may build up a circle of volunteers to support those patients who lack close friends and family at their time of need.
- Organisations in the field of health care using innovation to delivering outcomes such as education or empowerment that are beneficial, but not related to health. For instance, a GP surgery may decide to take on and train a young unemployed person to become a clerical worker through an apprenticeship scheme.
- Organisations and individuals not directly involved in health care who promote health benefits through activities to strengthen social ties and personal capabilities. For example, a swimming pool might introduce a regular women-only session, to assist those who are self-conscious or have religious beliefs about what they should wear when in the presence of men.

The rest of this chapter considers: examples of social innovation as applied to patients for differing types of health need; the process of growing such social innovations; the wider forms of value such innovations can achieve; the recipients of value; conflicts in value; and indications of the future for social innovation for health care.

Social innovation for differing levels of health need

Social innovations can achieve major improvements in health at very different stages of health (see Figure 3.1).

Prevention

Traditional forms of health care have often been poor at prevention. A 2008 survey in England on whether respondents had been given advice on public health issues by their GP found that 44 per cent were failing to get advice on exercise, 43 per cent lacked advice on diet, 27 per cent lacked advice on smoking and 23 per cent lacked advice on alcohol consumption.[12] Unfortunately, this appears to be a common shortfall and studies of German, UK and US provision of advice on prevention find Germany lagging behind on the agenda.[13]

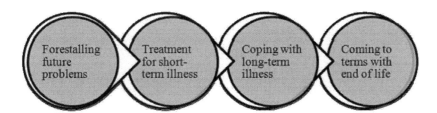

Figure 3.1 Different stages of health.

One explanation for these figures is that GPs feel uncomfortable in giving such advice. Research suggests that many GPs feel they lack the skills needed to deliver effective health promotion, or else are unconvinced that their efforts to advise patients on lifestyle issues will be effective in changing behaviour.[14] Perhaps this is not surprising given that for many doctors, medicine uses a 'reductionist' approach that 'speaks the language of deficit and illness'.[15]

Such findings have increased the urgency to understand the connections and drivers of change between social relationships and behaviour. For those connections are often strong – one study of what makes British women aged 16 to 19 take exercise regularly found that the unquestioned most enjoyable aspect was the social element – 'having a laugh' or 'being with friends' whether the activity was martial arts, hockey or walking.[16]

Recognising patients' wider interests

Many social innovations have harnessed the appeal of sport and connectedness to promote physical health and wider benefits. These range from the Disabled Golf Society, which facilitates links for disabled people who wish to play golf, through to the 'Homeless World Cup'. This latter organisation, which has links to more than 70 countries, supports homeless people (a group with often very poor health outcomes) to join the 'Team of Hope' and to train and play football – potentially reaching tournaments – while also gaining access to advice on issues from employment to education.

Other innovations pick up on the influence that religious leaders can have among members of their faith. For example, the Maslaha website resource for Muslims includes short videos from recognised religious authorities on the extent to which strict fasting is (not) required for those with diabetes problems during Ramadan.[17]

Action within communities

Local authorities have often taken the lead in promoting support through channels that are less formal and so more comfortable for members of the public. FLAG is a new kind of health information and advice service in Stockport, UK and is operated in collaboration with a range of voluntary and user-led organisations.[18]

Local authorities can also set the tone for facilitating relationships through planning and design – studies show that even a simple factor such as the level of traffic in a street can influence the average numbers of residents' friends and acquaintances in the area by a factor of two or three.[19]

Other social innovations have linked a sense of empowerment to better outcomes. One programme in rural areas of Japan actively sought to promote a sense of assertiveness and empowerment, in order to reduce high levels of suicides.[20]

Improved access to knowledge

Online communications are increasingly important in our lives. Advances in technology have brought information (if not always robust knowledge) much more within reach for those with curiosity on health issues. The most obvious source of change is through instant internet access to medical advice, but much more tailored information is available too, through such means as '23 and me'[21] that offers a genome sampling service. Nor is advice limited to agendas of physical health – the social enterprise 'Mindapples' specialises in 'care for the mind'.[22]

Short-term illness and injury

The point where a short-term illness or injury has occurred would appear to be one where social relationships should play only a negligible role in health care – but this is not, and indeed should not, necessarily be the case.

One social innovation introduced in Addenbrooke's Hospital in Cambridge in conjunction with Contact a Family is a 'hospital passport' for parents of disabled children, who tend to be recurrent users of health services.[23] The passports quickly provide key information on the child's medical condition, issues to bear in mind (such as sleeping patterns), and their preferences (such as disliked items of food).

Knowledge is a key theme too in relation to dosages of medicines. One in three older adults in England are unable to understand basic usage instructions on a medicine label;[24] and the effects of poor health literacy alone increase the risk of dying prematurely by around a quarter.

One promising social innovation to address the issue is through pamphlets ('photo-novelas') that tell a story with easy-to-read text alongside photographs – the authenticity of the message is often enhanced by having them written and designed in part by learners themselves.[25] A further route is to integrate adult learning with health literacy. The Community Health and Learning Foundation in the UK uses health issues to engage individuals on literacy skills, in settings ranging from probation hostels to homes for the homeless.

Knowledge and peer support are central to a new approach to mental health illness being trialled in the London Borough of Lambeth. This involves prompt discharge from hospital, with enhanced levels of community support and an easy route back in to see a consultant if the condition deteriorates. Lambeth is putting in place a range of 'low and medium level services' in the community, from a personalised 'navigator' service through to peer support groups, exercise groups and a network of mutual support provided through timebanks.[26]

Long-term illness

Empathy between medical staff and the patient and their family members is a vital element of good care in cases of long-term illness. One initiative aimed at promoting this link has been introduced in Vanderbilt Children's Hospital in Tennessee, USA. The hospital gives medical students the opportunity to stay for a period of time in the homes of family members dealing with an extended illness or episode of care.[27]

For those affected by extended illness, an ability to tap into support from those outside the medical sector becomes even more important. Various options have been successfully explored to help people cope with long-term illnesses, from peer networks, to supportive friends and community networks. Some of these options are about directly examining health requirements. An increasing variety of telemetry options are available – from pill dispensers checking if the right number of daily doses have been taken, to bed sensors monitoring the time spent out of bed during the night. Yet no matter how sophisticated the sensor, an essential ingredient is that the device has connections to care centres and/or families and friends, so that patients can maintain independence, while issues can be dealt with promptly and effectively without putting undue strain on carers.

Peer learning is central to more than a hundred 'Re-think Mental Illness' user groups in England, which have as their aim 'To work together to help everyone affected by severe mental illness recover a better quality of life'. Their sessions put an emphasis on sympathy, non-judgemental listening and depth of understanding.

Some options relate more to generalist support. RSM, for example, is a charity based in East Sussex. A charity given funding from the local council, it provides its members with drivers, handymen and classes in activities such as arts, crafts and computing. It also delivers bereavement counselling and guidance on issues ranging from benefits form-filling to instructions for medicines.

Some options provide support in an indirect way. Survivors' Poetry was created in 1991 in the UK, and uses poetry workshops, readings, performances, music and visual arts as ways to promote wellbeing among those who have 'survived' such issues as psychiatric illness, drug addiction, sexual abuse and mood-altering medication.

And some options involve radically shifting whole sets of relationships. San Patrignano is a drug rehabilitation community run and managed by 2,000 rehabilitating heroin addicts in the Emilia Romagna region of Italy. It has a hospital; an animal shelter where abandoned dogs are cared for and trained to be therapy and service pets; and a multitude of revenue-raising employment facilities, from furniture building to wine making, from web design to cheese production.[28]

End of life

Surveys suggest that, in Britain, more than six out of ten (63 per cent) would prefer to die at home with their family, with almost a further three out of ten (29 per cent) highlighting a preference for a hospice. While those figures shift as people age (for those over 75 years old, the preferences are 45 per cent for home and 41 per cent for hospice) it is clear that they are wholly out-of-kilter with the actual occurrence (53 per cent in hospital, 5 per cent in hospices and 21 per cent at home).[29] By contrast, it is estimated that in the USA, some 45 per cent of deaths were under the auspices of a hospice programme.[30]

Hospice, or palliative care, is the desire to make the experience of death a more dignified and spiritual one than is generally possible in a hospital. This represents an important social innovation and the proportion of patients dying in hospital in Britain has fallen in recent years. Partly this trend has been assisted by better

60 *Neil Reeder*

sources of advice on coping with the process of dying, such as through the 'Natural Death Handbook'.[31]

One further way to help patients 'make peace with death' is through video technology. A 2010 survey by Remember a Charity indicated that nearly two-thirds of people (63 per cent) in Britain would like to create a video to explain their formal will to family and close friends, provide messages of advice and say goodbyes.

Creating and growing value from social innovation

Social innovation can be introduced as a separate entity (with one or more social entrepreneurs in charge); designed and developed by one or more within an organisation ('intrapreneurship'); or designed and developed as part of a wider initiative within an organisation. Either way, research has outlined that each social innovation undergoes similar stages in terms of moving from a recognition that something should be done (stage 1) through to the systemic change (stage 6) that hallmarks substantive and important innovations (Figure 3.2).

Problems to overcome

Successful movement along the spiral is not easy. It is one thing to come up with a good idea. Developing that into a pilot then usually takes much time and effort – often achieved alongside 'the normal day job', with budgets kept low by use of volunteers and one-off donations of goods and services. Further progression is even tougher and requires a coalition of individuals and institutions willing to fulfil various roles in supplying and paying for the social innovation.

One-way progress along the spiral is far from guaranteed. My experience as an adviser at the Young Foundation has showed me that, in practice, growing a

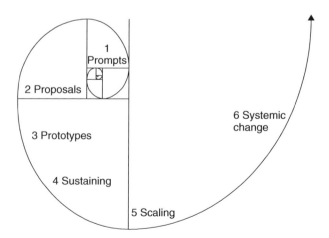

Figure 3.2 Stages of social innovation.

Source: Murray, R. et al. (2010) *The Open Book of Social Innovation*, London: Young Foundation.

social innovation can be like a game of snakes and ladders, with disappointments setting the team back or rare moments of serendipity moving the team swiftly forward. That is why resilience is so often quoted as a key determinant of success in entrepreneurs.[32]

One of the major sources of uncertainty will often be finding a good answer to the question: where is the money going to come from to pay for the social innovation? John Kotter has pointed out that a 'burning platform' is often a timely moment for decision-makers to reflect on what has gone wrong and begin to work out how to do better,[33] but social innovations do not always form at such timely moments.

As Bunt and Leadbeater (2012)[34] put it in their analysis of the 'art' of decommissioning in public services: 'Producers, consumers and politicians all have powerful reasons to want to protect patterns of provision with which they are familiar, rather than risk investing in less well established alternatives.' Without compelling business cases – and equally compelling narratives – social innovations generally fail to match their potential.

One example of the barriers that can be faced is the 'Ambulatory ICU' approach prototyped in the USA. The programme, jointly designed by a collaboration of doctors, nurses, managers and systems engineers, focuses on the 10 per cent of employees most likely to need intensive care in the future. Implementation has, however, been slow – not least because of hostility from those doctors and organisations that would lose substantial revenues if the approach succeeds.[35]

And, as noted earlier in the Introduction to this chapter, the 'clinic-based' perspective on health care is hard to shift. For example the UK government's 2011 innovation paper *Health and Wealth*[36] makes no references to social innovation, and where communities are mentioned, all references are to 'scientific' or 'business' communities, community pharmacies or data on communities.

Strengthening the supply of innovation

Having a vision and supportive economic case is only a start. It is important to be able to implement the vision – or implement even better visions if they are recognised along the way. A hallmark of good social innovators is listening closely to the customer, and adapting approaches if that produces a better outcome. As Samuel Beckett put it: 'Try again. Fail again. Fail better.'[37]

The 'Bell-Mason' framework lists a number of familiar key success factors[38] – including CEO, team and board; supply chains; infrastructure; marketing and sales; networks; cash; and products, services and communities of benefit. All these are clearly vital aspects to have under control in order to improve the chances of successful growth.

There is, however, another agenda that is sometimes overlooked, which considers the internal dynamics of the CEO, team and board. That agenda is of coping with uncertainty; a useful typology of skills comes from Ashridge research, which identifies seven core capabilities (Figure 3.3)[39]

Successful growth requires access to people who can put messages across simply and forcefully; people who can focus on getting the details right; people

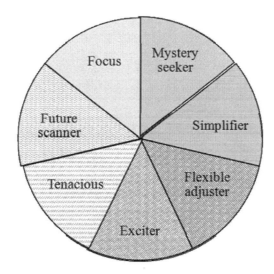

Figure 3.3 Seven core capabilities in coping with uncertainty.

who worry about things that 'don't seem right' and uncover unexpected results; people who can push for new solutions when conditions change; people who can highlight issues that may impact hugely without due attention; people who do not just give up easily, or at all; people who can inspire.

Willingness to invest and pay for services

No matter how strong the team, to be successful a social innovation requires organisations or individuals to 'put their money where their mouth is'. Without some source of resources, innovation cannot succeed.

Furthermore, resources can be paid over with very different expectations from the payer as to what will be received in return. Key questions to consider are:

- Are the resources to support capacity and capability and the development of the innovation, or are they about receiving a service?
- Are the resources paid on a philanthropic basis, or is some form of return expected?
- Are the resources paid to an 'intrapreneur' or to an external party?

Social innovations can take very different paths depending on the answers to such questions, with a selection of routes outlined in Figure 3.4.

Although many variants are possible, sooner or later the key issue is finding someone or some organisation to provide the resources required for the innovation to be put into practice. In doing so, close attention is required to the specifics of who plays what role in supporting health.

Creating value in health care through social innovation 63

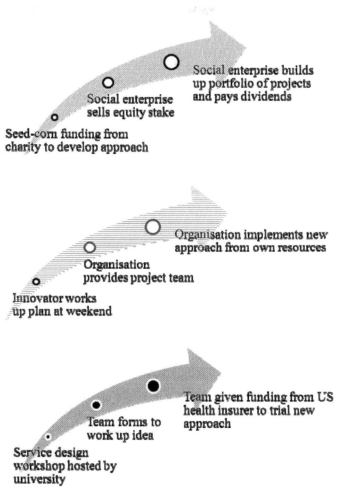

Figure 3.4 Possible pathways to success.

The USA has traditionally had monetary resources flowing from 'payers' to 'finance intermediaries' to 'providers' (hospitals, doctors and pharmacies) to 'producers' of health care (pharmaceutical companies, diagnosis machine makers, etc.). Insurance is a cornerstone of the system.[40] By contrast, the UK has a tightly integrated funding and delivery system for public health care, with a firm commitment to health care being free at the point of delivery (except for medicines prescribed by GPs). That leads to very different market environments for innovators; schemes based on tweaking insurance premiums in line with given behaviours[41] have little traction in the UK.

It is also important to pay close attention to the terms and conditions of the various sources of finances that a social innovator may call upon. Research and development subsidies, grants, debt and equity all have different pluses and minuses at different stages.[42]

Supportive culture

Advice and mutual support from peers, intermediary organisations and networkers can often be highly valuable in enabling social innovations to grow and develop. One approach taken in the past in England has been the use of health care 'collaboratives' – open groups with an interest in a topic such as renal care. The group's members are able to learn in detail about a well-honed approach to improvement, share benchmarking data in confidence, debate topics on a discussion board and identify hints and tips for change management.[43]

Such sources of knowledge – tested, debated and refined – are highly useful to designing and implementing social innovation. Delivery is often sensitive to the social context, for example:

- Rural versus urban – rural populations in poor countries can have huge difficulty in accessing medical advice. Medic Mobile in India runs clinics on the principle that patients should not have to travel to clinics, rather the clinic should come to their village.[44]
- Demographics – the Aconchego Program in Portugal draws strength from the existence of two different age groups with different requirements. Older people provide housing to university students in their homes, while students help older people to overcome loneliness and isolation.[45]

Social innovation is crucial in understanding how to use 'differences' as opportunities to make improvements to society. For example, the British sociologist and activist Lord Young of Dartington, one of the most successful social entrepreneurs of all time, emphasised speaking directly to those in need in generating his ideas that changed education (with the Open University) and health care (with advice through telephones – a forerunner of NHS Direct).[46]

Wider value

Like any other major employer and purchaser of goods and services, health services can do much to promote a social and environmentally sustainable society. A mental health service may decide to employ people with mental health problems to help deliver the service; a GP surgery may support a 'good neighbour' volunteer scheme – these have benefits above and beyond health.

Health services have, however, often given such wider action a low priority. Analysis of mission statements for Canadian hospitals found that 'concern for society' was given little prominence, and where it did appear the connection was to 'benefactors', rather than 'source of inspiration' or business definition.[47] Similarly, the 2008 guidance notes on world-class commissioning for the UK NHS[48] make reference only to health outcomes.

Creating value in health care through social innovation 65

There have, however, been some signs of change. The state of British Columbia in Canada has achieved a 'carbon neutral' public sector through action on buildings, transport, utilities and carbon offsets.[49] In the UK, the NHS has introduced a Carbon Reduction Strategy aiming to reduce carbon footprints by 10 per cent between 2007 and 2015,[50] and in turn that has facilitated a broader perspective, including a study producing toolkits to measure achievement of 'social value'.[51] Value is potentially obtained in one or more of seven categories:

- income (for example, nurses working in deprived areas may be able to give guidance to households on benefit payments that they may be eligible for);
- employment (such as signposting to charities that can assist with training);
- health (for instance, a focus on reducing excessive alcohol consumption);
- education (such as adult literacy/health literacy classes);
- housing (such as advising older people on retaining independent living);
- environment (for instance, reducing the number of unnecessary trips);
- crime (such as Accident and Emergency services sharing data with police).

Heartland Health in Missouri, USA, outlines how that broader perspective can be implemented in practice. Its initiatives include a partnership arrangement that educates parents about the importance of reading to children; a programme to educate children about being active citizens; and a dental clinic offering preventative and restorative care, with a specialist tasked to support young people with behavioural issues.[52]

One complex aspect of wider social value is the extent to which it is preferable that local employment is increased. Such an approach certainly reduces pollution, carbon emissions and time taken to travel. However, the impact on jobs is often overestimated, unless the area in question is one where there is social deprivation and a lack of job opportunities. This is because a protectionist approach to local jobs in local areas runs into problems when other areas behave in similar ways – buying fewer goods and services from elsewhere, and so taking jobs away in return. The net effect is that any gains tend to cancel each other out.[53]

Legislation for wider value

The Social Value Act 2012 has recently come into force in the UK. The Act requires public authorities (such as NHS trusts or local authorities) to take into account community benefits (such as environmental benefits), even though these were not stated in the contract specification, when deciding where to award a contract.

The Act has been welcomed by charities and non-profit organisations, with the National Council for Voluntary Organisations (NCVO) hailing it as a major opportunity for its sector.[54] However, it should be noted that the requirement is to 'consider' such wider benefits. The key question is whether health organisations have been particularly closed to recognising these; only then will the Act have an effect in counteracting the traditional priorities given to cost and health gains.

The recipients of value

The three main potential recipients of value achieved by a social innovation are:

- the social innovator and/or the organisation that they are part of;
- the staff that effect the innovation; and
- society, in terms of the people and the environment affected by the innovation.

The effects on each group are considered in turn.

Social innovator

The financial incentive to produce and disseminate innovation is strong when the product is tangible and so can be patented. This poses a problem to the field of social innovation, since much of its power is in the form of intangible relationships that apply in given localities and circumstances. Yet, although patents are problematic, the building up of trade-marks, professional know-how, reputation and copyrighted materials are all accepted as intellectual property and sources of value.[55] Provided that social innovations achieve either the same outcomes at lower costs and/or better outcomes at the same costs, this generates a surplus and hence value.

If and when successful, a social innovator stops thinking so much about such questions as: 'how do I survive?', and more about such issues as: 'how do we progress from here?' For the latter question, the most obvious answer is simply to grow the organisation that hosts the social innovation. However, alternatives such as franchising and licensing – or even giving away intellectual property on a Creative Commons basis – may also be worth considering.

Innovators can also adopt a deliberate strategy of being 'taken over' by a larger organisation.[56] Indeed where a social innovation is simple and readily transferable, yet other organisations would face internal resistance to adopting 'others' ideas', case study analysis suggests that this may be the best route to achieving the vision of the innovator.[57]

Staff

Changes in ways of working are often difficult for staff to adjust to. Social innovation does, however, have some facets that could potentially offset such fears:

- expanding the positive sense of 'being in a team',[58] by working more closely with stakeholders to achieve a beneficial result;
- increasing the extent to which positive feedback is given – a strong relationship exists between patients' perceptions of the quality of their care and employee satisfaction;[59] and
- increasing the sense of being able to assist, by being empowered to deploy a greater range of potential solutions.[60]

As a member of staff on a health literacy pilot put it:[61]

> We were really happy to be involved and get information from the group but also really pleased to be able to give information back and really what we found with the learners is that they're no different to any other group. They were struggling with information, struggling to know what was right and what was wrong . . . what information would be helpful.

An adaptable approach to meeting practical needs can be of great assistance to staff too. One striking example comes from Foote Hospital in the USA.[62] When a hospital employee lost three close relatives, her colleagues lobbied to change rules to allow them to donate vacation time – a change that was agreed, enabling them and others after to provide true support when needed.

Society

The recipients of public services have much to gain potentially, from an expansion of social innovation. For this entails moving from an 'illness service' to one designed to keep you healthy for as long as possible; moving from a 'do as I advise' approach to a 'let's talk through what should be done' process of jointly devised solutions.

Social innovation has the potential to transform expectations. It entails shifting from a situation in which an instruction leaflet can routinely assume that its readers are familiar with the term 'hypercholesterolemia'; it means that when posters on hospital say 'It's OK to ask', then staff really do have time and inclination to provide advice if and when asked.

Social innovation can break down silos between health services and the wider community. Medical staff command great respect (one recent Gallup poll in the USA had 85 per cent rating nurses as high or very high for ethics, compared to 8 per cent for car salesmen).[63] Yet, if health services act to conserve environmental resources, or promote trust in their community, or give job opportunities to those on the margins, this too is a major benefit for society. Health services can do more to improve transparency, just as businesses do through corporate social responsibility audits.

Conflicts in value

A range of definitions of what is meant by health outcomes exist, though each definition can fairly readily identify whether a particular element of health (such as mobility) is improving or getting worse. As such, health differs from criminal justice, where some outcomes (such as whether a prisoner likes or dislikes prison) are viewed in a very different way by different people.

There are, however, two particular agendas where conflicts can and do arise – issues around power and empowerment; and issues around mental health.

Power and empowerment

Social innovation harnesses and taps into resources in through networks, through peer relationships. That is very different from the traditional hierarchical approach of a doctor or nurse prescribing a plan of action to a patient. One explanation for resistance to change to a more co-designed approach comes from a former senior policy adviser:[64]

> One of the main barriers to the ability of medical staff to co-produce is that they hear the idea of co-production as one which removes health professionals from the scene . . . medical professionals work with very, very dependent people and . . . this strikes them as absurd (and they would be correct if that was what co-production was saying).

Instead, what social innovation and co-production approaches are really saying is that better health requires professionals and patients to work together in different ways. The right goal is to promote supported independence. That is not easy but can be done – from Australia's holistic Centrelink agency[65] to social exercise game Zamzee,[66] programmes that harness social innovation tap into relationships and empowerment.

Can *both* staff and users of health services feel empowered? Optimists would say yes. But finding a way for users, staff, communities, peers, family and friends to connect together more effectively is a major challenge for social innovations to address.

Mental health

Mental illness is more stigmatising than physical illnesses.[67] The sense of discomfort it can raise has long been an important issue for debate. In the 1960s, several controversial philosophers and psychiatrists (for example, R.D. Laing, in *The Politics of Experience*,[68] and Michel Foucault, in *Madness and Civilization*[69]) argued that simply because an individual is not living, speaking or acting in a way that society regards as 'normal', this does not mean that they are 'ill'.

And, as the historian Sarah Wise discovered of patients locked away in Victorian asylums (*Inconvenient People*[70]), sometimes motivations were centred on removing 'inconvenience' rather than promoting healing and adjustment. That clash between 'inconvenience' and adjustment still exists. Given a choice between or achieving a 'creative', 'alert' but somewhat 'ungraceful' outcome, or a 'numb' but quiet outcome, social innovations opt for empowerment.

Indeed, from Britain to Japan many mental health user groups provide valuable mutual support and help shape the provision of services.[71] And agendas such as art provide important alternative routes to empowerment. As one member of a survivors' poetry group puts it: 'Abuse continues alas even in the most celebratory of environments. Sometimes there seems more truth than poetry to write about; but our primary concern is to transmute that by acts of affirmation, healing, creativity and defiance.'[72]

The future

In western countries, health care has long adopted a clinical and technological-based approach. It focuses on curing illness rather than maintaining health. A doctor will far more readily advise consumption of a pill than suggest ways to reach out to friends and reduce loneliness. Health care services have been relatively poor at encouraging a true partnership between users, staff, communities and family and friends. Services have been relatively poor at empowering patients.

Yet there are some signs of encouragement for a social innovation approach. There is growing acceptance that care should be centred on the patient's needs;[73] there is growing awareness that a pure medical approach will neither achieve desired outcomes nor be affordable.[74]

By contrast, the value of social innovation lies precisely in what can be achieved for health, and for an array of other social benefits, when patients are empowered and relationships are strengthened. Social innovators have a crucial role to play if these opportunities are to be grasped.

Notes

1 Hussein, N. 'The role of the doctor: to diagnose and prescribe, or co-produce?' in *Working towards People Powered Healthcare* (2012). London: NESTA and the Innovation Unit.
2 Holt-Lunstad, J., Smith, T.B. and Layton, J.B. (2010) 'Social relationships and mortality risk: a meta-analytic review', *Public Library of Science – Medicine* 7 (7).
3 Christakis, N. and Fowler, J. (2008) 'The collective dynamics of smoking in a large social network', *New England Journal of Medicine* 358: 2249–58.
4 Randall, C. (2012) *Measuring National Well-being: Relationships in the UK 2012*, Newport: Office of National Statistics.
5 Self, A. et al. (2012) *Measuring National Well-being: Life in the UK 2012*, Newport: Office of National Statistics.
6 Perissinotto, C. et al. (2012) 'Loneliness in older persons: a predictor of functional decline and death', *Archive of Internal Medicine* 172 (14): 1078–84.
7 Tong, H. et al. (2011) 'Effects of social exclusion on depressive symptoms: elderly Chinese living in Shanghai', *Journal of Cross-cultural Gerontology* 26 (4): 349–64.
8 www.lho.org.uk/LHO_Topics/National_Lead_Areas/NationalSmoking.aspx.
9 Figures for levels in 2010 from www.cdc.gov/tobacco/data_statistics/fact_sheets/adult_data/cig_smoking/.
10 Ott, B. and Srinivasan, R. (2012) *Three in Ten Chinese Adults Smoke*, Gallup World, www.gallup.com/poll/152546/three-chinese-adults-smoke.aspx.
11 Rice, G. et al. (2008) 'Enhancing a primary care environment', *British Journal of General Practice*, www.ncbi.nlm.nih.gov/pmc/articles/PMC2441527/.
12 *2008 National Survey on Patients Experiences of Local Health Services*, London: Healthcare Commission.
13 Von Dem Knesebeck, O. et al. (2010) 'Differences in the diagnosis and management of type 2 diabetes in three countries (US, UK and Germany): results from a factorial experiment', *Medical Care* 48: 321–6.
14 Laws, R. et al. (2008) '"Should I and can I?": a mixed methods study of clinician beliefs and attitudes in the management of lifestyle risk factors in primary health care', *BMC Health Services Research* 8 (44).
15 Collins, A. 'Co-production and mainstream healthcare: an uneasy alliance?' in *Working towards People Powered Healthcare* (2012). London: NESTA and the Innovation Unit.

16 Cox, L. et al. (2006) *Understanding Participation in Sport: What Determines Sports Participation among 15–19-year-old Women?*, London: Sport England.
17 www.maslaha.org and, for more details on the case study by Diabetes UK, see https://www.diabetes.org.uk/upload/How%20we%20help/Magazines/Update/Share%20and%20share%20alike.pdf.
18 Duncan-Rees, C. 'Co-production, lessons from Stockport', in *Working towards People Powered Healthcare* (2012). London: NESTA and the Innovation Unit.
19 Hart, J. and Parkhurst, G. (2011) 'Impacts of motor vehicles on the quality of life of residents in three streets in Bristol UK', *World Transport Policy and Practice* 17 (2): 12–30.
20 Motohashi Y. et al. (2007) 'A decrease in suicide rates in Japanese rural towns after community-based intervention by the health promotion approach', *Suicide and Life Threatening Behaviour* 37 (5): 593–9.
21 http://en.wikipedia.org/wiki/23andMe.
22 http://mindapples.org/.
23 Contact a Family (2012) NHS parent carer participation case study, Cambridgeshire: Pinpoint and Addensbrooke Hospital.
24 Bostock, S. and Steptoe, A. (2012) 'Association between low functional health literacy and mortality in older adults: longitudinal cohort study', *British Medical Journal* 344: e1602. Note that the cited effect includes adjustments for age, socioeconomic position, baseline health status and health behaviours.
25 Cornett, S. (2009) 'Assessing and addressing health literacy', *Online Journal of Nursing* 14 (3).
26 *People Powered Health: Summaries of Pilot Programmes: Lambeth Living Well*, NESTA and Innovation Unit.
27 Shaller, D. and Darby, C. (2009) *Profiles of High Performing Patient and Family Centred Medical Centres: Vanderbilt Medical Centre*, Picker Institute.
28 San Patrignano Collaborative (2011) *San Patrignano Annual Mission Report 2010*.
29 Gomes, B. et al. (2011) *Local Preferences and Place of Death in Regions within England 2010*, London: Cicely Saunders International.
30 NHPCO (2012) *Facts and Figures: Hospice Care in America*, Alexandria, VA: National Hospice & Palliative Care Organization.
31 Natural Death Centre (2012) *Natural Death Handbook*, London: Strange Attractor Press.
32 See for example Hedner, T. et al. (2011) Entrepreneurial resilience, *Annals of Innovation & Entrepreneurship* 2: 7986.
33 Kotter, J. (1996) *Leading Change*, Boston: Harvard Business School Press.
34 Bunt. L. and Leadbeater, C. (2012) *The Art of Exit*, London: NESTA.
35 Newby, K. (2012) 'Against the odds', *Stanford Medicine*, Fall: 14–21.
36 NHS Improvement and Efficiency (2011) *Innovation Health and Wealth*, Leeds: NHS.
37 Beckett, S. (1983) *Worstward Ho*, London: Calder.
38 See case study in Murray, R. et al. (2010) *The Open Book of Social Innovation*, London: Young Foundation.
39 Hodgson, P. et al. (1996) *The Future of Leadership*, London: Pitman.
40 Pareras, L. (2011) *Innovation and Entrepreneurship in the Healthcare Sector: from Idea to Funding to Launch*, Phoenix, MD: Greenbranch Publishing.
41 As advocated by Regina Herzlinger, discussed in 'Health-care heretic', *Economist magazine*, 31st May 2007, http://www.economist.com/node/9254081.
42 Ibid.
43 'Renal improvement collaborative', Renal Association website, www.renal.org/whatwedo/JointActivitiesSection/ImprovementCollaborative.aspx.
44 'Mobile Medics Healthcare case study', Center for Health Market Innovations website, http://healthmarketinnovations.org/program/mobile-medics-healthcare.

45 'Aconchego case study', Social Innovation Exchange website, www.socialinnovationexchange.org/ideas-and-inspiration/health-and-wellbeing/case-study/aconchego-program.
46 Dench, G. et al. (ed.) (1995) *Young at Eighty: The Prolific Public Life of Michael Young*, Manchester: Carcanet Press.
47 Bart, C. and Hupfer, M. (2004) 'Mission statements in Canadian hospitals', *Journal of Health Organization and Management* 18 (2): 92–110.
48 Directorate of Commissioning, *How to Achieve World Class Commissioning Competencies: Practical tips for NHS Commissioners* (2008), London: Department of Health.
49 www.livesmartbc.ca/government/carbon_neutral/health_authorities.html.
50 NHS Sustainable Development Unit (2009) *Saving Carbon, Improving Health*, Cambridge: NHS.
51 Nelson, B. et al. (2010) *Social Value Commissioning Project Final Report*, CPC & NHS.
52 North West Social Value Foundation (2009) *Study Trip to Heartland Health*, Middlewich: North West Social Value Foundation.
53 HM Treasury guidance on appraisal and evaluation (*The Green Book: Appraisal and Evaluation in Central Government*, London: TSO, 2003) requires business cases to take into account substitution effects – 'Would the project attract scarce skills, or investment, that would otherwise have gone to other parts in the country?' 'If the policy involves support for local businesses, these may compete for resources and/or market share with non-assisted businesses.' Due to such effects it states 'The effect on net employment and net output is likely to be much smaller than the direct employment and direct output of the project'.
54 NCVO policy team (2012) 'What is the Social Value Act?', NCVO blogs and discussions, www.ncvo-vol.org.uk/networking-discussions/blogs/18452/12/07/02/what-social-value-act.
55 See discussion on intangible assets and firm performance in World Intellectual Property Organization (WIPO) (2011) *World Intellectual Property Report 2011 – The Changing Face of Innovation*, Geneva: WIPO.
56 Mulgan, G. et al. (2006) *In and Out of Sync: The Challenge of Growing Social Innovations*, London: NESTA.
57 Ibid.
58 Adams, A. and Bond, S. (2000) 'Hospital nurses' job satisfaction, individual and organizational characteristics', *Journal of Advanced Nursing* 32 (3): 536–43.
59 Atkins, P. et al. (1996) 'Happy employees lead to loyal patients', *Journal of Healthcare Marketing* 16 (4): 14–23.
60 Regan, L.C. and Rodriguez, L. (2011) 'Nurse empowerment from a middle management perspective', *The Permanente Journal* 15 (1): e101–7.
61 ALISS (Access to Local Information to Self-Support) – *Health Literacy Report* (2009), Edinburgh: Health Care Policy & Strategy Directorate, Scottish Government.
62 Dutton, J. (2003) 'Fostering high quality connections through respectful engagement', *Stanford Social Innovation Review* Winter: 54–7.
63 'Honesty/ethics in professions', Gallup poll Nov. 2012, www.gallup.com/poll/1654/honesty-ethics-professions.aspx.
64 Corrigan, P., 'Why co-production can seem absurd from a medical practitioner viewpoint', in *Working Towards People Powered Healthcare* (2012), London: NESTA and the Innovation Unit.
65 Darcy, M. and Gwyther, G. (2010) 'Centrelink's "place based services": can a national service delivery agency address local needs and conditions?' Paper presented to Social Policy Association conference.
66 Zamzee case study, Social Innovation Exchange, www.socialinnovationexchange.org/global/network-highlights/project/zamzee.

67 See Corrigan, P., et al. (2000) 'Stigmatizing attributions about mental illness', *Journal of Community Psychology* 28 (1): 91–102 and also Ando, S. and Thornicroft, G. (2012) 'Attitudes to mental illness in Japan and Britain' in Taplin, R. and Lawman, S. (eds) (2012) *Mental Health Care in Japan*, London: Routledge.
68 Laing, R.D. (1967) *The Politics of Experience and the Bird of Paradise*, [n.p.]: Penguin.
69 Foucault, M. (1964) *Madness and Civilization: A History of Insanity in the Age of Reason*, New York: Pantheon.
70 Wise, S. (2012) *Inconvenient People: Lunacy, Liberty and the Mad-doctors in Victorian England*, London: The Bodley Head.
71 Lawman, S. (2012) 'An overview of the user movement in Britain and Japan', in Taplin, R. and Lawman, S. (eds) (2012) *Mental Health Care in Japan*, London: Routledge.
72 Fuller, S. (2012) 'Update', in *Poetry Express* #40, Survivors' Poetry.
73 See, for example, the NHS Constitution (London: Department of Health, 2012) – 'NHS services must reflect the needs and preferences of patients, their families and their carers. Patients, with their families and carers, where appropriate, will be involved in and consulted on all decisions about their care and treatment.' And in the USA, Regina Herzlinger is a longstanding, strong advocate of 'consumer-driven health care'.
74 NHS Constitution (London: Department of Health, 2012) – 'The NHS works across organisational boundaries and in partnership with other organisations in the interest of patients, local communities and the wider population.'

4 The financial reporting of research and development costs and its signalling effects on firms' market values

Chin-Bun Tse and Andrew Ekuban

Value creation and research and development

Apple and Dyson show us the importance of product innovation in creating and enhancing the value of firms. This type of value creation happens when the products are in the marketplace and are generating cash for the firms. Such value creation or enhancement may be observed where the underlying fundamental value of a firm, as measured by share prices and dividend levels, changes as a result of increased cash generation. However, before the realisation of cash, the firms needed to spend a great deal on research and development (R&D) of the products. How should we report these R&D expenses in financial statements? How do investors see and react to the spending on R&D? Do they wait until they see the actual realisation of cash after the products are in the markets and then react, or do they react straight away when they know a firm has spent a large amount of money on R&D? Would the capital markets react differently to different ways of reporting R&D costs?

These are interesting questions that we attempt to address in this chapter. We first review the R&D accounting reporting requirements where R&D can be, in general, either *written-off* straight away in the income statement when it is incurred or *capitalised* as an asset on the statement of financial position. To capitalise it or not is an important question that the directors of companies need to think about. There are a number of conditions stipulated in the accounting standards to meet before the directors can decide to capitalise the R&D costs. However, we argue that the subjective nature of the conditions of capitalisation provides a potential opportunity to the directors to communicate to investors whether something good is ahead. This is, of course, a pure hypothesis. We do not know whether the directors really use the capitalisation as a tool to signal or not. We do not know whether the investors believe the signal or not. To look at this issue more deeply, we review the existing global empirical evidence reported in the literature.

Through the literature review, we are in a better position to understand the *practical* signalling roles of R&D reporting. We also hope to identify some knowledge gaps that are still occurring in the literature as well as the inconsistencies found in the literature. This will in turn meet the major objective of this chapter that is to stimulate further research for both practitioners and academics in order to have an even better understanding of the value relevance of reporting R&D costs.

Financial reporting requirements

On 19 July 2002, the European Parliament and the Council of the European Union passed Regulation (EC) No. 1606/2002[1] that had as its primary objective the adoption and use of international accounting standards within the European Community. The regulation required publicly traded companies to adopt the use of international accounting standards in preparing their consolidated accounts for financial statements commencing on or after 1 January 2005. Article 2 of the regulation defines 'international accounting standards' to include International Accounting Standards (IAS), International Financial Reporting Standards (IFRS) and related interpretations (standard industrial classification – IFRS interpretations).[2]

The standard that is directly relevant to the discussion here is IAS 38 *Intangible Assets*.[3] The corresponding standards under UK General Accepted Accounting Principles (GAAP) are the Statement of Standard Accounting Practice (SSAP) 13 *Accounting for Research and Development* and Financial Reporting Standards (FRS) 10 *Goodwill and Intangible Assets*.[4] However, as the discussion is primarily on R&D, the focus will be on the requirements and application of SSAP 13. Furthermore, since 2005, the requirements under IAS 38 *Intangible Assets* have largely been followed and applied instead of the requirements of SSAP 13.[5] The standard, IAS 38 *Intangible Assets*, applies to all intangible assets except in instances where the accounting treatment, either due to the nature of the asset or the transaction underlying the creation of the asset, is covered within the scope of another standard. An example, which is cited in the standard, would be intangible assets held by an entity for the purposes of resale in the ordinary course of business should be treated in accordance with IAS 2 *Inventories*.[6]

IAS 38 *Intangible Assets* establishes the general principles and criteria for the recognition and measurement of intangible assets. These principles and criteria are broadly similar to those under UK GAAP; however, there are some significant differences. SSAP 13 *Accounting for Research and Development* was originally issued in 1977 and revised in 1989, to provide guidance and establish the accounting practice to be followed in respect of R&D expenditure.[7] The basic concepts that underlie the determinations of the standard are the 'accruals' concept in relation to the matching of revenues and expenditures in the periods to which they were dealt with and the 'prudence' concept in relation to the recognition of revenues and profits.[8] The scope and objectives of FRS 10 *Goodwill and Intangible Assets* are to set out the principles of accounting for goodwill and intangible assets.[9] The requirements of the standard FRS 10 *Goodwill and Intangible Assets* apply to all intangible assets except those covered by SSAP 13 *Accounting for Research and Development* and within the scope of other standards.[10]

An intangible asset is defined by IAS 38 *Intangible Assets* as 'an identifiable, non-monetary asset without physical substance'.[11] The main features of this definition are captured within the following components:

- identifiable (suggesting that it is separable or separately transferable);
- an asset (the definition of which encompasses both the notions of future economic benefit and control).

The significance of the 'identifiable' characteristic lies in the fact that the International Accounting Standards Board (IASB) has determined that all assets that are 'separable', as per above, are identifiable and thus in a business combination such assets should be recognised separately from goodwill. However, the standard states that the separable nature of an asset in itself is not the only indication of it being identifiable as this criterion may be met in other ways, such as a legal right, giving rise to future economic benefit although not separable from the underlying business entity. However, it is the second component of the definition (an asset) that gives rise to the controversy surrounding this standard, for the determination of an asset – which is defined, essentially, by the ability to generate future economic benefit to the controlling entity – is rather uncertain and in many cases incorrectly forecasted when dealing with intangible assets. Intangible assets by their very nature present with a higher level of uncertainty pertaining to their ability to generate a future economic benefit than tangible assets. For example, whereas it is relatively simple to quantify the potential earnings from a physical machine of a certain maximum production capacity that is being built, this is not always the case with the creation, say, of a new technology that is yet to be brought to market. The higher levels of uncertainty as exemplified above, can lead to either significant errors in estimation or may simply be abused or manipulated by managers who may have a biased opinion of the future viability of their intangible creations and its earnings potential. The suggestion is that managers may use this opportunity not simply to inform investors of developments within the organisations but rather to give an overly optimistic view of the future earnings potential of the entities they manage, effectively using capitalisation as (or not) as a signal to the market about the future earnings potential of a firm. In an attempt to reduce the level of subjectivity in the exercise of determining what costs may be capitalised or not, the standard introduces and invokes a set of stringent criteria to be applied in ascertaining whether R&D expenditure may be capitalised.

The term 'research and development' is used to describe a wide range of activities. SSAP 13 *Accounting for Research and Development* defines R&D expenditure under three broad categories of activity, namely pure research, applied research, and development. These categories are consistent with the Organisation for Economic Co-operation and Development's (OECD) definition of the different types of R&D.[12] Pure research is defined as 'work undertaken primarily to acquire new scientific or technical knowledge for its own sake . . .' whereas applied research is defined as 'original or critical investigation undertaken in order to gain new scientific or technical knowledge and directed towards a specific practical aim or objective'.[13] However, such a distinction between pure and applied research is not made under IAS 38 *Intangible Assets*; instead the definition refers to research activities as being aimed at obtaining new knowledge and not related directly to any of the company's products or processes.[14] However, both standards define development expenditure in broadly similar terms, with each requiring that a new and recognisable asset should be the outcome of such expenditure. Examples of such output given in the standard include new materials, products, services or processes.[15] Essentially, R&D activity is identified separately from non-research-based activity by the existence or otherwise of a substantial element of innovation or even the breaking of new ground.

The accounting for R&D expenditure tends to fall into two broad treatments, namely to write-off expenditure that is not directly attributable to the creation of an asset and to capitalise expenditure that does. SSAP 13 *Accounting for Research and Development* requires development expenditure to be written off except where the following stringent recognition criteria are met. This includes the identification of a clearly defined project; separately identifiable expenditure and that the outcome of the project, in terms of its technical feasibility and commercial viability, can be measured or assessed with reasonable certainty; and that sufficient resources exist to complete a profitable project.[16] Similar recognition criteria are provided under IAS 38 *Intangible Assets*, in that if it is probable that future economic benefit that are attributable to the asset will flow to the entity and the costs of the asset can be measured reliably then it should be recognised in the financial statements.[17] However, research expenditure should be expensed as it is incurred; this is consistent with SSAP 13.

The requirements for capitalisation under IAS 38 *Intangible Assets* are not dissimilar from those provided under SSAP 13 as noted above. However, the main difference is that under SSAP 13, development expenditure may be capitalised where the recognition criteria are met, whereas IAS 38 requires capitalisation under similar circumstances, thus placing limits on management's discretion.[18] It is the subjective nature of these criteria that has given rise to much debate over their application. Take for example, the identification of a clearly defined project; it is the directors (managers) of a company who will invariably determine if a project is worth pursuing or not and only they have the full information to determine its technical feasibility and commercial viability. They could generate or compile sufficient accounting information that will enable them to satisfy the criteria for determining what costs are required to completion and prepare forecasts of future incomes that confirm the profitability of the project. One could argue that directors, being the holders of the fullest set of information pertaining to the project, are best placed to make any judgements concerning the technical and commercial viability, as well as the profitability, of their projects. However, the very uncertain nature of such projects and the high levels of estimation that are invariably required in forecasting future costs and income will undoubtedly leave much space for subjective judgements. It is this space that is given to subjective judgements that allows for the possible manipulation and abuse of the very criteria set to limit management judgements. But if the directors can, and arguably should, make these judgements about the future viability of their projects, then market participants are equally likely to take a view as to the future earning potential of a firm based on the accounting treatment of its R&D costs. Therefore, by capitalising R&D expenditure, directors are communicating to market participants their judgements concerning the inherent and anticipated value of the current R&D expenditure. Likewise, an immediate write-off of similar expenditure would signal to the market the directors' sentiments that the R&D expenditure to date had no capacity to generate future economic benefit. This effectively captures the signalling nature of the accounting treatment of R&D expenditure.

Another important difference in accounting treatment that exists between UK GAAP and IFRS is in the treatment of internally generated intangible assets. Whereas IAS 38 has a single set of stringent rules to cover the recognition of internally generated assets under both development expenditure and other intangible assets, under UK GAAP, internally generated intangible assets may not normally be capitalised. The impact of this discrepancy in accounting treatment is that some assets that could not be recognised in the statement of financial position under UK GAAP will be capitalised under IAS 38. Interestingly, Tsoligkas and Tsalavoutas,[19] citing Green et al.,[20] Stark and Thomas[21] and Oswald,[22] note that under SSAP 13 and prior to 2005 many companies did not capitalise their R&D expenditure. It would seem that the caution that directors took, even when faced with the potential to capitalise, has been eroded or completely removed by the change in requirement under IAS 38 for directors to capitalise their firms R&D costs once the criteria are met. By contrast, under US GAAP (Statement of Financial Accounting Standards (SFAS) No. 2) all expenditure on R&D must be expensed in the income statement as the view taken by the US regulator is that 'a direct relationship between research and development costs and specific future revenue' has not been demonstrated.[23]

This alternative view highlights a common underlying thread of concern in the minds of regulators as to the objectivity and reliability of estimates of R&D expenditure to be capitalised, and the associated opportunity for managers to manipulate earnings[24]

We observe from the above that the accounting treatment of R&D expenditure is by no means the same across various parts of the world. Where capitalisation of R&D expenditure is allowed or even required, the application of the conditions for capitalisation tends to be a rather subjective decision-making process. It may be argued that it is because of this subjectivity that decisions made by directors have such signalling effects on firms, with investors reacting accordingly. This interesting potential signalling effect has been investigated and reported in the literature. We review some of these global experiences in the following section.

Review of global experience

The last three decades have witnessed the unprecedented growth in R&D expenditure of which Apple and Dyson are recent examples from the US and UK respectively. Several authors (Garcia-Manjon and Romero-Merino,[25] Chan et al.,[26] Pyykkö[27]) have all observed that R&D expenditure is the driver underlying corporate and even national growth. Pyykkö assesses the international impact of R&D expenditure and finds that it is the underlying driver for mergers and acquisition (M&A) activity across international borders.[28] Garcia-Manjon and Romero-Merino, however, find that the benefits of signalling apply mainly to high-technology firms and that R&D is only essential for the growth and survival of certain businesses and industry sectors.[29]

In this section, we review evidence from around the globe to establish if managers are able to use R&D expenditure reporting as a signal to the markets about the future earnings potential of their firms. The review begins with the case of the US, where under SFAS No. 2, firms are not allowed to capitalise R&D expenditure except in limited instances such as software development costs (SFAS No. 86).[30] Aboody and Lev,[31] cited in Eccher,[32] conclude that whereas there is evidence that capitalising software costs, as a proxy for R&D capitalisation in the case of US firms, provides value-relevant information about the future earnings potential of firms, the accuracy of such forecasts is questionable. These findings are made all the more significant when one considers the Financial Accounting Standards Board's (FASB) thinking behind the requirement to write to the income statement all R&D expenditure, that 'a direct relationship between research and development costs and specific future revenue generally has not been demonstrated . . .'.[33] However, the fact that value-relevant information is provided, arguably at the expense of accuracy, does reopen the longstanding debate on the trade-off between relevance and reliability, which is also mentioned by Markarian et al.[34] The work by Aboody and Lev was prompted by the Software Publishers Association's (SPA) petition to the FASB in August 1996 to abolish SFAS No. 86.[35] They argued that the capitalisation of software did not benefit the investor but rather if all software costs were charged to the income statement then the reliability and consistency of financial reporting and financial statements will be improved. These findings are at variance with conclusions drawn from the works of Sougiannis et al.,[36] Lev and Sougiannis[37] and Chambers et al.[38] Furthermore, Lev et al. find that the requirement to write-off all R&D expenditure may be costly to both the firms and market participants. The costs are incurred initially by the prevention of management to publish private inside information that would reduce information asymmetry between them and investors. This leads investors and other participants to seek this additional information through alternative and usually costly means. The lack of relevant information may also lead to the mispricing of equity and the associated inefficient allocation of resources.[39]

In Europe, unlike the US, the implementation of IFRS means that firms are able and even required to capitalise their R&D expenditure where certain criteria are met. Following the study of some 754 firms in Europe, Garcia-Manjon and Romero-Merino provide evidence to support a positive relation between R&D and sales growth and conclude that for firms to increase their sales, grow and ultimately survive they must invest in R&D. They also find that the intensity of this relationship is enhanced in high-growth firms and heightened further in high-technology industries but this relationship is not clearly evidenced in low-technology firms.[40] This is consistent with the findings of Chan et al.[41] and Zantout and Tsetsekos[42] who also conclude that a strong positive correlation exists between R&D investment in high-technology industry firms and market responses and a negative correlation in the case of low-technology industry firms.

Buckley and Casson[43] and Caves[44] are proponents of the internationalisation theory that suggests that cross-border M&As are largely driven by the benefits and synergies arising from the R&D activities of both the target and acquirer firms. Pyykkö, extends the internationalisation theory using the ten most R&D active European countries and finds that 'cross-border M&As have a positive impact on the value that investors place on acquirer's R&D activity but only if both the acquirer and the target are technology firms'.[45]

The evidence from Italy provided by Markarian et al. posits the notion that management's motivation to capitalise R&D expenditure stems from the opportunity to use it as a tool for manipulating earnings or for earnings-management. Their work has contributed largely to the reliability side of the debate on the trade-off between relevance and reliability by identifying income-smoothing as being the determining factor for managers when considering whether to capitalise their R&D costs or not. They conclude that income-smoothing is an 'effective and efficient way to signal and communicate important information to the market' and so favour the requirement to expense all R&D costs if financial statements are to provide reliable information.[46]

In the UK, the adoption of IFRS has had a positive impact on the value-relevance of reported assets with Tsoligkas and Tsalavoutas[47] finding evidence in support of Barth et al.[48] and Ball[49] that the implementation of IFRS improves the reporting of companies' fundamentals. Reported R&D expenses though, were only found to be significantly value-relevant in large companies; this is in contrast to the findings of Shah et al.[50] but consistent with Zhao[51] and Cazavan-Jeny and Jeanjean.[52] In other words, where large firms failed to capitalise their R&D expenditure this was perceived as inefficiency by investors. The assumption here being that larger firms would be expected to make more efficient use of the R&D expenditure and gain a competitive technological advantage.

Cazavan-Jeny and Jeanjean[53] examine the value-relevance of R&D accounting treatment using a sample of companies listed in France. They conclude that capitalised R&D expenditure has a signalling effect evidenced by significant positive correlation with market prices for commercially successful firms and negatively correlated to the stock market returns or prices when R&D costs are expensed. However, Cazavan-Jeny and Jeanjean[54] and Cazavan-Jeny et al.,[55] find that capitalising R&D on the whole has a neutral or negative impact on future performance: 'When firms both capitalise and expense R&D costs, the expensed portion exhibits a stronger (and negative) relationship with future earnings.' These findings are in stark contrast to the evidence reviewed previously, which was largely in favour of capitalising R&D costs.

Value-relevance of R&D reporting – gaps in knowledge

Cazavan-Jeny et al. suggest possible reasons for the difference in their findings to previous evidence, which was in support of capitalising R&D expenditure. One of the main reasons proffered for this difference is the fact that the research carried out by Cazavan-Jeny et al. was based on real data as opposed to simulated data, which had been used previously.[56]

Ahmed and Falk, make a similar point when reviewing their findings in the light of previous studies. This is particularly true of research based on US data where under FASB accounting rules companies must expense all their R&D costs. Therefore, researchers are required to make a judgement in placing all R&D expenditure into appropriate 'capitalised' and 'expensed' categories. The argument here is that managers, given the choice, may not capitalise the same expenditure, thus making these categorisations highly subjective and questionable exercises.[57]

In countries where IFRS has been introduced, the adoption of IFRS has amplified companies' fundamentals but continued to confirm the value-relevance of R&D expenditure. This is particularly evident in countries such as the UK where the accounting treatment has not changed significantly from pre-2005. What is not clear is what the impact would have been if the accounting treatment had changed significantly from pre-2005.[58]

The studies by Garcia-Manjon and Romero-Merino, Chan et al. and Zantout and Tsetsekos suggest that the type of industry (high technology or low technology) and Ehie and Olibie the type of sector (manufacturing or service) will have a bearing on outcomes. Firms in the high-technology industry are more likely to benefit disproportionately from the effects of R&D expenditure as compared to low-technology firms.[59]

Chambers,[60] citing Ciftci et al.,[61] suggests that given the uncertain nature of the future earnings from R&D expenditure, firms involved in an innovative R&D strategy may find their stock mis-priced (generally under-priced) due to the anticipated and associated inherent risk in the R&D projects and a conservative estimate of expected future earnings.

Summary and conclusion

The two main accounting treatments are to either expense the R&D costs to the income statement or to capitalise R&D expenditure in the statement of financial position. In certain contexts, such as in the US, the accounting treatment is quite prescriptive with little or no room for management judgement. The required accounting treatment under US GAAP is to expense all R&D costs, as the standard-setter's claim there is no demonstrable relationship between R&D costs and specific future revenue. A considerable amount of research has been performed across the globe to provide evidence that a relationship does exist between R&D costs and specific future revenue. It is in the face of this mounting evidence that other standard-setters in the UK, Italy and France (pre-2005) and now throughout Europe, under IFRS, not only allow for the capitalisation of R&D expenditure but also require it where the conditions for capitalisation are met. It is these conditions for capitalisation that have been the subject of much debate as they are largely of a subjective nature and require a certain amount of management discretion. Much of the debate has centred on the value-relevance of the amounts recognised in the financial statements as either an expense or an asset and whether or not management are inclined to use R&D expenditure as a tool to signal to the capital markets the future earnings potential of their companies.

The evidence suggests that investors perceive firms that expense their R&D costs negatively whereas those firms that capitalise their R&D expenditure tend to see a positive reaction to their stock prices. This positive correlation between the capitalisation of R&D expenditure and market responses is further enhanced in high-growth and high-technology firms. Larger firms also tended to benefit relatively more due to the perceived efficiencies and synergies. However, a fundamental problem that pervaded the findings was that although there was a positive correlation between the capitalisation of R&D costs and market responses, the estimation of the perceived benefits or forecast of future earnings fell short of the reality.

However, a recent study by Cazavan-Jeny et al. based on a sample of French listed companies found evidence that capitalising R&D on the whole has a neutral or negative impact on future performance. These findings are in stark contrast to the evidence reviewed earlier, which was in favour of assertion that capitalising R&D costs invariably leads to increases in market values.

These conflicting empirical findings mean that it is difficult to conclude the value-relevance of accounting treatment to R&D expenditure despite in theory that capitalisation of the expenditure has a signalling value of a good future. It is safe to say that more research is required to work out where the missing links are in both theory and practice.

Notes

1 EU regulation is readily accessible from the following website: http://eur-lex.europa.eu/LexUriServ/LexUriServ.do?uri=CELEX:32002R1606:EN:NOT.
2 The issue and publication of IAS are the responsibility of the IASB. The IASB is the independent standard-setting body of the IFRS Foundation.
3 IASB, IAS 38 (Revised) *Intangible Assets* (London: IFRS Foundation, 2004), http://eifrs.ifrs.org/eifrs/bnstandards/en/2012/ias38.pdf.
4 Statements of Standard Accounting Practice (SSAPs) were originally issued by the Accounting Standards Committee. These standards were later adopted by the Accounting Standards Board (ASB) that took over the responsibility of standard-setting in the UK in 1990 and issued Financial Reporting Standards (FRSs). Since July 2012, the Financial Reporting Council has assumed responsibility for all accounting standards in issue in the UK. See http://www.frc.org.uk/Our-Work/Codes-Standards/Accounting-and-Reporting-Policy/Standards-in-Issue.aspx.
5 F. Tsoligkas and I. Tsalavoutas, 'Value relevance of R&D in the UK after IFRS mandatory Implementation', *Applied Financial Economics*, 21, 2011, 957–67.
6 IASB, IAS 38 (Revised) *Intangible Assets*, p. A1035.
7 Institute of Chartered Accountants in England and Wales (ICAEW), SSAP 13 (Revised) *Accounting for Research and Development* (Hertford: Stephen Austin and Sons Limited, 1989), http://frc.org.uk/Our-Work/Publications/ASB/SSAP-13-Accounting-for-research-and-development/SSAP-13-Accounting-for-research-and-development.aspx.
8 Ibid., p. 2.
9 ASB, FRS 10 *Goodwill and Intangible Assets* (Milton Keynes: ASB Publications, 1997).
10 Ibid., p. 12.
11 IASB, IAS 38 (Revised) *Intangible Assets*, p. A1036.
12 ICAEW, SSAP 13 (Revised) *Accounting for Research and Development*, p. 2.

13 Ibid., p. 5.
14 B. Elliot and J. Elliot, *Financial Accounting and Reporting*, 15th edn (Harlow: Pearson Education Ltd, 2012), pp. 493–7.
15 Ibid., p. 494.
16 ICAEW, SSAP 13 (Revised) *Accounting for Research and Development*, p. 6.
17 IASB, IAS 38 (Revised) *Intangible Assets*, pp. A1039–40.
18 F. Tsoligkas and I. Tsalavoutas, 'Value relevance of R&D in the UK after IFRS mandatory Implementation', *Applied Financial Economics*, 21, 2011, p. 959.
19 Ibid., pp. 957–67.
20 J.P. Green, A.W. Stark and H.M. Thomas, 'UK evidence on the market valuation of research and development expenditures', *Journal of Business Finance and Accounting*, 23, 1996, 191–216.
21 A.W. Stark and H.M. Thomas, 'On the empirical relationship between market value and residual income in the UK', *Management Accounting Research*, 9, 1998, 445–60.
22 D.R. Oswald, 'The determinants and value relevance of the choice of accounting for research and development expenditures in the United Kingdom', *Journal of Business Finance and Accounting*, 35, 1998, 1–24.
23 FASB, SFAS 2 *Accounting for Research and Development Costs* (Norwalk, CT: FASB, 1974).
24 B. Lev and T. Sougiannis, 'The capitalization, amortization, and value-relevance of R&D', *Journal of Accounting and Economics*, 21, 1996, p. 108.
25 J. Garcia-Manjon and M.E. Romero-Merino, 'Research, development and firm growth. Empirical evidence from European top R&D spending firms', *Research Policy*, 41, 2012, 1084–92.
26 S. Chan, J. Martin and J. Kensinger, 'Corporate research and development expenditures and share value', *Journal of Financial Economics*, 26. 1990, 255–76.
27 E. Pyykkö, 'Stock market valuation of R&D spending of firms acquiring targets from technologically abundant countries', *Journal of Multinational Financial Management*, 19, 2009, 111–26.
28 Ibid.
29 J. Garcia-Manjon and M.E. Romero-Merino, 'Research, development and firm growth. Empirical evidence from European top R&D spending firms', *Research Policy*, 41, 2012, 1084–92.
30 D. Aboody and B. Lev, 'The value-relevance of intangibles: the case of software capitalization', *Journal of Accounting Research*, 36 (supplement), 1998, 161–91.
31 Ibid.
32 E. Eccher, 'Discussion of the value relevance of intangibles: the case of software capitalisation', *Journal of Accounting Research*, 36 (supplement), 1998, 193–8.
33 B. Lev and T. Sougiannis, 'The capitalization, amortization, and value-relevance of R&D', *Journal of Accounting and Economics*, 21, 1996, p. 108.
34 G. Markarian, A. Prencipe and L. Pozza, 'Capitalization of R&D costs and earnings management: evidence from Italian listed companies', *The International Journal of Accounting*, 43, 2008, 246–67.
35 D. Aboody and B. Lev, 'The value-relevance of intangibles: the case of software capitalization', *Journal of Accounting Research*, 36 (supplement), 1998, p. 161.
36 T. Sougiannis, L. Chan, J. Lakonishok, 'The stock market valuation of research and development expenditures', *Journal of Finance*, 56, 2001, 2431–56.
37 B. Lev and T. Sougiannis, 'The capitalization, amortization, and value-relevance of R&D', *Journal of Accounting and Economics*, 21, 1996, p. 108.
38 D. Chambers, 'Discussion of "Is research and development mispriced or properly risk-adjusted?"', *Journal of Accounting, Auditing and Finance*, 2011, 117–20.
39 B. Lev, B. Sarath and T. Sougiannis, 'R&D reporting biases and their consequences', *Contemporary Accounting Research*, 22 (4), 2005, p. 1018.
40 J. Garcia-Manjon and M.E. Romero-Merino, 'Research, development and firm growth.

Empirical evidence from European top R&D spending firms', *Research Policy*, 41, 2012, p. 1085.
41 S. Chan, J. Martin and J. Kensinger, 'Corporate research and development expenditures and share value', *Journal of Financial Economics*, 26. 1990, p. 275.
42 Z. Zantout and G. Tsetsekos, 'The wealth effects of announcements of R&D expenditure increase', *Journal of Financial Research*, 17, 1994, 205–16.
43 P.J. Buckley and M. Casson, *The Future of the Multinational Enterprise, 25th Anniversary Edition* (New York: Palgrave Macmillan, 2002).
44 R.E. Caves, 'International corporations: the industrial economics of foreign investment', *Economica*, 38, 1971, 1–27.
45 E. Pyykkö, 'Stock market valuation of R&D spending of firms acquiring targets from technologically abundant countries', *Journal of Multinational Financial Management*, 19, 2009, p. 124.
46 Markarian et al., op. cit., p. 264.
47 F. Tsoligkas and I. Tsalavoutas, 'Value relevance of R&D in the UK after IFRS mandatory Implementation', *Applied Financial Economics*, 21, 2011, p. 959.
48 M.E. Barth, W.R. Landsman, and M.H. Lang, 'International accounting standards and accounting quality', *Journal of Accounting Research*, 46, 2008, 467–98.
49 R. Ball, 'International Financial Reporting Standards (IFRS): pros and cons for investors', *Accounting and Business Research*, 36, 2006, 5–27.
50 S.Z.A. Shah, A.W. Stark, and S. Akbar, 'Firm size, sector and market valuation of R&D expenditures', *Applied Financial Economics Letters*, 4, 2008, 87–91.
51 R. Zhao, 'Relative value relevance of R&D reporting: an international comparison', *Journal of International Financial Management and Accounting*, 13 (2), 2002, 153–74.
52 A. Cazavan-Jeny and T. Jeanjean, 'The negative impact of R&D capitalisation: a value-relevance approach', *European Accounting Review*, 15 (1), 2006, 37–61.
53 A. Cazavan-Jeny and T. Jeanjean, 'Value-relevance of R&D reporting: a signalling interpretation', *CEREG* working paper 12, 2003, 1–25.
54 A. Cazavan-Jeny and T. Jeanjean, 'The negative impact of R&D capitalisation: a value-relevance approach', *European Accounting Review*, 15 (1), 2006, p. 59.
55 A. Cazavan-Jeny, T. Jeanjean and P. Joos, 'Accounting choice and future performance: the case of R&D accounting in France', *Journal of Accounting and Public Policy*, 30, 2011, 145–65.
56 Ibid.
57 K. Ahmed and H. Falk, 'The value relevance of management's research and development reporting choice: evidence from Australia', *Journal of Accounting and Public Policy*, 25, 2006, 231–64.
58 F. Tsoligkas and I. Tsalavoutas, 'Value relevance of R&D in the UK after IFRS mandatory Implementation', *Applied Financial Economics*, 21, 2011, p. 959.
59 I.C. Ehie and K. Olibo, 'The effect of R&D investment on firm value: an examination of US manufacturing and service industries', *International Journal of Production Economics*, 128, 2010, 127–35.
60 D. Chambers, 'Discussion of "Is research and development mispriced or properly risk-adjusted?"', *Journal of Accounting, Auditing and Finance*, 2011, p. 117.
61 M.B. Ciftci, B. Lev and S. Radhakrishnan, 'Is R&D mispriced or properly risk-adjusted?' *Journal of Accounting, Auditing and Finance*, 26, 2011, 81–116.

5 Value–energy interrelationship and dynamic added value taxation

Victor Bartenev

Introduction

Physical macroeconomics is an interdisciplinary research direction dedicated to the study of physical and bio-developmental foundations of economy. This chapter introduces the basic concepts of physical macroeconomics, re-conceptualizing where value can be derived from the economy in an innovative manner assessing the added value of energy consumption.

The original idea[1] was that there is a principle of "value–energy equivalency" and that the economy enlarges the added value[2] by the consumption of external (primary) energy. A similar process occurs in the electric power amplifier.

The identity of the value and energy is obvious when we pay for electricity. We pay just for the energy (kWh) rather than, say, for the amount of consumed current (amp-hours).

Therefore, generally speaking, you can set the price of any product not in money but in energy units. For example, based on the electricity price in a certain region of the country (p_e, USD/kWh) and on the loaf of bread price in the same region (p_b, USD/loaf), the price of a loaf can be expressed in energy units: p (kWh/loaf) $= p_b/p_e$. This price is the amount of energy used to produce a loaf in the long production chain, from cereal breeding to cashier work.

Comparison of the economy with the amplifier was very useful simplification. For example, using the analogy of the concept of the electric amplifier efficiency, we defined a calculable magnitude of the economic efficiency. This magnitude is a ratio of added value created in the region, to the amount of the primary energy consumed by the region, including the food energy.

The law of energy conservation is expressed in economics in the form of balance equation:

$$S \text{ (sales)} = E \text{ (expenses)} + G \text{ (gain)} + T \text{ (taxes)} \qquad (1)$$

The balance equation is the basis of accounting.

A more detailed examination[3,4] shows that, instead of the ordinary value–energy equivalency principle, there is a system similarity (isomorphism) between added value and the thermodynamic free energy. By producing added value (gross domestic product (GDP)), a socio-economic system reproduces and increases its "free energy" as any living system does to maintain its viability.

Thermodynamic free energy change is a consequence of the law of energy conservation (the first law of thermodynamics). Similarly, starting from the balance equation, you can get a mathematical expression for added value.

To do this, one should divide the expenses E into two parts – the internal expenses E^{int} (create added value) and external expenses E^{ext} (external payments to suppliers). Then the added value created by producers within the annual tax period is:

$$\Delta S_+ = S - E^{ext} = E^{int} + G + T \tag{2}$$

Total added value produced by the economy (GDP) is obtained by summing ΔS_+ through all producers.

The socio-economic system produces added value by the joint efforts of producers and society. Produced added value is divided between society and the producers through taxes. Both producers and society spend energy to produce added value. Corresponding energy costs should be offset by a balanced distribution of added value between them. This can be achieved by properly organized added value taxation.

In fact, any multi-tax system, perhaps with overlapping tax bases, is reduced to added value taxation. Accordingly, we shall imply below that the T item in equation (2) is a *system-defined* added value tax. Other ancillary taxes[5] should be included in the values of E and G.

Harmonious and sustainable balance in nature is maintained by a balanced distribution of free energy through dynamic metabolic feedback. In the economy, the distribution of added value between producers and society is currently out of balance, leading to instability. The reason for the imbalance is that the existing static taxation (with constant tax rates) cannot fulfill the function of feedback.

A possible solution is that the destabilizing static taxation should be replaced by a dynamic added value taxation (DAVT). In an abbreviated form, the DAVT theory is given at the end of the chapter.

On a system-wide perspective, the DAVT is a stabilizing negative feedback. Positive and negative feedback loops are in the list of general living system principles noted by Bertalanffy.[6]

Physical macroeconomics argues that there are no so-called "capitalistic," "socialistic" or "communistic" economies. Only one economy exists – it is a social living system functioning in accordance with economic analogs of physical and bio-developmental laws. Any economic policy must take into account these laws and principles.

Economy and general living system principles

General living systems principles are applicable to the economy, and include:

Openness. All living systems are open, because they exchange energy, matter and information with the environment and with other systems. Therefore, the second law of thermodynamics (the entropy increase in a closed system) does not apply to them.

Living systems, including the economy, remain viable through the consumption of external (primary) energy. Inside a living system primary energy is converted into the energy of secondary energy carriers that are suitable for in-system use.

Vitality of a living system depends on the thermodynamic free energy of the system. The free energy is continuously consumed and reproduced by the system.

Therefore, the efficiency of the system can be numerically defined as the ratio of the amount of free energy created to the amount of the primary energy consumed by the system.

Isomorphism. Basic properties of living systems are similar to the properties of the systems that are evolutionary older and simpler. In physical macroeconomics, the main principle is an added value and free energy isomorphism.

Feedbacks. Within living systems distribution of free energy is balanced. Balance is achieved through dynamic feedback (nutritional and metabolic).

In the economy, total added value (on an annualized basis, GDP) is distributed between producers and society through the tax system. But under the current static taxation this distribution is unbalanced, leading to social and economic instability.

In essence, the proposed DAVT is a stabilizing negative feedback, in addition to objectively existing negative feedback in the form of demand function.[7]

Steady state. The steady state of a living system is a state of sustainable development, regulated by feedback. If positive feedback in the system is not compensated by negative feedback, the system becomes unstable. As a result, for example, finance bubbles occur in the economy.

The above system principles are the basis of physical macroeconomics. In the following sections we will discuss the basic relations and give some estimates.[8]

We pay attention to the fact that only current prices are used below. Money in the economic system does not lose its "purchasing power" – it is an illusion. In reality, there is a growth of "free energy" of the system, and namely the current prices adequately describe the growth.

Efficiency indicators

The economy increases the added value by the consumption of primary energy. In such a way, the economy functions as an added value amplifier. Efficiency is the main characteristic of the amplifier. Consequently, physical macroeconomics is to give the definition of economic efficiency.

Economic efficiency definition

The regional socio-economic economy efficiency R is defined in physical macroeconomics as the ratio of total added value (GDP) produced by the region to primary energy H consumed by the region, including food energy:

$$R = \text{GDP} / H \tag{3}$$

The magnitude of economic efficiency is expressed in monetary/energy units. Therefore, this magnitude can be used as a correlation coefficient that links the monetary and energy units of added value.

Efficiency and electricity price

The price of electricity p_e has the same dimension as the efficiency magnitude R. This suggests that the magnitude of the efficiency and average price of electricity $<p_e>$ vary in line with the trend:

$$<p_e> \rightarrow R\uparrow \tag{4}$$

If so, then the average electricity price can serve as an empirical efficiency indicator for economies with independent electric energy systems.

The difference in the price of electricity in the US, in fact, demonstrates the existence of a correlation between the average electricity price and the relative level of economic development (Figure 5.1).

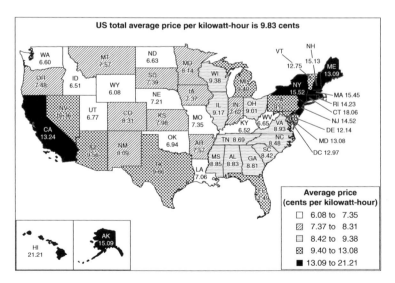

Figure 5.1 US electricity prices, 2009.

Source: US Energy Information Administration. Form EIA-861. "Annual electric power industry report."

Note: Data are displayed as five groups of ten states and the District of Columbia.

88 *Victor Bartenev*

The following sections will show that the definition (3) and the trend (4) are adequate and correct, provided that the amount of primary energy is calculated correctly.[9] The fact is that at present this amount is completely wrong.

Primary energy

In order to adequately assess the amount of primary energy consumption, it is necessary first of all to correctly define the boundaries of the system.

Energy sources of the world economy

At present, the energy sources of the world economy are classified in accordance with the scheme, which in general terms is shown in Figure 5.2.

This scheme is wrong because "renewables" are classified in the scheme as the primary sources. But in reality, "renewables" are made within the boundaries of the socio-economic system. The economy is producing "renewables," consuming the energy of solar radiation.

Consequently, biomass, hydro, solar and wind energy must be classified as secondary sources. Instead of "renewables," the scheme must contain "solar radiation."

The world economy consumes a huge amount of solar radiation, especially for food biomass production. This amount is much higher than the current value of "primary energy consumption (H_0)." In fact, the value of H_0 is only a small fraction of the real amount H of the primary energy consumption. Therefore, if you use the H_0 magnitude as the amount of the primary energy consumption, the evaluation of economy efficiency will be greatly overestimated. For example, the $R_0 = GDP/H_0$ magnitude for the US is five times higher than the average electricity price (Table 5.1).

So, the scheme shown in Figure 5.2, should be reviewed.

In fact, for the world economy, the primary energy is the energy of the Sun. A small part of this energy was conserved billions of years ago and is now used

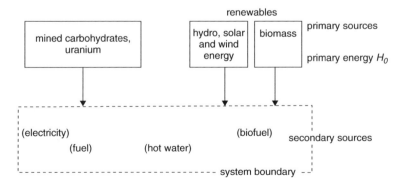

Figure 5.2 The current scheme of world economy energy sources.

Table 5.1 The R_0 magnitudes for world and US economies in 2010

Economic system	GDP (USD/capita/hour)	H_0 (kW/capita)	$R_0 = GDP / H_0$ (USD/kWh)	$<p_e>$ (USD/kWh)
World	1.0	2.2	0.4	—
US	5.2	9.6	0.5	0.10

mainly by the consumption of hydrocarbons and uranium. But the prevailing part of the external energy inflow is not "from the past" – it is obtained due to current solar radiation inflow. Thus, the correct energy scheme must first contain solar radiation.

The world economy obtains the bulk of solar radiation energy directly, and the rest of the energy is obtained indirectly, through interaction with Earth's climate system (Figure 5.3).

It makes little sense to term the sunlight as "renewable," so the term "renewable primary energy" in general should be avoided. Otherwise, you can come to a curious conclusion, that sunrise and sunset are "renewable phenomena."

By replacing the "renewables" with solar radiation we do not just refine the classification. Namely this replacement allows us to estimate the real value of the primary energy consumption.

The world economy consumes most of the solar energy for food biomass production, which will now be discussed.

Food factor in primary energy

Food biomass is the most important, vital secondary energy carrier. The amount of solar energy consumed by the economy for food biomass production, can be identified as H_f.

At present, this energy is not taken into account in the value of "primary energy" H_0. Therefore, the actual amount of primary energy can be estimated[10] as:

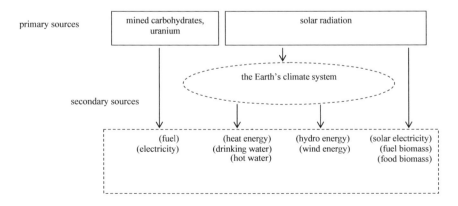

Figure 5.3 Primary and secondary energy sources of the world economy.

$$H \approx H_0 + H_f$$

How do we evaluate the H_f magnitude?

Man consumes about 2,000 kcal of food energy per day. Taking into account that 1kcal $\approx 1.2 \times 10^{-3}$ kWh, one can evaluate food energy consumption power as:

$$2{,}000 \text{ kcal/capita/day} \approx 2000 \times 1.2 \times 10^{-3} \text{ kWh/capita/24h} = 100 \text{ W/capita}$$

This energy is very small compared with the H_0 magnitude (2.2 kW/capita, see Table 5.1), so that, at first glance, it seems the "food energy factor" can be ignored. But that would be a wrong conclusion.

Food biomass is a secondary energy carrier and its production requires much more of sunlight energy than the amount of chemical energy stored in the biomass:

> The efficiency with which energy or biomass is transferred from one trophic level to the next is called ecological efficiency. Consumers at each level convert on average only about 10 percent of the chemical energy in their food to their own organic tissue. At the lowest trophic level (the bottom of the food chain), plants convert about one percent of the sunlight they receive into chemical energy.[11]

Consequently, the world economy consumes for food biomass production 100 times more sunlight energy than 100W per capita, namely, about 10kW. The human being – it is a serious sunlight-consuming machine!

In order to estimate the H_f magnitude, it is necessary to recalculate the food chemical energy in the sunlight energy consumed in agriculture and fisheries (H_a and H_s respectively). That is:

$$H_f = H_a + H_s$$

The bulk of food biomass is produced by agriculture. It is reasonable to assume that H_a magnitude is proportional to the total production of grain and soybeans. The world production of the "grain basket" (wheat, rice, corn, barley and soybeans) is rather stable and amounts to 0.95 kg/capita/day (Figure 5.4). Beginning in 2003, this figure began to grow; growth clearly linked to biofuels production. Note that the "grain basket" price was almost unchanged ($\approx$ 0.14 USD/kg) for 30 years.

Production of the "grain basket" satisfies the human need for food energy (100W/capita). Based on the energy efficiency of crops production ($\sim$ 1 percent) we can estimate the H_a magnitude as

$$H_a \sim 100 \times 0.1 \text{ (kW/capita)} \times Q_a = 10 \text{ kW/capita} \times Q_a$$

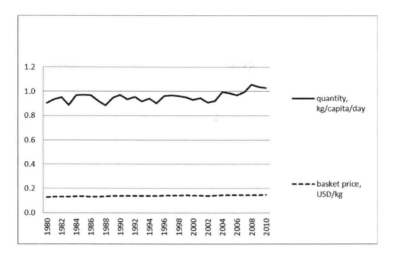

Figure 5.4 The world production of the grain basket.

where Q_a is a number of "grain baskets" per capita per day produced in agriculture (one basket contains approximately 1 kg of grain and soybeans).

Besides agriculture, for some countries (e.g. Japan and Norway) seafood production is very important, fishing being the most important. Fish is on the next level of the food chain after the water-inhabiting plants, so energy efficiency of fish biomass production is about 10 percent of the green biomass production efficiency. Consequently, the energy efficiency of seafood production can be roughly estimated as 0.1 percent.

Accordingly, the sunlight energy consumption power for seafood production can be evaluated as

$$H_s \sim 1{,}000 \times 0.1 \text{ (kW/capita)} \times Q_s = 100 \text{ kW/capita} \times Q_s$$

where Q_s is a number of "fish baskets" per capita per day produced in fisheries (one basket contains 1 kg of fish).

In sum, for the total primary energy consumption power, we have the following evaluation:

$$H \approx H_0 + H_a + H_s$$

which should be used for economy efficiency estimations.

Efficiencies of largest economies

Table 5.2 summarizes our estimates to compare the economic efficiency and primary energy consumption magnitudes in the world major economies. The US

Table 5.2 Efficiency R and primary energy consumption magnitudes in the world, US, EU, Japan and China economies, 2010

Economy	GDP (USD/capita/hour)	H_0 (kW/capita)	H_a (kW/capita)	H_s (kW/capita)	$H (H_0 + H_a + H_s)$ (kW/capita)	$R = GDP / H$ (USD/kWh)	$<p_e>$ (USD/kWh)
World	1.0	2.2	10	4	16	0.06	N/A
US	5.4	9.8	43	3	55	0.1	0.1
EU	4.0	4.7	14.4	1.4	21	0.2	0.24
Japan	4.8	5.3	2.4	9.9	18	0.3	N/A
China	0.52	2.5	10.3	3.2	16	0.03	N/A

economy consumes in agriculture much more solar energy per capita ($H_a = 43$kW) than other economies. As a result, the value of efficiency of the US economy ($R = 0.1$ USD/kWh) is two times lower than for the European Union (EU), and is three times less than that of Japan.

The Japanese economy consumes a relatively small amount of solar energy in agricultural production ($H_a = 2$kW), but at the same time a lot of solar energy is spent for seafood ($H_s = 10$kW).

Note that, according to our estimates, the largest amount of solar energy consumption per capita is in Norway – about 130 kilowatts!

Statistical data on the average price of electricity is freely available only for the US (see Figure 5.1). In 2010 the average price of electricity in the US was 10 cents per kilowatt-hour, which is in line with our estimates of US economy efficiency.

Among statistics presented at the Europe Energy Portal, there are no data on the average electricity price in the EU. The price listed in Table 5.2 (0.24 USD/kWh) was evaluated as the average electricity price for households in Germany, France, the UK and Italy.

For comparison, Figure 5.5 shows the graphs of the average electricity price and the economy efficiency in the US, starting in 2003 (after the California electric crisis). As one can see, the trend (4) is actually observed in the US economy.

It should be noted that the dynamics of economic efficiency depend mainly on the change in GDP, not the change of the primary energy consumption. The reason is that the GDP value per capita is changing much faster than the consumption of primary energy.

For example, the global economy's GDP per capita increased fivefold, from 1980 to 2011. At the same time, the primary energy consumption per capita increased slowly and grew only by about 20 percent (Figure 5.6).

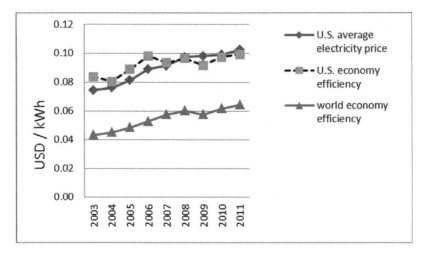

Figure 5.5 Comparative dynamics of economic efficiency and the average US electricity price.

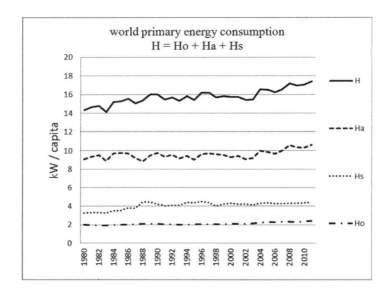

Figure 5.6 The growth of primary energy consumption per capita in the world economy.

Figure 5.7 shows the rise of the efficiency of the world economy and the US economy from 1980 to 2010. Annual fluctuations of the efficiency in the case of the US economy are due to differential sizes of crops. For the world economy, these fluctuations are evened out. The efficiency dynamics of the world economy is the most important trend, which allows us, in particular, to assess the global trends in world energy prices.

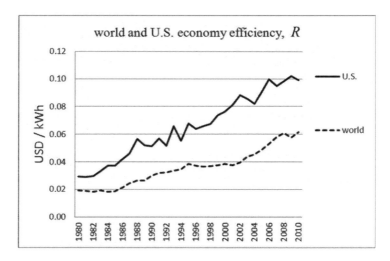

Figure 5.7 The dynamics of the US and the world economy efficiency.

Energy and information components of GDP

Physical macroeconomics argues that added value production is similar to thermodynamic free energy change. That is, both the added value, and the price of any commodity, contains two components – "useful energy" and "negative entropy" (or "information"):

$p =$ "*useful energy*" $+$ "*information*"

The "useful energy" item objectively characterizes the commodity as an energy carrier, while the "information" item is a subjective society's assessment of commodity's informative features.

The principal role of "society" in the socio-economic processes is to interpret and assess the information item in commodity prices. Without such an assessment, say, the paperback price would have been equal to the cost of energy that may be obtained by the paperback burning. Thus, society is a real, albeit indirect, added value manufacturer.

To keep the economy in a steady development state, distribution of added value between producers and society must be balanced, that is proportional to their energy expenses in the production process.

The "useful energy" item in carrier price (in monetary units) is an objective magnitude that is equal to carrier energy content h (in energy units) multiplied by value–energy correlation coefficient R:

"*useful energy*" $= h\,R$

Hence, prices of energy carriers with large energy content (as compared with the "information" item) must increase with economy efficiency growth.

Then other commodities prices, with dominant "information" item, most likely also will increase due to increased energy expenses. Thus, there are two constituents of inflation – a leading "useful energy" inflation and an induced "information" inflation.

A full inflation gives rise to increased GDP, consequently, to increased efficiency magnitude R, and then the next inflation circle starts. *Moderate inflation and economic efficiency growth are closely interrelated notions.*

Is there a limit to the growth of economic efficiency?

The human demand for useful energy is limited mainly to their need for food, warmth, water and transport. The demand of humans for information is rapidly growing, and it can be assumed that it is limited only by the computing power of the human brain. So, perhaps economic efficiency will rise until the brain processing power is exhausted.

Unfortunately, the demand for information includes not only the demand for such products as "green energy" and useful medication. It also includes a demand for ever more sophisticated weapons and drugs. Moreover, some people consider the new weapons production and free drugs circulation as increasing stability and harmony.

Thus, the value of information component in the value of the final product depends to a large extent on the "state of mind" of society. Accordingly, the efficiency R magnitude also depends on the society's state of mind. Similarly in physics, the entropy value depends on the observer's choice of the set of system parameters that describe the system. But, of course, once the set is strictly defined then the observer can see that the second law of thermodynamics is true.

By summarizing values of all final products produced by the economy during one year we get the GDP value:

$$\text{GDP} = R \, \Sigma h_i + I$$

where I is an information item of GDP and Σh_i is a total energy content of the final product. Taking into account that $R = \text{GDP} / H$ we obtain:

$$I = \text{GDP} \, (1 - \Sigma h_i / H)$$

i.e. the percentage of information component in the GDP value correlates with the magnitude of the $\Sigma h_i / H$ energy ratio.

The energy content of final product differs for concrete regional economies and is determined mainly by the energy contribution of the following final energy carriers:

Food energy carriers. The food energy content of the world economy final product is relatively small (≈ 0.1 kW/capita), in accordance with human need for food energy.

Energy carriers for households (electricity, gas, hot water). For advanced economies, the corresponding power can be roughly estimated as 1 kW/capita. Due to the development of energy-saving technologies, this power is expected to diminish.

Transport fuel for households. The energy content of transport fuel is correlated with the quantity of cars sold and is rapidly growing in the world economy.

Public energy carriers (for transport, institutions and army). Unfortunately, reliable statistics are simply not available.

Weapons. These final energy carriers are still produced in large amounts. Worldwide shooting, bombing, explosions and continuing sophisticated weapons production give us very little hope that the weapons contribution to final energy consumption could diminish in the nearest future.

In principle, the maximum information content in GDP value would be achieved if the list of final energy carriers contained only food products, that is, in the case of the pure agro/aqua economy. In this case, the magnitude of the $\Sigma h_i/H$ ratio would be about 1 percent, in accordance with energy efficiency of food biomass production (~1 percent in agriculture and ~0.1 percent in seafood production).

Accordingly, the percentage of the information component in GDP value would be very high – about 99 percent.

At first sight, the conclusion that the agro and aqua-oriented economy produces the added value with the highest information component seems to be discouraging. We used to think that engineers and workers in the industrial economy produce much more technologically advanced product than farmers and fishermen do. But actually grain, and a fortiori fish, are much more complex and informative products than any industry output.

Every seed is a tiny nanotech factory. Placed in appropriated conditions, this factory unpacks/produces several dozen similar factories and does not pollute the environment. Moreover, it improves ecology by consuming carbon dioxide and extracting oxygen.

The overall multistage process, programmed by a DNA nucleotide sequence, is very complex and requires some energy consumption at every stage. Finally, only about 1 percent of consumed solar radiation energy is stored in seeds in order to begin the next production cycle.

People are far from creating similar industrial technologies. They can only improve, for their own purposes, some of the details of the natural process by means of breeding and genetic engineering.

Grain basket price

With regard to non-final energy carriers on the market, crude oil and grain are practically important sources of energy.

The main difference between these energy carriers is that oil is the main energy source for transport and industry, while the grain is the most important and irreplaceable source of food energy for society.

The results of calculations of the world economy efficiency dynamics (see Figure 5.7) leads to some important conclusions concerning oil and grain world prices.

Grain is a secondary energy carrier that has two properties that are essential to global economic and social stability (see above Figure 5.4):

1   grain production of cereals and soybeans per capita is approximately constant, in accordance with the need of people in food energy (~1kg/capita/day);
2   the average world price of grain basket is low and flat (~0.14 USD/kg), thus guaranteeing minimum livelihood for the majority of the population of the Earth.

These properties can be challenged for the following reasons.

First, in view of the fact that the world economy efficiency magnitude grows, the "useful energy" component of grain basket price is also growing and reached the observable world prices (Figure 5.8).

Second, because the grain basket price is low and energy demand is increasing, it became profitable to use grain not only for food purposes, but also for the production of biofuels.

If the efficiency of the world economy will continue to grow, the "useful energy" component of the basket price may exceed the observed price. The observed price

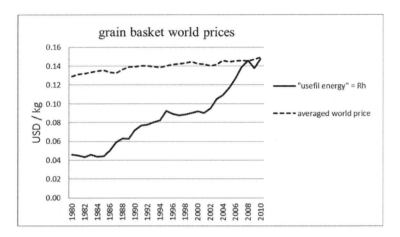

Figure 5.8 The dynamics of the grain basket world price.

Note: The food energy content h of the basket is equal to 2,000 kcal/kg, in accordance with the human need for food energy.

cannot be lower than its component for far too long. So, you'd expect a drop in the efficiency of the global economy or a sharp rise in grain prices.

The second, more optimistic possibility means that the world economy could undergo a "phase transition" to a new steady state with sharply increased GDP ($\equiv$ free energy level) and with a substantially increased agriculture sector.

Unfortunately, there is a real danger of mass starvation in poor countries during the transition period. To help them and to prevent food speculation, the international community should take measures in advance.

In particular, the global DAVT should be introduced. DAVT has powerful stabilizing characteristics and confronts pure speculative financial activity (see DAVT section).

A significant portion of the tax revenue from global DAVT should be devoted to the worldwide development of agriculture, for the sake of global socio-economic stability.

Crude oil prices

Unlike grain, oil is not a vital energy source. In principle, oil could be replaced by the other sources of primary energy. In fact, unlike the prices of the grain basket, world oil price has shown a sharp and variable dynamics in 1980–2010 years (Figure 5.9).

The "useful energy" value, which is proportional to the world economy efficiency, showed steady growth when the world oil price was relatively low (from 1985 to 2008 year).

In 2008, the world oil price had reached a "useful energy" value. One would expect that, in the case of subsequent more or less sustained growth of the world

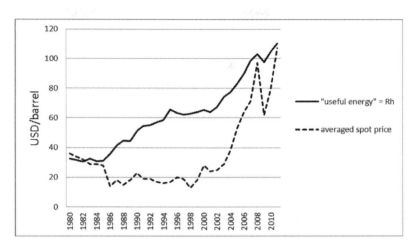

Figure 5.9 The magnitude of "useful energy" component of oil price and observed prices.
Note: The crude oil energy content $h = 1.7$ MWh/barrel.

economy, the world oil price will fluctuate around the "useful energy" value. But if there is a "phase transition" of the world economy to a new equilibrium state (see previous section), the oil prices dynamics during the transition period would be unpredictable.

DAVT

The DAVT paradigm[12] was proposed as the only feasible alternative to existing static taxation, which is a destabilizing factor in the economy.

In order to compare the qualitative output characteristics of dynamic and static tax systems, it is enough to compare the output characteristics of the proposed DAVT and the current VAT.

Basic relations

The magnitude of added value tax T in balance equation (1) is

$$T = N(G + E^{int}) \tag{5}$$

where N is a tax rate.

The above formula indicates that T is a tax on internal production. It should be noted that VAT is a tax on internal consumption since its amount is defined as $N/(N+1)$ part of the sales value S, debited by VAT amount paid by suppliers. The VAT definition is correct if only the VAT tax rate N is the same for all producers (i.e. if there are no preferential tax rates). In reality, VAT cannot exist without preferential tax rates due to the extremely harmful VAT influence on the low-profit producers. So, we shall assume below both for DAVT and for VAT the tax amount is defined in accordance with correct definition (5).

Let's introduce an important dimensionless parameter – "internal profitability"

$$\lambda = (S - E) / E^{int} \tag{6}$$

Internal profitability and normal profitability $\beta = (S - E) / E$ are related by equation $\lambda = \beta E / E^{int}$.

Then from relations (1), (5) and (6) one can easily obtain:

$$G = E^{int} (\lambda - N) / (N + 1)$$
$$T = E^{int} (\lambda + 1) N / (N + 1) \tag{7}$$

Therefore,

$$G/T = (\lambda - N) / (\lambda + 1) / N$$

As you can see, in the case of the static VAT (N = const):

- the production is unprofitable if $\lambda < N$, i.e. profitability threshold exists;
- the T/G ratio (which is the reverse of the G/T ratio) is equal to infinity if $\lambda = N$ that means a serious economy distortion;
- the added value distribution is misbalanced in favor of high-profit producers: with internal profitability increasing from profitability threshold to infinity, the G/T ratio increases from zero to $1/N$.

Profitability threshold elimination and balanced added value distribution can be achieved if N is directly proportional to the dynamic output characteristic – namely, to the internal profitability. That is, for DAVT we get:

$$N = n\lambda$$

where n is constant coefficient ($0 < n < 1$). Therefore,

$$G/T = (1 - n) / n / (\lambda + 1)$$

As contrasted with VAT, under DAVT:

- the profitability threshold does not exist; consequently, all producers are legal DAVT payers (so the shadow sector of the economy is shrinking);
- the T/G ratio has no singularities so there are fewer distortions in the economy;
- the added value distribution is no longer misbalanced in favor of high-profit producers.

DAVT eliminates the inherent destabilizing features of static taxation – the profitability threshold and disparity of added value distribution.

DAVT accounting

As it follows from the equations in (7), under DAVT the gain and tax magnitudes are defined by formulas:

$$G = E^{int} (1-n) \lambda / (1 + n\lambda)$$
$$T = E^{int} n (\lambda + 1) \lambda / (1 + n\lambda) \quad (8)$$

The above formulas are useful primarily for theoretical considerations. As for practical purposes, primarily for accounting, it is more convenient to rewrite these formulas in a form that does not contain uncertainties with any internal expenses.

To do this, let's introduce dimensionless parameter "y" that describes the expenses structure. Namely:

$$E^{ext} = yE$$

and accordingly:

$$E^{int} = (1 - y) E$$

The internal profitability λ is linked to the normal profitability β as follows:

$$\beta = (S - E) / E = \lambda E^{int} / E = \lambda (1 - y)$$

If external expenses are absent ($y = 0$), then $\lambda = \beta$. Therefore, instead of formulas (8) we obtain:

$$G = (1 - n)(1 - y) E (S - E) / [(1 - y) E + n (S - E)]$$
$$T = n (S - E)(S - yE) / [(1 - y) E + n (S - E)] \quad (9)$$

so for the current taxation period there is no need to calculate the internal profitability magnitude.

At the same time, the chief accountant must not fear making a loss (as in the case of VAT) because production is unprofitable only if total expenses exceed the sale. In such a case, the DAVT payment should be deferred until the next fiscal period.

Unlike VAT accounting, DAVT accounting is much more simple:

- producers are equal, because the tax coefficient n is the same for all of them;
- complex schemes of preferential taxation are no longer needed;
- since DAVT is a tax on domestic production, all exporters are its contributors. Therefore, the problem of VAT refunds completely disappears. Pseudo exporting also disappears.

- when replacing the VAT on the DAVT, the tax burden is shifted from low-profit producers to high-profit producers so the income tax could be abolished.

Productive economy stimulation

Unlike VAT, DAVT stimulates development of a productive, not speculative economy (Figure 5.10). In a VAT-using economy, the more external expenses percentage, the more profit. Such an economy encourages mediation rather than its own production.

Under DAVT, profit falls with increasing proportion of external expenses. The DAVT-using economy is a production-oriented one. Moreover, under DAVT, the profit extraction is impossible if internal expenses are absent. Consequently, purely speculative financial activity, with zero internal expenses, is meaningless: the entire amount of income ($S - E$ value) shall be paid as DAVT. DAVT is really an effective way to combat financial speculation, as opposed to financial transactions tax,[13] which is now being discussed in the EU.

Maximum profitability restriction

DAVT does not allow you to make money "out of thin air." A pure speculative activity, with negligible internal expenses and, consequently, with infinite internal profitability, is unprofitable.

Moreover, the maximum profitability magnitude is limited to the value of $1/\sqrt{n}$. We illustrate this conclusion by using equations (9).

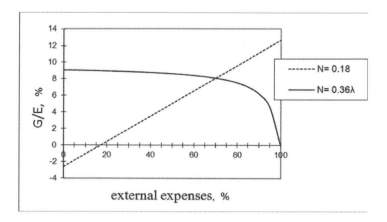

Figure 5.10 Two different economies: the G/E graphs for the low-profit enterprise, $(S - E)/E = 15$ percent.

Note: In the case of VAT ($N = 0.18$) the G/E ratio linearly grows with increased percentage of external expenses. Under DAVT ($N = 0.36\lambda$) the G/E ratio diminishes with the growing external expenses percentage and equals zero in the absence of internal expenses.

Value–energy interrelationship and dynamic added value taxation

As one can see, the G magnitude equals zero if expenses are absent ($E = 0$) or equal to sales ($E = S$). The profit maximum is reached with some optimal expenses value $E = \varepsilon S$, where $0 < \varepsilon < 1$. Then, from the condition $\partial G / \partial \varepsilon = 0$, we get the equation for the optimal ε_m magnitude:

$$(n' - 1)\varepsilon_m^2 - 2n'\varepsilon_m + n' = 0, \text{ where } n' = n/(1-y)$$

Thence, $\varepsilon_m = \sqrt{n'}/(1 + \sqrt{n'})$ and corresponding profit value is

$$G_m = S(1 - n)/(1 + \sqrt{n'})^2$$

This value is biggest if $y = 0$, that is, with zero external expenses (so $\beta_m = \lambda_m$). Finally, we get expressions for the gross profit, expenses, DAVT and profitability magnitudes at the point of maximum profitability:

$$G_m = S(1 - \sqrt{n})/(1 + \sqrt{n})$$
$$E_m = T_m = S\sqrt{n}/(1 + \sqrt{n})$$
$$\beta_m = \lambda_m = 1/\sqrt{n}$$

For instance, if the tax coefficient $n = 0.36$ (that corresponds to our reasonable estimates), then the maximum profitability is 167 percent – more than enough for a productive economy.

Theorem on stability

Some "grey" financial schemes involve a fictitious enterprise fragmentation (consecutive or parallel) in order both to diminish the VAT payments and to extract super-profits. Under static taxation such schemes create further instability in the economy. In a DAVT-using economy the instability decreases dramatically, which is proved by the following theorem:

> *Theorem on stability.* Let there be an enterprise with internal profitability λ, gain G and DAVT (or VAT) value T. Suppose that this enterprise is fragmented to a group of enterprises with parameters λ_k, G_k and T_k, the sum of internal expenses being kept. Also, both the sales and the external expenses are equal for the initial enterprise and for the group of enterprises. Then under DAVT ($N = n\lambda$) the inequalities $\Sigma G_k \leq G$ and $\Sigma T_k \geq T$ are true, equalities being fulfilled if only $\lambda_k = \lambda$.
>
> As to the VAT-using economy, the system is indifferent to any subdivision, i.e. $\Sigma G_k = G$ and $\Sigma T_k = T$.

The proof of the theorem, presented in the Appendix, clearly demonstrates the usefulness of the concept of internal profitability.

Therefore, the DAVT-using economy is stimulated to decrease excessive mediation and fragmentation. Nevertheless, this stimulation is not a monopoly promotion because only the length and thickness of production chains are forced to be shortened, but not the number of chains.

Market equilibrium

In order to assess the DAVT properties with respect to the market equilibrium, one should take into account that in this case the *S* and *E* variables in equations (9) are not arbitrary variables, because their magnitudes are defined in line with demand function.

For qualitative estimates it can be assumed that all producers are self-sufficient, so external expenses are absent ($y = 0$). Consequently, the internal profitability (λ) and usual profitability (β) magnitudes coincide ($\lambda = \beta$).

At first let us consider a non-taxable economy ($N = 0$ or $n = 0$). Market equilibrium in the economy is maintained due to demand function, which should be considered as an objectively existing nonlinear negative feedback.

The demand function can be approximated by dependency

$$Q = k / p^\alpha$$

where Q is sales quantity, p is commodity price (so $S = pQ$), α is demand parameter ($\alpha = 0$) and k is some coefficient. Under this approximation, price elasticity of demand is constant and equals to $p / Q \, (\partial Q / \partial p) = -\alpha$.

Bearing in mind that $S = pQ$ and $E = p_0 Q$, where p_0 is a cost price, we get for sales and expenses at market equilibrium:

$$S = k / p^{\alpha-1}; \; E = k p_0 / p^\alpha$$

If commodity price is equal to its cost price then sales amount equals $S_0 = k / p_0^{\alpha-1}$, therefore, $k = S_0 p_0^{\alpha-1}$ and we obtain:

$$\begin{aligned} S &= S_0 / x^{\alpha-1} \\ E &= S_0 / x^\alpha \end{aligned} \qquad (10)$$

where dimensionless parameter $x = p / p_0$.
Profitability $\beta = (S - E) / E = x - 1$. The profit magnitude is equal to

$$G0\,(x) = S - E = S_0 \, (1 / x^{\alpha-1} - 1 / x^\alpha)$$

Note that if the cost price is not varying, then the dependency of *G0* on $x = p / p_0$ actually means its dependency on price *p*. With rather good approximation it may be implied in most cases: the cost price is a conservative variable, while price can always be fixed at any level.

Under this approximation (so S_0 = const), the maximum of *G0* is reached if $x_m = \alpha / (\alpha - 1)$, so the optimal profitability magnitude is

$$\beta_m = 1 - x_m = 1 / (\alpha - 1)$$

Consequently, the non-taxable system is stable if demand parameter $\alpha > 1$. In the range of extra high demand ($0 < \alpha \leq 1$) the maximum profit magnitude does not exist that means economic instability.

If VAT (N = const) or DAVT ($N = n\lambda$) are introduced into the system then the corresponding maximum profit magnitudes G_N or G_n are defined by formulas (7) or (9) combined with expressions (10).

After taking derivatives, from the condition $\partial G / \partial \beta = 0$, we get equations for the optimal profitability magnitudes:

$$\beta_N = (1 + \alpha N) / (\alpha - 1)$$

in the case of VAT, and

$$\alpha n \beta_n^2 + (\alpha - 1)\beta_n - 1 = 0$$

in the case of DAVT.

Of course, if $N = 0$ or $n = 0$, in both cases we get the same magnitude of optimal profitability: $\beta_N = \beta_n = 1/(\alpha - 1)$. Unlike the magnitude of β_N, the β_n is less than $1/(\alpha - 1)$ and diminishes with n growth (Figure 5.11).

Qualitatively similar trends exist for optimal prices level. Thus, as distinct from VAT, the use of DAVT leads to diminishing of market prices.

An important DAVT feature is that DAVT stabilizes the economy in the extra-high demand range (that is, in the range of $0 < \alpha \leq 1$). For instance, if $\alpha = 1$ then we get the finite optimal profitability magnitude for DAVT: $\beta_n = 1/\sqrt{n}$, while in the case of VAT the corresponding β_N magnitude is equal to infinity.

Both the non-taxable economy and VAT-using economy are unstable in the extra-high demand range.

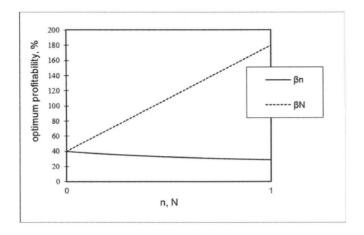

Figure 5.11 Opposite trends of the optimal profitability magnitudes in the DAVT- and VAT-using economies ($\alpha = 3.5$, $y = 0$).

DAVT as a stabilizing feedback

The examined DAVT features allow us to consider this tax as a stabilizing negative feedback introduced into the economic system in addition to the objectively existing demand function.

The DAVT concept was initially suggested by analogy with the electric negative feedback amplifier.[14] A crucial negative feedback feature is that the negative feedback sharply improves the amplifier stability while the amplification factor is diminished.[15]

The magnitude N of the DAVT "tax rate" is defined as $N = n\lambda$. Since the internal profitability λ can be very large, the N magnitude can also be more than unity.

Hence, the N magnitude should not be considered as a tax rate. Instead, the N magnitude should be considered as a feedback factor, which in principle can reach infinite values.

The internal profitability is directly proportional to profitability and inversely proportional to internal expenses percentage:

$$\lambda = \beta / (1 - y)$$

Consequently, the feedback factor N increases with increasing profitability, and it increases with decreasing internal expenses percentage.

As a result, the DAVT: (1) does not allow profitability to be too high, as well as (2) it does not allow internal expenses to be too small.

The first property, in particular, leads to the restriction of the maximum profit by $1 / \sqrt{n}$ magnitude.

Due to the second feature, the internal expenses percentage is stimulated to increase. Consequently, the DAVT stimulates, not a speculative but a productive economy. The type of the economy (productive or speculative) can be characterized by the average percentage of external expenses, namely, by the value of

$$\langle y \rangle = \Sigma \, y \, \Delta S_+ / \Sigma \, \Delta S_+$$

If this percentage becomes too large, then the economy may be destabilized due to insufficient own production.

The final conclusion is that DAVT is able to stabilize the economy both in relation to profitability and expenses structure, because the negative feedback factor ($n\lambda$) dynamically depends on both these output characteristics.

If the internal profitability magnitude increases to infinity, then the feedback factor also increases to infinity. In this case, the entire amount of income shall be paid as DAVT.

Dynamic versus static taxation

So, the stabilizing properties of DAVT are the result of the feedback function performed by this tax. The static taxes cannot play a feedback role in principle. If new static taxes are introduced or rates of existing static taxes are increased, then economy distortions and instabilities will grow more.

The most important DAVT stabilizing feature is balanced added value distribution between producers and society. Any static taxes, including financial transactions tax (which is actually an additional sales tax), cannot ensure the balanced added value distribution and, consequently, economy stabilization.

A static tax rate increasing is harmful first of all for low-profit producers. In particular, the suggested increasing of VAT rates in some EU countries means an increased profitability threshold and, consequently, a diminished number of legal tax payers. Hence, again, increased economy distortions, asymmetries and instabilities.

Differences in the properties of DAVT and VAT qualitatively reflect the difference between static and dynamic taxation in general. This characterizes qualitative difference between dynamic and static taxation paradigms as a whole. The main differences between DAVT and VAT are summarized in Table 5.3.

Global DAVT

DAVT simplifies and unifies domestic tax systems, which should help its global application. In particular:

- DAVT is a tax on internal production, while VAT is a tax on internal consumption. Consequently, exporters are DAVT payers, so a tax return is not required any more. Fraudulent pseudo-export completely disappears.

Table 5.3 The VAT and DAVT comparative features

Tax characteristics	VAT	DAVT
Tax rate	N = const	$N = n\lambda$
Tax accounting	$N/(N+1)$ part of the sales value S debited by VAT paid by suppliers	in accordance with expressions (9)
Tax type	internal consumption	internal production
Tax exempts	exporters and privileged producers	no exempts
T/G ratio	$(\lambda + 1) N / (\lambda - N)$	$n(\lambda + 1)/(1 - n)$
Profitability threshold	$\lambda = N$	no threshold
Maximum profitability	unlimited	$1/\sqrt{n}$
Economy instability range	super-high demand, $0 < \alpha \leq 1$	no instability
Tax-stimulated economy activity	intermediation and speculation	own production
Resistance to tax fraud	indifferent and provokes export tax return fraud	high resistance, export tax return does not exist
Market prices with respect to non-taxable economy	increased	diminished

- Under DAVT the profitability threshold does not exist, so there is no need for sophisticated schemes of preferential taxation. All producers are equal: the tax coefficient n is the same for all of them.
- Most of the existing static taxes, with overlapping tax bases, can be replaced by a single DAVT.

Due to the simplicity of the tax and its increased resistance to the "grey" financial schemes, DAVT introduction into regional economies promotes a global DAVT, instead of complicated and incompatible domestic tax systems.

The global DAVT would facilitate a more balanced distribution of the world GDP value in order to improve global socio-economic stability.

Symmetry and harmony in the economy

The economy, as a social living system, operates in accordance with laws of physics and bio-evolution. In addition to these laws, there are principles of symmetry and harmony, which are applicable to living systems as well as for their non-living environment.

State of sustainable development of the living system is maintained by the continuous reproduction of the thermodynamic free energy and its subsequent balanced distribution within the system. Balanced distribution of free energy occurs because of the existence of dynamic metabolic feedback.

In the case of unbalanced free energy distribution, mainly due to failure or the damage of negative feedback, the system develops distortions, asymmetries and instabilities, which can lead to disease of the system or even to its death.

In inanimate nature, there is also a symmetry and harmony. We admire the snowflakes and jewels, rainbows and the Northern Lights.

But symmetry principles are not laws and symmetry cannot be met in nature. The DNA helix is a right one, not the left helix. The proteins contain only L-amino acids, and there are no D-amino acids, etc. Life on the Earth has chosen one of the possible mirror worlds.

Although not a law, the principles of symmetry hold certain limitations that confront the confusion and chaos in the universe.

Thus, a variety of crystal structures is limited to 230 groups of symmetry; the sequence of colors in the rainbow is the same; solar systems are always flat; the chemical elements can be placed in the periodic table; and so forth.

Symmetry and structural order of the thermodynamic systems are quantitatively characterized by the entropy: the more structural order in the system, the lower the entropy. Therefore, the term of "information" in the theory of information is associated with the term "negative entropy," which means "reduced uncertainty."

Throughout biological evolution, living systems increased their structural and functional information content, becoming more complex, primarily due to the consumption of solar energy.

The thermodynamic free energy is the main factor that characterizes the vitality of the system, i.e. its capacity for dynamic behavior and development, in particular, for the maintenance of chemical reactions.

The higher the level of free energy, the more vitality. Therefore, living systems tend to increase the free energy level and maintain the level as long as possible. A steady state of the living system is the state with the maximum free energy.

On the contrary, the stable state of the inanimate system is characterized by a static order with minimal free energy.

Symmetric crystal structure is formed from disordered molecules, when free energy minimum is achieved that depends upon both useful energy and entropy factors.

Life is an "aperiodic crystal," according to Schrödinger's definition.[16] But in contrast to the crystallization process, in which the minimum of free energy is eventually reached, living systems tend to a maximum free energy.

However, in both cases, the state of harmonious equilibrium is formed by balancing the free energy distribution between the numerous degrees of freedom of the system. The difference lies in the fact that the crystal structures are in a state of static equilibrium, while the living systems are in a state of dynamic sustainable development.

Thus, based on the above physical analogy, we can conclude that a balanced distribution of added value ($\equiv$ free energy) is a basic condition for the stability and harmony of the socio-economic system.

Balanced distribution of added value in the large economy can only be achieved through dynamic taxation; DAVT provides that opportunity.

Under static taxation, there are obvious disparities and asymmetries in the economy: some producers are not able to legally pay taxes because of the existence of a profitability threshold, while other producers extract super-high profits due to the possibility of an infinite internal profitability. But living systems cannot be defined by infinite quantities!

In a DAVT-using economy, all producers are equal, there is no profitability threshold, added value distribution is balanced and maximum profitability is $1 / \sqrt{n}$.

Prosperous, evolutionary advanced economies of relatively small Nordic countries demonstrate that sufficiently balanced added value distribution can be achieved by static taxation with high tax rates.

But in the global economy, the level of social responsibility is much lower than, for example, in Norway, which consumes the greatest amount of primary energy per capita. Therefore, in order to reduce the socio-economic instability in the world, a global DAVT should be introduced.

It should be emphasized that, in order to stabilize the economy, a balanced added value distribution is needed, but not a limitation of personal income. Why so?

1 First, personal income is only part of the total added value.
2 Second, the human desire for high personal income has deep psychological and socio-psychological roots. Despite the remarkable words of Keynes ". . . that avarice is a vice, that the extraction of usury is a misdemeanour, and the love of money is detestable . . .," there is a maximum profit principle associated with psychologically caused demand function.
3 Third, in the future, people will start to limit their love of money.

In fact, there are some signs that the "state of mind" of society is changing in the direction of real feelings for harmony, which is opposed to greed. People understand that harmony is foremost for the unity of man and nature, as evidenced by the huge success of James Cameron's film *Avatar*.

Moreover, some international entrepreneurs are beginning to comprehend the importance of symmetry and harmony in the global economy.[17]

The natural human tendency to harmony is particularly evident in people's love of music. Perhaps the electromagnetic oscillations in the brain correspond to the major–minor rules of musical harmony. If so, then we can assume that music is a reflection of the universal harmony of the world.

Of course, it is too early for economists to study musical harmony to restore economic stability and add overall value to the global economy through a DAVT tax efficient system. It seems best to start with a review of pretty outdated economic theory based on the findings of physical macroeconomics.

Appendix – Theorem on stability: the proof

For initial enterprise we have: $E = E^{ext} + E^{int}$, and internal profitability is equal to

$$\lambda = (S - E) / E^{int} = (G + T) / E^{int}$$

The total sales value of the group of enterprises is equal to the sales value S of the initial enterprise and satisfies balance equation:

$$S = \Sigma(G_k + T_k) + \Sigma E_k^{int} + E^{ext}$$

Taking into account that internal expenses are kept, i.e. $E^{int} = \Sigma E_k^{int}$, we get equations

$$(S - E) = \Sigma(G_k + T_k) = \Sigma \lambda_k E_k^{int}$$

hence,

$$\lambda E^{int} = \Sigma \lambda_k E_k^{int}$$

Thereby, by introducing a "sales vector"

$$\boldsymbol{S} = \{\lambda E^{int}, E^{int}\} = \{G + T, E^{int}\}$$

the theorem conditions can be rewritten as $\boldsymbol{S} = \Sigma \boldsymbol{S}_k$.

The DAVT or VAT magnitudes are respectively equal to:

$$T = N(G + E^{int}), \; T_k = N(G_k + E_k^{int})$$

Under VAT (N = const), for the first component of the sales vector we get

Value–energy interrelationship and dynamic added value taxation 111

$$G + T = G + N(G + E^{int}) = (N + 1)\Sigma G_k + N \Sigma E_k^{int}$$

consequently, for VAT-using economy $\Sigma G_k = G$ and $\Sigma T_k = T$. Under DAVT ($N = n\lambda$), in accordance with formulas (8),

$$G = (1 - n) E^{int} \lambda / (1 + n\lambda)$$

It may be seen that the proof of inequality $\Sigma G_k \leq G$ is equivalent to its proof for the case of two enterprises, with sales vector $S = S_1 + S_2$. In such cases, the inequality to be proved, $G_1 + G_2 \leq G$, can be transformed into the following inequality:

$$za / (1 + na) + (1 - z)(b - za) / [(1 - z) + n(b - za)] \leq b / (1 + nb)$$

where $a = \lambda_1$; $b = \lambda$; $z = E_1 \, int \, /E^{int}$. By reducing to a common denominator, we get

$$nz(a - b)^2 \geq 0$$

The equality is fulfilled if only $\lambda_1 = \lambda_2 = \lambda$, QED.

Notes

1 Bartenev, V.N. (2009), Value–energy interrelationship and Dynamic added value taxation, *Journal of Interdisciplinary Economics*, 21, 2, pp. 273–94.
2 There are three terms used in the economic literature with the same qualitative meaning: "added value," "value added" and "surplus value." We use only the "added value" term.
3 Bartenev, V.N. (2011), Physical macroeconomics: energy and evolutionary grounds, *Interdisciplinary Journal of Economics and Business Law*, 1, 2, pp. 53–78.
4 Bartenev, V.N. (2012), Discussion papers. Reply to Jean-Jacques Pernet, *Interdisciplinary Journal of Economics and Business Law*, 1, 4, pp. 131–40.
5 We do not consider at all a simplified version of VAT – the sales tax, because it contains a serious system defect, namely, multiple taxation of the same base (added value) in the production chain.
6 Bertalanffy, L. (1968), *General System Theory: Foundations, Developments, Applications*, New York: Braziller.
7 Progressive personal income tax creates a stabilizing negative feedback loop, but it is insufficient because personal income is only a part of the total added value.
8 All the sources of data for the tables and figures in the chapter are in the public domain (portals eia.gov, fao.org, energy.eu, cia.gov, worldbank.org, bp.com, economywatch.com).
9 Bartenev, V.N. (2013), Indicators of efficiency and primary energy consumption in physical macroeconomics, *Interdisciplinary Journal of Economics and Business Law*, 3 (in publication).
10 The global economy consumes a relatively small amount of sunlight energy for the fuel biomass production, so this amount is negligible as yet.
11 *American Heritage Science Dictionary* (2005), Boston: Houghton Mifflin Company.
12 Bartenev, V.N. (2009), Value–energy interrelationship and dynamic added value taxation, *Journal of Interdisciplinary Economics*, 21, 2, pp. 273–94.

13 Intrinsically, the financial transaction tax is a usual sales tax, that is, a simplified version of VAT.
14 Bartenev, V.N. (2009), Value–energy interrelationship and dynamic added value taxation, *Journal of Interdisciplinary Economics*, 21, 2, pp. 273–94.
15 Palumbo, G. and Pennisi, S. (2002), *Feedback Amplifiers: Theory and Design*, Dordrecht: Kluwer Academic.
16 Schrödinger, E. (1946), *What is Life?*, New York: Macmillan.
17 Pernet, J.-J. (2012), From symmetry to harmony. A proposal for universal ethics, http://pernethique.ch.

6 Residual value insurance in the maritime sector

Stephen Allum

Subprime shipping sails into view

Everyone in the industry is aware that shipping experienced a buoyant market in the first few years of the new millennium, leading to profits that should, by now, be safely re-invested. The boom in shipping has its roots back in the 1990s and, helped by new global trade patterns, continued relatively untroubled towards peaks in rates for all asset classes.

Financing the boom was also relatively easy. With the demand for tonnage running high, second-hand vessel prices were sustained and shipyards continued to expand to meet the requirement. Used vessels commanded premiums above the cost of newbuilds as prospective owners sought to capitalise on demand. Scrapping of vessels was at a historical low and orders for new ships achieved new highs of US$200 billion in 2007.

The capital markets were also helping by playing the game. The dual attraction of the buoyancy of the shipping market, coupled with the availability of investment funds that did not have an attractive alternative, meant that financing was readily available to any shipowner with ambition and a half-sensible business plan.

At the beginning of 2007, whether you were borrowing a billion dollars to buy a company or a few million to buy a ship, lenders were prepared to lend 100 per cent of the purchase price with no questions asked.

When loans were used to buy assets, these loans pushed up the value of assets. This rise in the value of assets sparked yet more lending, which in turn pushed up asset prices further.

But the storm clouds were already gathering. In 2006, the danger to shipping from the US mortgage market was evident. But that warning was not then focused on the availability of credit, it related more to the domino effect fallout that the mortgage issues would have on the shipping industry. Pushed by the subprime mortgage issues, the first domino to fall would be US consumer confidence, quickly followed by a decrease in US consumer spending. That proved to be true; in early December 2007, the US consumer confidence index plunged to its lowest level since just after Hurricane Katrina in 2005.

This spending reduction initially found its way through to the shipping market via a reduction in US imports from China, with the resulting redeployment of vessels trading on the Asia–North America routes impacting rates around the world as the supply/demand balance readjusted.

The second domino effect of the impact of the US subprime mortgage market on global credit was less obvious. If reports are to be believed, few people anticipated it. To be fair, however, a shipping credit crunch has been talked about for many years – the programme for the Marine Investments Financing Forum in 2001 started by asking 'Is there a credit crunch for shipowners?'

Superficially, at least, it appears that the credit crunch we are now experiencing had little immediate impact on the shipping market. Perhaps shipping was initially still seen as a relatively safe haven by the financiers. Faced with the raw statistics, it was difficult to be pessimistic. But the game had become slightly more complex.

What started in the US now plays out on a global stage, fuelled by a credit crunch spiral that paralysed financial markets. The consumer confidence domino chain is no longer restricted to North America. Major high street names across the globe have seen massive falls in their share prices; some have gone into administration. The economic outlook is still darkening. Forecasts for gross domestic product growth in America and Europe were written down again earlier this year, while inflation forecasts are moving in the opposite direction.

There is universal agreement that economic conditions are going to be difficult for some time to come. Consumers will continue to tighten their belts. The volatility, which makes it so hard for shipowners and investors in shipping companies to plan, is unlikely to dissipate.

Red for danger

Any serious analyst of world economy will be well versed in China, the Asian powerhouse. Home to 25 per cent of the world's population, China's 1.3 billion people inhabit 30 cities with population over 5 million. The nation is expanding its infrastructure to accommodate an expanding and more prosperous population who want a better diet, advanced communications, bigger homes, better utilities and the freedom afforded by a private car.

Even before the global downturn, which seemingly China largely ignored, China was the number one consumer in the world for copper, platinum, steel, zinc and iron. They produce more steel than Japan and the United States combined. China's appetite for everything from oil to copper to soybeans is driving the prices of many commodities.

Go back a few years to 2007; global shipping was under pressure for different reasons. Hyundai Heavy Industries in South Korea boasted the world's largest shipyard, where nine dry docks were occupied with partially built ships over its 1,000-acre home site. They had orders to build 180 ships, and were highly selective. Demand outstripped supply all across shipyards in northeast Asia. The volume of ship orders in Korea more than doubled in one year, to the highest levels since 1973.

On some routes, freight rates quadrupled in the same year. They were unprepared, however, for the new demanding kid on the block – China. Suppliers and customers operating 'just in time' logistics had high anxiety. BHP Billiton, an Australian mining firm, claimed lack of ships represented a serious threat to its operation.

Seaborne trade accounts for 90 per cent of world trade, which in 1998 was up by half from 1990. A barometer of prices for the dry bulk freight market, the Baltic Dry Index, tripled in 2008. Dry bulk includes iron coal, grain and ore and is dominated by steel processing supply lines. Longer voyages to China added further pressure on already high container rates.

Out of the ashes: the state of shipping

Yet, all was not rosy in the garden: although forecast, the rapidity and depth of the plunge in freight rates in 2008 came as a shock to many (Figure 6.1). It has yet to recover.

There is room for some optimism in the container ship business, as witnessed by the number of loaded containers going into the ports on the US West Coast. Here, demand increased by 1.7 per cent during 2012, more than making up for the fall in demand in 2011. This uplifting result was achieved in spite of a strike, which heavily affected imports into the port of Los Angeles in November and December.

In the chartering market, time charter rates for tonnage in the range of 1,100 to 4,250 TEU (twenty-foot equivalent unit) have slipped back below the early 2012 levels following a brief flash of optimism at the middle of 2012. This new level is pushed down on the back of low demand for these vessel types.

Large container ships operate in a different environment than the small ones, and charter demand for ultra-large container vessels (ULCVs, greater than 10,000 TEU) remains healthy. Supply is still relatively scarce, which is why the charter

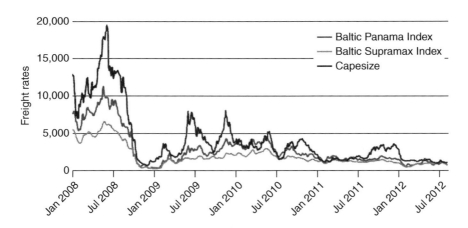

Figure 6.1 The decline in freight rates from 2008 to 2012.

Source: Bloomberg.

116 *Stephen Allum*

rates for these vessels are not under the same pressure as the smaller vessels with higher unit costs and an abundant number of uniform alternatives to choose between for charterers.

As demand for cargo grows sluggish and the supply of tonnage constantly hovers around 6–8 per cent annual growth, something has to give. That something is the asset prices. According to VesselsValue.com asset prices for 2013-built tonnage in the range of 2,500 to 13,000 TEU have dropped by 17.7–20.7 per cent over the past year. This value erosion only becomes exacerbated the older the tonnage gets. Corresponding asset prices for 2006-built tonnage have dropped to the extent of 22.4–25.2 per cent over the past year.

The container ship fleet is off to a flying start regarding supply, as the fleet has already been expanded by over 110,000 TEU during January (see Figure 6.2). This reverses the trend of low-scale deliveries that took place during the second half of 2012. For the full year of 2013 the Baltic and International Maritime Council (BIMCO) expects a level that will surpass that of last year and come in around 1.4 million DWT (deadweight tonnage); a level that will lift the total available TEU by 7 per cent after the elimination of obsolete tonnage sold for recycling.

On the demolition front, January saw a significant amount of container tonnage being sold for recycling; third only to two peak months in mid-2009.

Contracting activity has also started 2013 fairly fast, with new orders for over 113,000 TEU being placed in January, much impacted by two orders in particular: 4 × 10,000 TEU at one Chinese yard and 5 × 14,000 TEU at a South Korean yard.

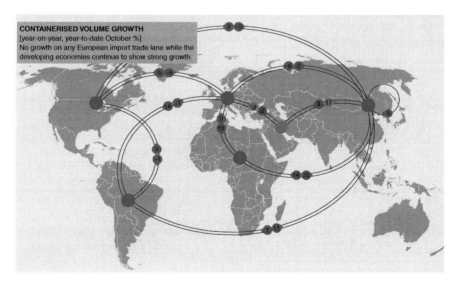

Figure 6.2 Containerised volume growth (year-on-year, year-to-date October %).

Source: Raconteur/Seabury Global Ocean Database.

Note: No growth on any European import trade lane while the developing economies continue to show strong growth.

Residual value insurance in the maritime sector 117

The industry expects ordering during 2013 to exceed the level of 2012 that came to a total of just 446,564 TEU.

China's five-year plan (2011–15) prioritised shipbuilding; at the start of this period time, China accounted for one-third of the total production. The global slump was accompanied by a collapse of the ships on order; from a peak of about 250 Chinese shipyards with reasonable prospects, currently only around 150 Chinese shipyards have an orderbook. Those that have orderbooks have seen the numbers decline. Overall, there has been a fall of 47 per cent in DWT of vessels waiting to be built.

A total of 475 vessels remain on the orderbook for delivery between 2013 and 2016. With half of them scheduled for delivery in 2013 alone, the container ship segment is expected by BIMCO to hold up best. In this respect, the container ship situation differs from that of tankers and bulkers, where the share of the orderbook that is scheduled for delivery in 2013 represent 61 per cent and 71 per cent respectively. Slippage ratios in those two segments to the extent of 25 per cent and 30 per cent are still anticipated (Figure 6.3).

In the course of 2012, no less than 51 ULCVs were launched into the active fleet. In 2013 that number is likely to go down. The impact from this will be felt in particular on the Far East to Europe trading lane, where these vessels are almost

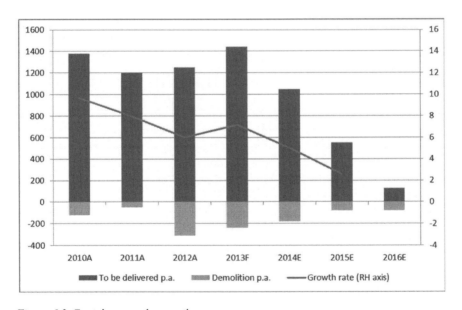

Figure 6.3 Container supply growth.

Source: BIMCO.

Note: A is actual, F is forecast, E is estimate (which will change if new orders are placed). The supply growth for 2013–16 contains existing orders only, and is estimated under the assumptions that the scheduled deliveries fall short by 10 per cent due to various reasons and 15 per cent of the remaining vessels on order are delayed or postponed.

exclusively heading. This will mean that more than four full strings (of ten vessels each) will be added. They are likely to be put to work instead of smaller vessels on this trading lane, which will then be cascaded onto other trades in a snowballing effect across the market. This is relevant to the charter rates for feeder tonnage, as these ship sizes can get into an even more difficult situation during the cascading process.

In the lead-up to the Chinese New Year, the amount of idle container ship tonnage went down slightly to 754,000 TEU (4.6 per cent of total container ship fleet). Going forward, idling of tonnage is expected to stay rather flat as the higher rates incentivise no-one to lay up their vessels.

One light on the horizon is that the conditions will be right for scrapping of vessels that are long past their best by date, leading to a refreshing of the fleet. Many owners see an opportunity to capitalise on the current soft market and attempt to modernise their fleets, buying efficient, low-emission ships at rock-bottom prices; however debt financing options will remain difficult.

The perfect storm

This is a downturn like no other we've seen in recent memory, for two reasons: it's global; and its primary cause is well documented: the bursting of a massive debt bubble.

Since then, falling asset prices are leading to losses for those who borrowed to buy those assets. As they struggle to pay debts, they sell other assets, driving down the price of those assets and causing losses for other borrowers. And when they can't repay banks, the resources of banks are depleted, which means there's less credit available – and no 100 per cent ship mortgages or other loans – driving down asset prices further, which leads to a further contraction of lending, and so on in a vicious cycle of decline.

But new vessels, ordered during the peak years, were coming out of the shipyards and flooding the market. An increased number of vessels chasing a potentially reduced market will have the obvious effect of unbalancing supply and demand, and therefore reducing rates. Second-hand vessel values also suffered a 'correction'.

This reduced ability to pay and falling asset values, together with the ever increasing costs of fuel and the more recent higher costs associated with manning, produces a recipe for a perfect storm.

With a credit crunch that refuses to be just a blip, and eager not to be associated with 'subprime shipping', financiers have restricted their involvement with the industry. Banks have been forced into reducing their dependence on diminishing sources of wholesale funds, which is why they've been lending less. They also have increased burdens of managing and retaining regulatory risk capital to cope with.

For those shipowners that have not seen traditional sources of credit retreating, they will have encountered significantly higher lending rates for anything less than 'A-rated paper'.

With the end of easy credit and the downturn in rates, shipowners have to consider other options to manage risk and develop their businesses.

Bold shipowners could, of course, look to a stock exchange listing as an alternative source of funding. Even as the credit markets seized up in the second half of 2007, many corporations were still able to float equity – and plenty of it. The global initial public offering market raised a record $275 billion by the end of November 2007, with October and November being the biggest issuance months.

Greek shipping company Paragon Shipping was one company that entered the public market in August 2007, just as the credit crunch started to bite. The stock initially priced at the low end of expectations, raising over $160 million, but soon after peaked at around 30 per cent premium.

In financial year 2011, Paragon wrote down a $277 million impairment loss in an effort to make their book values closer to actual market levels. Paragon killed their dividend in Q1-2011, and since then the stock has dropped 67.2 per cent.

Others have taken the same route with varying degrees of success. In 2004, the fleet of publicly-quoted companies was 193m GT (gross tonnage), growing to 293m GT by November 2007, representing over 40 per cent of world tonnage.

It's uncertainty, not tight credit

Some bankers indicated that fear has seized the market, chilling business owners who might otherwise want to take on new debt. The concern is that the way the current crisis has been talked up has led them to pull back, and to not want to move forward with plans of expansion.

Other bankers perceive increased lending; they believe the banking industry is prepared to provide liquidity to the markets ready and willing, but there's a crisis of confidence that is holding shipping back.

But that is not the experience of the shipowners. Even big name shipping banks are asking good owners with good business cases to wait for funds. If the unfettered movement of capital, goods and services is going to survive, if there's not going to be a reverse-globalisation that could impoverish the future of shipping over the longer term, there will have to be a new model.

What is universal, and is key, is that the financial institutions want to ensure that they do not replace the subprime risks that have been offloaded to governments and taxpayers with other toxic risks. Capital is still flowing and loans can be provided although the bar has been set a lot higher.

So what can shipowners with ambition do now to make sure they are first in the queue for any money banks still have to lend?

In addition to the various financing options (cash reserves, equity and debt financing), lease financing is an important tool for acquiring durable goods and it accounts for nearly a third of the new industrial and commercial equipment sold annually.

Broadly speaking, a lease contract transforms a risky new real asset into two components, a front-end financial asset with fixed periodic payments over a known term, and a back-end residual physical asset that covers its economic life beyond lease termination.

In general, the residual value refers to the expected value of the used physical asset at the end of the lease. The main source of uncertainty embedded in the back-end residual asset is the risk that the future market value of the underlying asset at lease termination will vary from the projected residual value. This price fluctuation is commonly known as residual value risk.

A lease is thus a loan of an income-producing physical asset that depreciates in value over time: it exposes the lessor (lender) not only to default risk on the contractual lease payments but also to fluctuations in the lease-end residual value of the underlying asset.

It unbundles the risk of economic ownership of a new real asset into a hybrid structure consisting of front-end fixed-rate periodic lease cashflows and an uncertain final (balloon) payment. In so doing, it allows the lessor to restructure the time profile of ownership risk into two tranches:

1 a near-term debt-like security typically with lower risk (analogous to a senior tranche in a collateralised debt obligation (CDO)); and
2 a deferred equity representing residual economic ownership (similar to the junior or equity tranche in a CDO).

As compared with credit risk and interest rate risk, the residual value risk is the greatest uncertainly in lease financing because forecasting residual value several years in advance is fraught with difficulty.

The magnitude of the residual value at risk decreases with the term of the lease as a fraction of the economic life of the underlying asset (whereas default and interest rate risks tend to increase with the lease term). While the owner of the asset, called the lessor, typically bears the default and interest rate risks associated with the contractual lease payments, the allocation of residual value risk depends upon the type of lease contract.

In an open-end lease, the user of the asset, called the lessee, is obligated to compensate the lessor if the market value of the underlying asset at lease expiration drops below the projected residual value. In other words, the lessee is required to guarantee the underlying asset at lease maturity at the fixed residual value even though its market value may be lower.

The lessee issues a residual value guarantee, which is essentially a real put option, to the lessor in exchange for a real call option to purchase the underlying equipment at the residual value at lease termination.

These embedded real options expand the lessor's core portfolio to include:

1 the present value of lease payments (the front-end asset); and
2 the deferred residual asset bracketed by the put and call options.

The bundle of assets in (2) can be characterised as one resembling a long position in a stock with a value equal to the present value of the residual value of the underlying real asset, a long position in a put option on the underlying equipment with a strike price equal to the residual value and term identical to the lease period, and a short position in a call with an identical strike price and term to expiration to that of the put option.

If one makes a reasonable assumption that the residual value is set equal to the forward price of the equipment for delivery at lease termination, it is possible to show that the package comprising the long residual asset, long put and short call, is comparable to a riskless bond.

Thus a lessors overall portfolio covering both (1) and (2) positions consists of the sum of present values of a riskless maturity zero-coupon bond and a coupon-like bond representing the lease cashflows.

The net effect of these arrangements is that the lessor is returned to a position very similar to the one associated with outright sale of the underlying asset on credit.

In contrast, a closed-end lease contract exposes the lessor to residual value uncertainty. The classic example of a closed-end lease is a consumer automobile lease contract with two- to five-year terms.

The consumer most often encounters residual value risk when financing the purchase of a new car. Residual value guidebooks show what passenger vehicles are worth, depending upon the model, from about 20 per cent to 50 per cent of their initial purchase price after five years. Therefore, unlike the typical equipment lease contract, the consumer lease for new automobiles exposes the closed-end lessor to sizeable residual value risk; the risk that the market price of the leased vehicle at the end of the lease period varies from its predetermined residual value.

Even credit risk associated with the fixed monthly lease receipts is ignored, the closed-end lessor holds an undiversified risky position in the underlying residual asset. In contrast, the residual value guarantee issued by the open-end lessee in the equipment segment is typically a small part of his or her overall portfolio and hence relatively more diversifiable.

Similar to an open-end equipment lease, a closed-end lease typically grants a purchase option allowing the lessee the right to buy the leased asset at the fixed residual value at lease termination. Consequently, the core portfolio of a lessor contains a long position in the present value of lease payments, another long position in the present value of the residual value of the underlying assets and a short position in the call option.

Setting aside the stream of lease payments, the remaining two elements of the portfolio are analogous to the standard covered call writing strategy on financial options. As a writer of a call option on the used car, the closed-end lessor sacrifices not only the upside potential of market value exceeding the residual value of the used vehicle but also faces the downside risk – the risk that the terminal market value drops below the residual value.

Again, the lessor's core portfolio can be characterised as one resembling a long position in a riskless bond with a value equal to the present value of the residual value and a short position in a put option with a strike price equal to residual value and term identical to the lease period.

In other words, his long residual asset/short call position is similar to holding (risky) debt subject to default risk if the residual value varies from the forward price of the underlying asset. It is worth emphasising that this default risk inherent in the portfolio in (2) is separate from the credit risk attributable to the lessee in package (1).

The written put option reflects that the lessor is effectively self-insuring against the residual value loss. Evidently, a short put position can entail huge losses when the put exercise price is high (relative to the forward price of the used asset), the lease term is long and the underlying used asset price suffers a sustained sharp decline. Notice that the lessor's counterpart who sells the durable good outright on credit does not face the risk associated with a short put position.

Rescued by the dark arts

Risk management still seems to be viewed by many in the industry as a dark art that should be shunned, but shipowners who want to prosper in the current climate might do well to revisit the management of financial risks.

Amongst these are charterers' default insurance and residual value insurance (RVI). The former would protect the income stream of the owner should falling rates leave the charterer temporarily 'financially embarrassed', while the latter underpins the future value of the vessel as an asset.

Used in its widest sense, the management of risk is the management of uncertainty, and good risk management will help maximise the upside and opportunity risks, as well as minimising or eliminating the downside risks.

Good risk management will help with both credit financing and public listing. Regulatory requirement notwithstanding, demonstrating to investors that the company has identified the risks, has a thorough understanding of them and has adjusted its business plan and strategy to embrace them is a proven way of increasing the chances of success for an initial public offering.

By the same token, for credit financing, properly enumerating and managing the risks will help create 'A-rated paper'. By so doing, a shipping company should have access to funding at better rates than those still saddled with the spectre of the subprime market, and it only takes a small change in rates to have a huge effect on profits over a vessel's lifetime.

So the message is not to be afraid of the dark arts. The storm may be raging around, but by utilising risk management to underpin future value and create 'A-rated paper', it is possible for a shipping company to ride out even the perfect storm and come out the other side in better shape than its competitors.

Smoke and mirrors: solutions for meaningful asset valuation

As mentioned above, for shipping, the financial crisis that exploded in the third quarter of 2008 had the impact of choking off the supply of bank credit that would normally support purchases of second-hand vessels or resale of new ships about to be delivered from shipyards.

Until the market disruption, a steady flow of transactions provided the raw information for asset appraisers to evaluate changes in vessel prices. In turn, these values would serve as the basis for periodic asset valuations used in measuring requisite coverage ratios for shipping loans, with the loan-to-value (LTV) ratio being the best known.

Although new lending activity contracted in late 2008, bankers were still faced with the task of monitoring borrower compliance with covenants in existing credit facilities. A number of brokers who had provided guidance on values of standard vessel types through market reports and client circulars ceased doing so around this time, although some were still providing values to their bank clients on a bespoke basis. At one stage on www.shipvalue.net, the online service of major broker Clarkson Valuations Ltd, a disclaimer read:

> Because of current market conditions we are having difficulty in monitoring values. The values in the system were last updated on 3 October 2008 and have not been updated since. Until we have been able to update our values as a guide to present values, please do not use the system.

Where a vacuum of value information exists, those doing the talking built an audience: value assessments led to more visibility for the Baltic Exchange. One recent analyst report noted that asset values remain a concern in general for the tanker market, with rates for all vessel classes at depressed levels, tanker values have been assessed sharply lower by the Baltic Exchange, representing over a 40 per cent decline from the 2008 peak.

These dislocations in vessel asset markets – or lack thereof – have figured prominently in companies' negotiations with banks.

Questions surrounding valuations figure prominently in ship finance seminars. Compass Maritime has continued to provide valuations of vessels, mainly in relation to LTV computations for existing vessels. Until the end of 2008, most valuations were done by looking at recent sales. Since that time things have changed and the markets have become illiquid with big spreads between bid and asked.

Valuation standard

The valuation standard refers to the definition of value tied back to the valuation purpose. The most common valuation standard is the 'fair market value' (FMV) standard, which is commonly defined as the price at which a willing buyer and a willing seller would transact, with each party having access to all relevant information and with neither party under the compulsion to transact (Figure 6.4).

The alternative method of valuation, looking at replacement cost, which is applicable for new vessels, has also been problematical, because there were so few new orders in 2009 and 2010.

With these disruptions, long-standing practices related to valuations are now being contested. Up until very recently there was little evidence of borrowers challenging valuations. However, as the market has worsened and certain banks have issued reservation of rights letters, borrowers have begun to challenge valuations.

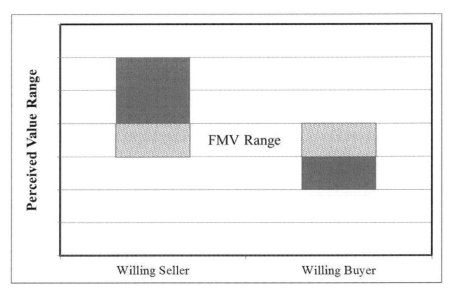

Figure 6.4 Fair market value.

A third appraisal method – the income method – answers the question of what can be earned from an asset; the method has seen more usage lately. But it is not an exact science; it is a theoretical exercise and just because the value is *x* today, it may be different tomorrow. Appraisers adopting this method are using rational but low expectations of the freight markets going forward. The risk of charter default is also an issue with the methodology, particularly where the current charter is significantly above the present market rates.

The income method of appraisal is becoming more established. The Hamburg Shipbrokers Association (HSA), a 100-year-old organisation in one of the world's leading shipping centres, reported that the 2008 crisis caused a virtual standstill in the main segments of the ship sales and purchase market. HSA added that transactions that have been reported might well be unreliable as a basis for proper valuation because they were forced sales.

German *Kommanditgesellschaft* (KG) funds, without deep-pocketed parents or investors willing to meet additional calls for equity capital, have indeed been forced to sell vessels under distress conditions. In one well-documented case, investors in a KG fund watched the prices on offer for a 1997-built, 2,900 TEU vessel dip in value to levels below those needed for investors to pay taxes due.

The HSA proposed an alternative mechanism for assessing the long-term asset value (LTAV) of vessels. The association's methodology, applicable across all shipping sectors, is the discounted cashflow (DCF) approach. Even though DCF has been around for decades in other asset classes, the proposal broke new ground in seeking to establish how and when it should be applied to maritime assets.

Of course, the devil is in the detail: the guidelines are applied through an equation for calculating the LTAV of a vessel over a ten-year timeframe. In spite of the apparent precision of the approach, much is left to individual judgement, which can result in 'spurious accuracy'. Suggestions for deriving two very important components of the calculation – operating costs and residual value – point to long-term averages.

Financial purists will enjoy the fact that a simplistic approach to determining the applicable discount rate is based on a weighted average cost of capital. The HSA recommended a 6.6 per cent cost of capital, based on 70 per cent bank finance at Libor plus 137.5 basis points and 30 per cent equity costed at 7.63 per cent.

While many may disagree with these assumptions, the methodologies underpinning the LTAV, which have been developed in conjunction with the German finance community, may point the industry towards a more objective approach to asset valuation.

Market participants are still getting used to the LTAV concept, which is meant to guide rather than replace appraisers: essentially it is just a net present value, calculated with specific assumptions. Although launched into a container ship marketplace, if data are available, it should also be applicable to all vessel categories including tankers and bulk carriers.

In ship finance, loan documentation always requires the use of one or more independent shipbrokers that are either appointed by or approved by the banks. Sometimes a panel will be scheduled. The formula approach could fail standard documentary requirements because valuations are usually predicated on a charter-free sale basis as between a willing buyer and a willing seller, which would indicate that recent sale and purchase activity should be the most appropriate measure.

Experience from other asset classes

In the aircraft sector, valuations still blend art and science but benefit from guidelines issued by the International Society of Transport Aircraft Trading, which also offers a rigid certification programme for asset appraisers. Commercial aircraft valuation has developed into a very complex business from very simple beginnings. Prior to the ascendancy of the leasing giants, appraisals were primarily built around the value of the last similar transactions. The advent of professional operating lessors, financing their fleets with complex, often tax-driven financial instruments, demanded better appraisals.

In the maritime sector, listed lessors include GSL, Danaos Corporation and Seaspan Corporation, amongst others. Privately held ship lessors include Sea Change Maritime LLC, which owns and operates a fleet of medium-size container ships to serve as a leading supplier of vessels to operators worldwide.

The first of two main methods used by aircraft appraisers is FMV – the price that would likely be agreed between a willing buyer and seller, without distress conditions. A second method – the 'securitised value' or 'lease encumbered value' – reflects the prevalence of operating leases for set periods where rentals are known in advance.

Where rental income is known, one can forecast the likely residual value, and a reasonable assumption can be made on the discount rate. Operating lessors, investors and hedge funds may well have a target rate of return that will form the implicit basis for the discount rate.

A mechanism for dealing with default risk is the key downfall in utilising LTAV more extensively. In shipping, the risk of charterer default or renegotiation is very real. LTAV guidelines to ship appraisers may need more definition in treatment of defaults.

Requests from banks to value entire portfolios rather than individual vessels for LTV purposes have also emerged, but so far there has been no sign of panicked sellers dumping ships onto the market.

What makes an asset market dysfunctional?

The HSA has defined what constitutes a dysfunctional market:

1 An uncharacteristically low number of sales candidates in comparison to the overall fleet with one category of vessel over a period of at least three months means that there is a severe imbalance between willing sellers and willing buyers.
2 Transactions in which either seller or buyer are knowingly under time pressure, constraint or in urgent need to conclude a deal driven by personal or corporate distress. Prices do not reflect vessel characteristics.
3 A difference of 30 per cent or more between current transaction prices and LTAV lasting for at least three months.
4 An uncharacteristically low number of market participants, based on total number of parties within a market over a three-month period.
5 Absence of essential, regular market conditions, such as the unavailability of debt financing for a large number of market participants.

The valuation of a maritime businesses remains closer to an art than a science, computer modelling and forecasting notwithstanding. Increasingly, bigger and more transparent companies created since the early 1990s have positioned themselves as 'industrial shipping' companies and have adapted a more corporate approach to business. A handful has attained public listing, while many have remained in the hands of families or private equity interests. In between the lines, companies are describing more stable business practices than the swashbuckling asset traders of days gone by, and company missions of forging long-term relationships with cargo providers.

Valuation premise refers to the underlying assumption on how the asset in question will be exploited in the future. Will the use of the asset remain as is? Alternatively, the asset may be valued under a specific use that differs from the historical usage, such as an acquisition. A common premise is the 'best use' concept, which values the asset at the highest value under foreseeable circumstances, regardless of current usage.

An area where premise is of crucial importance is in bankruptcy, where the distinction between an orderly disposition and a distressed disposition can have a significant impact on valuation.

A new paradigm: guaranteed residual values

Light at the start of the tunnel

The world is full of interpretation. Every day a trawl through the media will uncover any number of learned economists and financial experts taking the same data as conclusive proof that the global economic recovery will take one shape or another, or even that it is not happening at all.

One of the constant elements, however, is the continued lack of finance available to acquire new assets. Recently FORTIS Bank Nederland said that a brightening bond market is likely to become of increasing interest to shipowners seeking to cover financing requirements in the absence of bank finance, which is currently scarcely available.

With all elements of the value chain looking to manage asset risk, one positive step forward is to utilise RVI, a mechanism to manage and control the residual value risk of assets.

A growing class of insurance due to increasing underwriting capacity, RVI provides the asset owner and their financiers with asset value certainty at a predetermined time in the future, and is therefore an invaluable means of balancing exposures in volatile markets and removing asset risk from the balance sheet.

Any transaction where the payment stream does not amortise the full principal amount can benefit from RVI. For example, a shipyard may guarantee the future value of an asset to differentiate against the competition. The guarantee may result in the transaction being accounted for as a lease. However, with RVI, the manufacturer can still recognise the transaction as a sale for accounting purposes.

This class of business takes in many areas of asset-based finance including energy and marine, aviation, rail equipment, manufacturing, industrial and commercial equipment and commercial property.

For many years, the shipping industry was not amongst those. Traditionally, RVI and shipping have not been easy bedfellows. For many years the banks internalised much of their asset risk, and the only risks presented to the insurance market were those requiring additional capacity, or because they had complexity, or because – to be frank – the assets were difficult to give a value to. At the same time, the RVI market had a reputation of being niche, for being difficult and for not paying claims.

Insurers saw ships as assets that have high volatility, therefore assess a higher likelihood of a claim, and consequently responded by setting high deductibles and even higher rates. Potential buyers of the insurance perceived that price as too high for the apparent value.

Much of that has now changed. Banks no longer want to hoard asset risk, and would like to get much of it off their books. Certainly few of them are accepting new asset risk; and that provides an opportunity for RVI to help. RVI is an excellent tool to manage and control the residual value risk and, when introduced early in the structuring of a financing deal, it can expand sources of funding. RVI often provides the cornerstone of an asset financing programme.

The RVI markets are also in the process of transformation. There is more capacity for shipping now than has been available for some time; and there is significant interest from risk capital providers wanting to offer additional capacity. The vast majority of policies are now written on a proceeds basis, rather than on the FMV basis, one of the issues that gave the industry a poor reputation some years ago.

But RVI is not a derivative. The insurer is guaranteeing the quality of the appraisal. The record of the appraiser must be reviewed and understood and the variance measured.

Crucially, for the shipping markets, the biggest change in RVI has been the recent introduction of a shipping analyst to the RVI carriers. Several of the insurers and banks are now using Maritime Strategies International Ltd reports to help them as part of the analysis of the risks and assessment of the attachment and rate on line.

A lesser, though still important, aspect is the current state of the shipping market. As values are low, the theory is that they are unlikely to get much lower and so the volatility argument becomes a one-sided bet. Well, perhaps it is not as secure as that, but at least actuaries should feel far more comfortable in assessing the risk of insuring future asset values and giving realistic attachments and rates.

In many ways, therefore, the value of RVI to the shipping industry is inversely proportional to the health of the industry. Perhaps that's not ideal, but that is where we are.

Meanwhile, the insurers see a relatively narrow window where there will be sufficient overlap of interests in the value of RVI and its cost to allow most deals to work and then, having completed a few deals, they will be keen to complete more in order to diversify their portfolio.

Good news travels fast, but bad news travels faster. The good news is that the RVI markets are open for shipping business. The bad news is that demand will still vastly exceed supply. So whisper it quietly, and grab the opportunity while you can.

The preconditions for bringing an asset to the RVI markets are:

- the asset must be tangible;
- the asset must be specific and named;
- the date is a single point in time.

As before, RVI indemnifies the lessor if an asset is returned at term and it is worth less than its booked residual value. Assets that are not returned in agreed condition at term are not covered. A large amount of due diligence is undertaken prior to policy placement; think of RVI as being more akin to structured finance than insurance. Having said that, once the due diligence is complete, if there is a claim, then it is more likely that the claim would be paid promptly.

The most important part of RVI pricing is identifying all of the potential exposures and charging for them accordingly. Specific issues that the insurer has to consider include data quality, moral hazards, threat scenarios, aggregation of risk and cost of capital. Other asset specific issues can include:

- obsolescence (computers);
- liquidity (railroad);
- performance guarantee (wind turbines);
- property (specialty equipment);
- environmental (oil wells);
- popularity (SUVs);
- political risk (ships).

Projecting the values

Estimating forward-looking values for 10 years, or more, does require a combination of art and science, however all residual value calculations require this information on the basis of:

1. FMV – change of ownership;
2. forced market value;
3. absolute worst case for both sale (using a 1 in 100 value) and scrap.

In addition, stress testing of valuations in the years around the term (or tenor) of the policy would be required based on the following variables:

1. new building prices;
2. scrap prices;
3. recessionary environment;
4. changes in the life expectancy of the vessel based on legislation and/or technological changes;
5. composite of any or all of the above.

The estimated valuations so derived therefore take into consideration a wide range of determining factors, including the technical specification, operational capability, replacement cost and demolition pricing.

As well as the quantum values produced through such analyses, the insurer would want to understand the nature of the risk factors through commentary on what might influence these projections, and both the liquidity and volatility in relation to other vessel types.

Data are key

Data for the analysis of fleet and vessel prices are usually derived from proprietary economic models and in-house databases, supplemented by information from various broker reports and Lloyd's Register Fairplay.

130 *Stephen Allum*

Residual value drivers

The drivers of second-hand price cyclicality can be broken down into four, largely independent, components: newbuilding prices, scrap prices, earnings expectations and life expectancy.

> *Residual value = fn (replacement cost risk, scrap price risk, earnings, life expectancy)*

These are now discussed in turn.

The market ceiling – newbuilding prices

Substantial variations in newbuilding prices over the last 20 years have meant that a vessel's historic cost (or current book value) has been largely irrelevant to its future market resale value. What matters is the contracting price or replacement cost of an equivalent vessel at the time of resale.

Current shipyard contract prices effectively (with some rare but notable exceptions) impose a ceiling on prices for second-hand tonnage. This is, of course, hardly surprising: the price of an older asset (with a shorter working life) is unlikely to exceed that of a new one. The exception to this rule is where the owner/operator believes that there are short-term gains to be made through utilising an asset now, rather than waiting for one to two years while a shipyard manufacturers a new asset; in other words an opportunity premium can artificially distort the market for a period of time. This was a feature of the main shipping sectors during the 2005–8 China-led trade boom.

In general terms, however, whereas the second-hand prices for vessels of different ages generally move in the same direction as each other, this is not necessarily the same direction as those of yard prices; a pattern that is demonstrable across a wide-range of shipping sectors.

This is because yard prices only set an upper bound on second-hand prices. However the asymmetry in the relationship is actually of great importance in the evaluation of the residual risk.

On the one hand, if newbuilding prices increase dramatically, the price of second-hand ships may rise if arbitrage causes sufficient demand to switch into the sale and purchase market. On the other hand, if newbuilding prices plummet below those for modern second-hand ships, resale prices would definitely fall, because, as noted above, the value of a used asset will almost always be lower than the cost of replacement by a new one with a longer working life expectation.

This implies that the replacement cost risk to future resale values is influenced only very indirectly by the future condition of the asset. Shipyard prices are dictated by the economics of shipbuilding, including the balance between aggregate newbuilding capacity and forward orderbooks and shipbuilding costs. The latter are a function of productivity, steel plate and equipment prices, wage inflation and exchange rates.

In summary, the replacement cost risk relates to the possibility that, over the forecast period, yard prices will plunge so far below current levels that they will drag down the second-hand value of nearly-new ships. The origin of this risk lies outside the confines of any specific maritime sector, but could impact any sector, even if the charter rates for the sector are good.

The market floor – residual scrap values

The residual scrap value effectively sets a floor to its resale value. The level of this market floor – as with the ceiling – is determined largely by forces external to shipping markets. Steel scrap is a commodity like any other, and commodity prices are driven by the global supply and demand for that commodity, market forces that are totally removed from the shipping sector, shipping being only a marginal supplier of scrap steel.

Scrap prices typically follow the fortunes of the steel industry, which in turn closely follow the economic cycle. As a consequence, the risks to resale prices posed by movements in residual scrap values is not exclusively or even primarily a maritime sector specific risk.

Scrap steel demand is boosted thanks to its importance as a feedstock into electric arc furnaces, which are steadily replacing traditional ore-fed blast furnaces in steel-making. It remains, however, a relatively low value commodity and, when compared to other sources of scrap, such as automated vehicle crushing plants, the technology of shipbreaking is basic and very labour-intensive so as to be viable only in regions with low wage costs, such as the Indian subcontinent.

Such countries are typically constrained on foreign exchange, which therefore limits the USD upside for demolition prices. Prices can also fall when a glut of vessels, particularly large vessels, is available for demolition.

The standard measure of shipbuilding prices is $/LDT. Light displacement tonnage (LDT) is, essentially, a measure of the steel content of a vessel. The scrap price of a vessel is determined by multiplying the LDT by the prevailing scrap price for that type of vessel. Vessels with additional equipment, such as tankers, will command a slight premium due to the resale and recycling value of onboard items other than steel.

The past few years have seen the $/LDT prices move out of historical norms as demolition volumes first plummeted to exceptionally low levels coinciding with the Asian economic boom raising steel prices. An average of around US$450/LDT for the period 2004–9 compares with a typical range of US$100 to US$265 over the 20 year period to 2009.

With an increasing number of ships entering the breakers yards after 2008, and with steel prices sliding, the $/LDT values did return temporarily towards their historical averages, but the number of vessels available for scrap continues to fluctuate, with periods of stability interspersed with periods of volatility as buyers and sellers both attempt to beat the averages – prices are only agreed once the vessel arrives at the yard.

Despite all the volatility, the scrap price remains a low percentage of the value of a ship in the first half of its life and variations in scrap values are only really important in the residual value calculation if the asset under consideration is exceptionally old, and most insurers shy away from deals where the asset has less than half its working life left at term.

Of much greater impact than the level of the market floor are the risks that could cause resale values for all ages of ship to spiral down towards it. These are covered in the next two sections.

Future discounted earnings expectations

The gap between the market ceiling and market floor offers plenty of room for resale prices to fluctuate significantly and, as argued above, these fluctuations have not always been in the same direction as those of the floor or ceiling.

Ships, like any other income producing asset, are valued by fair markets on the basis of their anticipated earning power or, to be more specific, the discounted sum of their future net earnings stream. This, of course, is a prediction that tends to change in response to changing expectations about future trading conditions, the anticipated length of working life and other factors.

These expectations are primarily influenced by recent experience, the longer and stronger that earnings have been rising and how long the trend is expected to continue. Hence vessel resale prices are typically highest at the top of their earnings cycle and lowest at the bottom.

In order to net out the effect of changes in newbuilding and scrap prices and to capture the impact of earnings variations on resale prices, second-hand prices net of scrap values are normally used and are benchmarked as a percentage of current contracting prices (also net of scrap value).

When applied to working assets in a peak earnings environment, the analysis would indicate that the depreciation tends towards a straight line; conversely, a trough earnings environment results in a more pronounced sag to the depreciation curve.

Life expectancy

As a vessel ages, the more its condition influences the residual value. A vessel of advanced years that has been well-maintained, operated in benign environments by an A-class operator will command a premium relative to a vessel of a similar age that has not enjoyed these benefits.

Key influences on projected values

When assessing what may influence projected values, they can be categorised into 'replacement cost/newbuilding' risk, and 'life expectancy/saleability' risk. There could be upside and downside risks associated with each. It is stressed that these are not predicted to occur; they are, however, possible issues that need to be considered in any analysis:

Positive influences/possible risks

- A drop in newbuilding contract prices attracts cash-rich investors back into the market.
- The price of steel plate for shipbuilding continues to outperform the general steel market, raising the floor for newbuilding costs and prices.
- Exchange rate fluctuations can have a major impact over the short term; over an extended period Far Eastern currencies tend to appreciate against the USD, putting upwards pressure on ship prices in USD terms.
- The ordering boom of a few years ago resulted in a substantial expansion of shipbuilding capacity, especially in China and Korea. The impact of capacity rationalisation following the reduction in order numbers will raise the floor of newbuilding prices during the next three to five years, and hasten a recovery in newbuilding prices and asset values.

Negative influences/possible risks

- Newbuilding contract levels remain relatively low during the remainder of the downturn, and fail to pick up again during the next macroeconomic upturn.
- Increasing shipbuilding and steel plate capacity primarily in China.
- Any government intervention in Korea and China that seeks to save shipyards from bankruptcy, thereby maintaining artificially high capacity levels.
- Global recovery in the macroeconomic environment fails to materialise over the next five years.
- Further amendments to safety and/or environmental regulations administered by the International Maritime Organisation either reducing life expectancy or alternatively resulting in the associated costs acquired to meet new legislation.
- Global, regional or individual government legislation regarding the age of vessels deployed reduces useful life expectancy, reducing re-deployment potential.

Benchmark rating

Assuming the data are unbiased, then there is a 50 per cent chance of loss. The historic accuracy and variability of data changes by asset class; aircraft may be as low as –10 per cent to +10 per cent; shipping is usually much wider.

Take a case where the data uncertainty is –20 per cent to +20 per cent. The average loss, given that there is a loss, is 10 per cent, the likelihood of the asset being returned is 90 per cent and the duration of the residual value (RV) cover is seven years with a discount rate of 6 per cent. The calculated risk premium comes in at around 3.2 per cent on top of which the frictional costs of the insurer and the cost of holding regulatory capital must be paid for. RVI on a seven-year cover results in the insured borrowing the insurers' balance sheet for seven years; and each year must be paid for.

No wonder, then, that the one-off cost of purchasing an RV policy can be upwards of 7 per cent.

For the insured, the $ cost of residual value = $ future value × residual value, and for most it is as simple as that. But for some, games were played:

- The first RVI policies insured each asset individually. But, the insureds learned how to increase the variance of the risks, increasing the losses.
- Later policies insured the pool as a whole. But, the insureds then learned how to cherry-pick the better risks out of the portfolio, leaving only the assets with losses.
- Rules were then implemented to prevent cherry-picking. More recently, insureds have been understaffing their remarketing departments.

RVI is a valuable tool to guarantee future price, but 'price' is affected by everything. The asset financing industry has a sophisticated understanding on how to manipulate prices. It is therefore critical that the motivation of each party is understood by the insurer and incorporated into the pricing.

7 From co-creation to entrepreneurialism

Mobile apps and other examples

Valeria Corna

The co-creation trend

Consumer engagement in value creation and value delivery processes has been explored extensively within the academic literature over the past decade. From value co-creation to knowledge co-production, from co-design to co-ideation, it has been recognised that the consumer plays a very active role in a variety of business processes, and that such involvement can help organisations better meet customers' needs, improving the overall business performance.[1]

From an organisational perspective, the key assumption behind the rise of the co-creation trend is that interactions in which consumers are involved as co-creators generate more value than traditional buyer–seller transactions in which consumers play a 'passive' role. By involving consumers in their value creation and delivery processes, companies can acquire new knowledge, establish more meaningful relationships with their customers, improve existing processes, reduce costs, innovate more effectively and achieve a better understanding of the overall market. From the consumer perspective, drivers of involvement in value creation processes can vary from strong product engagement to mere curiosity; from dissatisfaction with current products to idea sharing; from an intrinsic interest in innovation to receiving extrinsic rewards.

The increasing relevance of consumers' participation in value creation and delivery is widely recognised in the service field,[2] in particular the impact that self-serving technology can have on cost reduction and customer satisfaction. Innovation is another area where the importance of consumer engagement has been acknowledged. From providing consumers with innovation toolkits,[3] to involving lead users in the idea generation process,[4] there are several ways in which companies can involve consumers in their innovation processes in order to explore new customer needs and spot innovation opportunities. Customers can play an active role in the initial stages of the innovation process by identifying latent needs or generating ideas for innovation. They can also be involved in the following stages of the innovation funnel by helping companies co-design products and services, or testing propositions before they are launched and brought to market. Consumer involvement in the innovation process is not as recent as we may think. Traditionally consumers were – and in some cases still are – involved in testing products for a variety of companies. This type of engagement, however, in addition to being less creative, provides consumers with limited opportunities to be actively engaged. They act as users and testers rather than as co-creators and even if they can influence the product evolution, they rarely feel part of the innovation process or the company as a whole.

The recognition that more active and engaging activities could lead to a more effective consumer contribution, combined with advances in information technology and with consumer willingness to collaborate more intensively have led to the emergence of multiple initiatives for consumer engagement. Most of these, rather than relying on face-to-face interactions, encourage collaboration through the use of online platforms.

Technology as an enabler of consumer involvement and crowdsourcing

Technological progress, combined with increased and ubiquitous connectivity, has created new opportunities for consumers' engagement in innovation. Thanks to tools such as online communities, forums, online panels and live chats companies now have multiple opportunities to engage with customers on an ongoing basis, to establish a meaningful and open dialogue, and to improve their understanding of the market and customer needs. Like never before, firms can leverage technology to tap into the 'power of the crowd' and source ideas for new products and services that feed into their innovation process. This phenomenon, also known as 'idea crowdsourcing' is being leveraged by organisations to improve the effectiveness of the ideation process as well as to establish deeper relationships with the most engaged consumers.

Dell Idea Storm

In 2007, Dell launched Idea Storm,[5] an online platform that allowed customers to brainstorm ideas with other customers as well as with Dell. Promoted as the platform that can 'help everyone turn their ideas into reality', Idea Storm hit the 16,000 ideas mark and implemented almost 500 ideas – according to its website. Since its launch, new features have been added to the platform. In 2009 Dell introduced 'Storm Sessions' where customers can submit ideas and respond to specific challenges posted by the company. In 2012 a new feature called 'Extensions' was also added in order to enable ideas to evolve over time through the collaboration of others. The feature allows customers to incorporate a comment someone else made on their idea into its final iteration.

My Starbucks Idea

Similarly to Dell, Starbucks launched 'My Starbucks Idea',[6] an online community aimed at engaging customers in the innovation process. Everybody is encouraged to submit their own ideas on Starbucks products, services or experiences as well as to browse the ideas submitted by others and comment on them. Ideas are reviewed by Starbucks employees and those considered to have the highest potential are implemented.

Both platforms allow Starbucks and Dell to collect a number of ideas for product creation and improvement, while enabling customers to feel part of the process and potentially see their idea implemented. Both, however, leverage customers' intrinsic motivation to collaborate as they don't provide participants with any form of compensation if their idea is used. In Dell's case, users must agree to the platform's terms and conditions – which grant Dell a perpetual and irrevocable royalty-free licence to use any of the users' ideas. Similarly, participants of My Starbucks Idea do not receive any form of compensation if their idea is used, with the exception of being credited on the Starbucks website.

The lack of extrinsic rewards from these companies may restrain many consumers from getting involved. However, for some users (potentially the ones most engaged with the brand or those with the highest interest in innovation) contributing to the success of a company they love or seeing one of their ideas implemented may be enough to drive intrinsic motivation.

Other platforms recognise the role that extrinsic motivation can play in encouraging customer collaboration and provide them with rewards or monetary compensations. The Kraft 'Collaboration Kitchen'[7] for instance, recognises that customers' ideas may be protected through copyright and suggests the development of agreements with idea creators, as well as potential remunerations to regulate the use of their ideas. Other platforms aim to engage consumers in solving specific business problems or challenges and provide winners with an extrinsic reward. Both Netflix Prize[8] and Lufthansa Innovation Challenge[9] are examples.

Kraft 'Collaboration Kitchen'

Kraft encourages customers to participate in the idea generation process by submitting their ideas on ingredients, packaging, processing, complete products and technology solutions to the 'Collaboration Kitchen' platform. User ideas are then reviewed by the Kraft Open Innovation team, and potentially by research and development teams. Kraft acknowledges that some ideas submitted may be protected through copyrights and suggests the development of specific agreements with the ideator in order to regulate its use. Furthermore, if Kraft is interested in using an idea that is not protected, it may (at its discretion) compensate the ideator with a maximum remuneration of $5,000.

Netflix Prize

Netflix provides a great example of how companies can tap into the power of the crowd to solve a specific challenge. Back in 2006, they launched the Netflix Prize: a competition with a 1 million dollar prize for the individual or group that could help Netflix substantially improve the accuracy of their algorithm and predict how much someone would enjoy a movie based on their movie preferences. Teams from more than 150 countries submitted algorithms and challenged one another up until 2009 when the competition was closed and the winner announced.

Lufthansa

Lufthansa also launched a challenge (2nd Air Cargo Innovation Challenge) inviting customers and other users to submit ideas on how customer service in the cargo business should look and function in the coming years, with emphasis on customer touch points. The winners in this case received flight simulation training at the Lufthansa Flight Simulation Centre.

From ideators to innovators to entrepreneurs

Thanks to advances in information technology and multiple company initiatives, crowdsourcing has become a great enabler of consumer participation in the innovation and ideation process. In most cases, however, crowdsourcing does not allow consumers to participate actively in the implementation and commercialisation of their idea. Such activities are left to the company itself. In other words, consumers participate as ideators, but are not provided with opportunities to become innovators and/or entrepreneurs. Their demand for being recognised as such, however, is on the increase. Consumers don't just want to be given credit for having a brilliant idea, they want to become able to fund it, turn it into reality and manage it successfully. Several companies, especially start-ups, have acknowledged the emergence of this trend. Large corporations are no longer the only ones tapping into the power of the crowd. Start-ups that make use of crowdsourcing within their business model are emerging. In addition to providing a platform that allows customers to submit their ideas, these companies also help them see their idea realised and potentially monetised upon.

Threadless

Threadless[10] is an e-commerce website selling t-shirts created by a community of designers and artists. Launched in 2000, the community allows anyone with a great idea for a t-shirt to design it on the website either individually or by collaborating with someone else in the community. Designs are then voted on by the general public and the best ones are selected for production, to be sold on the Threadless website. Designers receive a commission for every t-shirt with their design sold via the website. Once their design is printed Threadless earns the rights to print and sell it on any product. However, the individual is free to use it for any other commercial purpose and can also request their rights back. According to the Threadless website $7,120,000 has been awarded to 1,455 artists so far, with 2,431,150 global community members and 265,339 designs submitted to date.

The Wine Foundry

The Wine Foundry[11] is an online community that allows anyone with a passion for wine to create and sell their own wine. The company provides access to vineyards while enabling consumers to take charge of the rest of the process. After having selected a vineyard, users build a plan covering the entire process from fermenting to blending. They then monitor the vineyard, create the wine, design the packaging and define the pricing strategy. While the Wine Foundry provides access to the resource that most consumers lack, a vineyard, users are left as ultimate decision makers across the entire process from fermentation to ageing, to bottling and labelling. Once created, the Wine Foundry helps them launch and operate their wine business without the typically high cost of starting one's own winery.

Online communities providing consumers with the resources they need to turn their ideas into reality and generate revenue are not the only start-ups emerging around individuals' need to become innovators. Platforms that enable consumers to become entrepreneurs and maintain full rights to use their idea while collecting funds are also coming to the fore.

Kickstarter

One of the most successful examples is Kickstarter.[12] Described as 'the world's largest funding platform for creative projects' the Kickstarter website and community allows anybody with a creative idea to submit it to the platform and find potential funders. If an idea is successfully funded Kickstarter collects a 5 per cent fee from the project's total funding. However, neither funders nor Kickstarter takes any percentage of ownership or intellectual property as this remains fully with the ideator of the project. Being a form of commerce and patronage, and not an investment community, the platform also ensures that users will never need to give up their ownership or pay back any funds raised through Kickstarter.

The example of mobile applications

The mobile application (hereafter apps) market has grown enormously over the past few years, and this growth is not expected to slow down. According to Gartner, almost 25 billion apps were downloaded globally in 2011 and downloads could reach the 80 billion mark by the end of 2013.[13] Downloading and using apps has definitely become a part of consumers' everyday life, but what role do consumers play in the app development process?

Most mobile developers create mobile apps with little or no consumer involvement. Telecom companies recognise the critical role of developers in driving brand preference and device sales and have been investing heavily in developer marketing and engagement activities. They acknowledge the relationship between developers and consumers, but typically perceive them as two 'distinct species' that need to be targeted with different marketing activity.

Increased customisation, consumer co-creation and crowdsourcing are key trends that have affected multiple industries over the last few years. Consumers are taking a more proactive role in the creation of products and services they use; in some cases they have become an integral part of a business' value chain.

Recent events indicate that these trends are entering the app development industry too – in effect blurring the boundaries between consumers and developers. In the near future, we could all become mobile app developers of some sort, and even monetise from it generating revenue from app downloads, advertising or subscriptions. This convergence could transform developer marketing strategies as well as the industry's monetisation models.

How blogs evolved, will apps follow suit?

In 1994 Justin Hall created Links.net, the first ever blog. During the early stage of blogging one had to be a programmer and create his or her own custom blogging platform to have a weblog, as it was called at that time.[14]

It was only in 1999 that Blogger launched, paving the way for blogging to become mainstream. Thanks to services such as Blogger and Wordpress authors no longer needed to be programmers, web or digital specialists to create a blog, causing a dramatic increase in the number of blogs. Anyone with a computer and an internet connection could shift from being a blog reader to a blogger, from being a pure consumer to a creator of content.

Many individuals used blogs as a channel of communication with friends, family or the rest of the world. Others, typically the most tech savvy, began to monetise on them through advertising and affiliate marketing; some have made blogging their main profession.

Similar opportunities could open up in the app world. Consumers who are not only interested in creating the ideal app for their friends, but also in developing apps that address universal needs will have the potential to monetise their app.

A whole set of new monetisation opportunities could open up for this type of user/developer. These could include existing monetisation models such as advertising, or go beyond what is currently offered to focus on enabling peer-to-peer payments.

When consumers were just consumers

When the mobile app market emerged, consumers played their traditional value chain role. They were not involved in the app creation or innovation process and were acting purely as app downloaders and users. Despite this lack of involvement on the consumer side, the demand for apps was high and the market booming. The first apps to be launched addressed some of consumers' most basic mobile needs such as accessing train times, reading books, using social networks, all while on the move. Smartphone users eager to make the most of their latest technology became heavy downloaders and the countdown to the first billion app downloads started.

Even if the number of downloads kept increasing, the industry soon started to realise that the number of apps staying on consumers' phone for more than one week was fairly limited. Similarly, only a few apps were actually used after being downloaded. This could have been sustainable on a 'pay per download' business model. However, at this time, advertising-funded apps were the most popular implying that no app usage equalled no revenue for developers. With many mobile developers unable to sustain their business through app revenue[15] and smartphones getting increasingly cluttered by multiple apps, developers' interest turned to understanding the key ingredients for making a successful app. A unique and definitive formula for app success has not been found yet. Although the industry has moved on from its infancy and is becoming more sophisticated, its fast and constant evolution implies that success ingredients change as well. There is, however, one ingredient that has emerged as being key, if not even a pre-requisite to success: a successful app must address relevant consumers' needs and desires and improve their daily lives. After basic needs such as accessing train times, bank accounts, news and weather have been addressed, being able to launch a successful app requires the identification of users' needs that no one has been able to spot yet – maybe not even consumers themselves – and therefore it means innovating.

Placing consumer needs at the centre of app development

In the quest to ideate new apps that leverage market opportunities and address latent consumer needs, app development companies and individual developers are beginning to recognise the importance of placing consumers at the centre of the app creation process.

In the simplest case, consumers are involved in an 'indirect way', meaning that they are not contributing to app ideation or innovation, but their needs and behaviours are considered key inputs in such processes.

Multiple are the examples of innovative apps that have succeeded thanks to their ability to address in a more effective way universal user needs. These are apps that make us safe, improve our knowledge or save us time in ways that could not be contemplated in the non-mobile era.

Flipboard[16]

With the advent of e-readers, smartphones and tablets many readers have abandoned the paper version of magazines in favour of the digital format. In a similar way, many have stopped reading news from newspapers or websites and instead access news content when on the go. Up until the arrival of Flipboard, however, most readers were not able to access a unique and personalised source of content; they still had to rely on multiple magazines or news sites to read their preferred content. Flipboard realised that technology was making news personalisation much more cost-effective than in the paper-based era and launched an app able to provide consumers with access to a 'personalised magazine' pulling news and content from all their favourite sources. Thanks to its ability to simplify and personalise the user experience like never before, the app has been a great success, hitting 20 million users in August 2012.[17]

Hailo[18]

The Hailo app is another great example of innovation in the mobile apps market. The app, available in London and eleven other major cities worldwide, allows users to easily find and pay for black cabs thereby reducing waiting time, improving safety and simplifying the payment process. By partnering with cab drivers and providing an easy to use interface, Hailo has been able to address the travelling needs of many mobile users. Consumers using the app do not need to look for a taxi on the street anymore. Using the app, they can locate the Hailo cab closest to them, book it, track its movement and check how long it will take for the taxi to reach their location. In addition to ensuring a safe return home, the app allows users to link their credit cards to their Hailo account enabling them to easily pay for the drive with no need to withdraw any cash. According to their website, Hailo is now the largest app-based taxi network in any city in the world.[19]

Ocado and Tesco Home Plus

Thanks to advances in information technology and increasing broadband penetration online shopping boomed at the beginning of the twenty-first century. From clothes to groceries, from holiday packages to books, from furniture to financial services products, there is barely anything that we cannot buy online. The internet has re-shaped the retail market allowing thousands of e-commerce companies to emerge. Supermarket chains have been relatively quick to jump on the e-commerce bandwagon and many provide their customers with the opportunity to shop online. It is only, however, with the advent of grocery shopping mobile apps, that shopping 'on the go' has become a reality. Ocado is an internet retailer specialising in home-delivered groceries in the UK. The public company was founded in 2002 to enable users to shop online for a variety of products and have them delivered to their doorstep. In 2009, the company launched its mobile app for the iPhone.[20] This enables customers to do their grocery shopping without the need for a computer. Online shopping and home delivery were already providing users with substantial time savings. However, now that shopping for groceries is only one smartphone or tablet away, users can save even more time doing their groceries on the tube, train or in any other situation in which they need to kill time or have an opportunity to take a break. Ocado is only one of many apps to have emerged in this space. In South Korea, Tesco went a step further by launching an app that brings the company's supermarket to time-poor consumers. Home Plus – Tesco's branch in South Korea – has built virtual supermarket aisles on train platforms, allowing consumers to do their grocery shopping while waiting for the train to arrive. By using their mobile phones, commuters can scan products they wish to buy, add them to their basket and get them delivered directly to their home, even on the same evening. In addition to allowing users to save precious time, Tesco's solution has the advantage of making mobile shopping a more visual experience bringing some of the advantages of offline back into the online and mobile world.[21]

From co-creation to entrepreneurialism   143

Shazam[22] and SoundHound[23]

How many times have we been listening to music at home, in a bar or restaurant, on the radio or at a party thinking that we really like the song, but without any chance to discover its title or singer? A need that is definitely more trivial than safety or time-saving, but a universal one. Irrespective of where we live or how engaged with music we are, we have all found ourselves at least once in a similar situation. Thanks to the diffusion of 3G – and now 4G – technology and increasing smartphone penetration this need can now be easily addressed. Shazam is a mobile app created to specifically resolve this universal need. Mobile users interested in knowing more about a song when they are on the go now just need to 'Shazam it'. The app leverages the mobile phone's microphone to collect a sample of the music being played. It then compares it with a central database of songs in order to identify the right match. Once the match is found, information on the artist, title, album lyrics and concerts are provided back to the mobile users. The consumer can then decide whether to access any of the content, share it via email or social network or buy the song from the Apple iTunes store. SoundHound is an app very similar to Shazam with the exception that it also allows users to 'hum' a song in order to retrieve information about its title or artist.

Spotify[24]

Shazam and SoundHound have not been the only apps tapping into users' need to listen to their favourite music anywhere they are. After having revolutionised the music market with its desktop solution, Spotify, the commercial streaming service that provides music content from a variety of record labels, has launched its mobile app, now available across a variety of app stores. Thanks to the app, Premium Spotify users not only can listen to any song or artist they like, they can also access Spotify content from their mobile device in any place with data connection. Furthermore, they can download and store their favourite songs on their smartphone for offline access.

Nike Plus

Nike Plus[25] is not only an app that targets users' needs for self-monitoring and self-tracking in the sport and fitness space, it is also an exemplary case of how consumers can co-create their consumption experience through app usage. Runners with Nike Plus enabled shoes can download the Nike Plus running app for their iPhone or Android device to map their runs, track distance, pace, time and calories burnt as well as receive audio-feedback as they make progress. They can also create challenges, share their progress on social networks and receive 'virtual cheers' from friends as well as activate motivational songs during their workouts co-creating their ideal running experience. More recently, Nike launched a similar app, this time connected to the Nike Fuel Band rather than running shoes. By wearing the fuel band on their wrist and accessing the related app, users can track their daily activity, set fitness goals and track their progress leading to an overall

144 *Valeria Corna*

healthier lifestyle. The experience is gamified through the addition of Nike Fuel points, which users acquire as they progress. Points can unlock achievements that consumers can share with friends.

App crowdsourcing and crowdfunding

Apps created with more direct involvement of consumers in the process are also emerging. Consumers can now share their ideas through communities such as the IdeasProject, which helps app ideas to become a reality. Founded on co-creation through open innovation, the IdeasProject[26] online community has allowed apps such as Blood Sprint and mGraffiti to come to life.

The first – Blood Sprint[27] created by Viafo – is a free app for blood donors that helps charities, hospitals and other healthcare organisations to manage blood supplies more effectively. On the one hand, hospitals and health authorities can sign up to Blood Sprint via a web service where they can post their needs for blood donations. On the other hand, donors who have signed up to the service have a mobile app that leverages GPS functionality and is therefore aware of their location. Whenever their blood type and a local need for blood correspond, they receive an alert through the app.[28]

The second app – mGraffiti[29] – allows everyone to create their own graffiti without the negative impact on city walls. Once users have located virtual walls around them, they can create the graffiti they like and share it with friends.

Consumers can also become app investors and fund apps with potential through websites such as AppStori,[30] also known as 'the Kickstarter of mobile apps'. The website is described as a 'crowdsourcing and funding platform for mobile apps'. The site enables a higher degree of connection and collaboration between developers and consumers. From funding to testing, from promotion to communication, consumers and developers can build an open and direct dialogue without the intermediation of any app store. Consumers, on the one hand, can participate in the development of apps more actively and, through funding, make their contribution to help take the app to market. Developers, on the other hand, in addition to raising funds for their projects, can leverage consumer participation to beta test their apps and promote their projects (called 'stori' on the website). Depending on their level of contribution, consumers can receive a variety of benefits from the developer they have funded. However, money is exchanged only if the project is able to meet its overall funding goal. In addition to this the AppStori website deducts 7 per cent of the total collected funds, while an additional 2–3 per cent is deducted by Amazon Payments to cover processing.

AppStori is not the only platform of this kind. AppsFunder[31] is a similar funding platform 'connecting mobile entrepreneurs and developers with funders to realise great apps together'. Developers, on the one hand, can describe and even pitch their app via the website to an expert panel to encourage visitors of the website to fund their project. Those apps that are rated highly by the expert panel also receive a certified label that can increase their chances of being funded. Consumers and other investors, on the other hand, can fund the apps they like the most and get rewarded if the project succeeds. A 'gold fund' allows them to receive a reward pack as specified by the project owner. A 'platinum fund' entails a return on app revenue based on the amount initially invested. Similarly to AppStori, funders are charged only after the project has reached a specified milestone.

The democratisation of app development

There are strong indicators that democratisation is one of the avenues the fascinating app industry could take. Not only can consumers move from being pure downloaders and users to become part of the innovation process, they can now also create their own apps. Tools that allow anyone to create an app without coding, technology or design experience are emerging and are expected to become ever more popular.

For example, Appmakr[32] allows users to create their own iPhone or Android app with no need for coding experience. Users can create their app for free, or pay to upgrade in order to access premium features and customisation tools. In addition, users have access to an app analytics dashboard, can push notifications to users, monetise their app with advertising and publish it in app stores.

Yapp[33] is a simpler tool that aims at 'democratising' the development of mobile apps by allowing users to create personalised apps for key events such as birthdays, weddings, poker tournaments and many more. The service can be accessed for free and users are able to share their customised apps with friends, family or potentially the entire world via Twitter or other social networks. Users can choose from a variety of pre-existing app templates and add pages and content to their apps, send push alerts and upload photos.

Other similar DIY tools include MIT App Inventor[34] that allows anyone with a Google account to create their own app; Andromo[35] that lets users create native Android apps with no need for coding skills; and TheAppBuilder[36] that lets anyone create an app for iPhone, Android or Windows Phone in simple and easy steps. According to Andromo's website more than 200,000 individuals have already created apps relying on Andromo and thousands of apps have been uploaded on the Google Play app with an ad-funded business model thus generating revenue for their creators.

The quality of apps developed using DIY tools is still up for debate. As blogging has demonstrated in the past, there is reason to believe that emerging platforms will improve, with the potential to match the quality of professional apps. The increasing involvement from consumers in app creation, however, will have strong implications for equipment manufacturers and operating system providers. First, they will need to consider launching tools and templates that allow users to create their own apps. Similar to what Google did with Blogger, or even with Google Sites, most consumers will need standard templates, easy to populate and personalise, in order to make the app creation process simple and efficient. Second, a single strategy leveraging the synergies between consumers and developers could improve the effectiveness and efficiency of marketing activities of major operating system (OS) providers. Instead of targeting developers with communication focused on the technical tools available and consumers with advertisements focused on devices and services, OS providers could focus on the creation of more integrated marketing campaigns that place apps and consumer involvement in their creation at the centre of the process.

App development consumerisation: the implications

With app co-creation, crowdsourcing and, potentially, full app creation and ownership emerging as opportunities for consumers, new tools, solutions and business models will potentially come to the fore. In order to foster co-creation and crowdsourcing an increasing number of development companies and major Telcos are likely to involve consumers in some stages of the app innovation and creation process. Platforms such as the likes of IdeasProject and AppStori will become more prominent involving consumers in multiple ways from idea generation to beta testing. However, as consumers have the opportunity to become app entrepreneurs new business models and distribution channels may emerge. Currently, advertising funded, pay-per-download and subscriptions are amongst the most common business models. App stores are the most typical distribution channel. With the advent of app entrepreneurs, however, these are likely to evolve and potentially include peer-to-peer distribution and payment models.

Notes

1 See, among others, C.K. Prahalad and Venkat Ramaswamy, *The Future of Competition: Co-creating Unique Value with Customers*, Boston: Harvard Business School Press (2004); Adrian F. Payne, Kaj Storbacka and Pennie Frow, 'Managing the co-creation of value', *Journal of the Academy of Marketing Science*, 36: 83–96 (2008); Solveig Wikström, 'The customer as co-producer', *European Journal of Marketing*, 30 (4): 6–19 (1996); Deborah Roberts, Susan Baker and David Walker, 'Can we learn together? Co-creating with consumers', *International Journal of Market Research*, 47 (4): 407–27 (2005).
2 See, for example, Stephen L. Vargo and Robert F. Lusch, 'Evolving to a new dominant logic for marketing', *Journal of Marketing*, 68 (1): 1–17 (2004).
3 See, for example, Eric Von Hippel and Ralph Katz, 'Shifting innovation to users via toolkits', *Management Science*, 48 (7): 821–33 (2002).
4 See, for example, Eric Von Hippel, 'Lead users: a source of novel product concepts', *Management Science*, 32 (7): 791–805 (1986); Eric Von Hippel, *Democratizing Innovation*, Cambridge, MA: The MIT Press (2005).
5 See http://www.ideastorm.com/.
6 See http://mystarbucksidea.force.com/.
7 See http://www.kfcollaborationkitchen.com/EN/WHYINNOVATE/Pages/Home.aspx.
8 See http://www.netflixprize.com/.
9 See https://innovation.lufthansa-cargo.com/start.php.
10 See http://www.threadless.com/.
11 See http://www.thewinefoundry.com/.
12 See http://www.kickstarter.com/.

From co-creation to entrepreneurialism 147

13 See Set Fiegerman, 'Mobile app market to almost double this year to 45 billion', *Mashable*, http://mashable.com/2012/09/11/45-billion-apps-downloaded-201/ (2012) reporting data from Gartner, September 2012.
14 See http://en.wikipedia.org/wiki/History_of_blogging.
15 See Matos Kapetanakis, 'Developer economics 2012 – the new app economy', *Vision Mobile*, http://www.visionmobile.com/blog/2012/06/report-developer-economics-2012-the-new-app-economy/ (2012).
16 See http://flipboard.com/.
17 See Sarah Perez, 'Flipboard hits 20 million users, 3 billion flips per month', *TechCrunch*, http://techcrunch.com/2012/08/28/flipboard-hits-20-million-users-3-billion-flips-per-month/ (2012).
18 See https://hailocab.com/.
19 See 'Hailo receives $17M investment led by Accel Partners to expand globally' https://hailocab.com/boston/press-releases/hailo-receives-17m-investment.
20 See http://en.wikipedia.org/wiki/Ocado; http://www.ocado.com/webshop/startWebshop.do?dnr=y.
21 See Olivia Solon, 'Tesco brings the supermarket to time-poor commuters in South Korea', *Wired.co.uk*, http://www.wired.co.uk/news/archive/2011-06/30/tesco-home-plus-billboard-store (2011).
22 See http://www.shazam.com/.
23 See http://www.soundhound.com/.
24 See https://www.spotify.com/uk/.
25 See http://nikeplus.nike.com/plus/products/gps_app/.
26 See https://ideasproject.com/.
27 See http://www.bloodsprint.com/bloodsprint/Home.php.
28 See http://conversations.nokia.com/2011/12/12/organising-the-world%E2%80%99s-blood-donors-through-mobile/.
29 See http://www.windowsphone.com/en-gb/store/app/mgraffiti/33485415-2259-4326-bc08-22d973c05d7d.
30 See http://www.appstori.com/.
31 See http://appsfunder.com/en/?couponcode=GESTUpRaeCR.
32 See http://www.appmakr.com/.
33 See http://www.yapp.us/.
34 See http://appinventor.mit.edu/.
35 See http://www.andromo.com/.
36 See http://www.theappbuilder.com/features.html.

8 Big Data and innovation

David Rankin and Adrian Fry

The Big Data landscape is becoming increasingly clear. It has become a topic of conversation everywhere, faster than any other technology-driven buzzword in recent memory.

The concept of Big Data has gained broad acceptance and, in its latest manifestation, has reached a level of maturity that suggests enterprises of almost all sizes can benefit by better understanding the value that Big Data can bring to insight generation or development of goods and services.

This chapter will shed light on the actual benefits of Big Data to both consumers and corporations. It provides an understanding of the level of maturity that the Big Data market has reached, and explores the factors that will increase growth in the market as well as those that may limit acceptance and reduce the benefits that enterprises can receive from Big Data.

While we extol the benefits of Big Data to business in general, and specifically to marketers and consumers, we also suggest that some of its negative associations are based on misunderstandings, or simply the failure to recognise the value of the concept. There are, of course, some genuine risks, and we offer some clues as to how they are likely to be resolved.

Introduction

Big Data is a reality for most major businesses and an emerging issue for smaller firms, whether they know it or not. However, awareness of the concept, or its benefits, is generally low for many mainstream consumers.

The emerging trends that defined the past four years – financial and technological convergence, maturity of the web and full emergence of mobility – are gathering even greater momentum. The growth of each is facilitated to varying degrees by emergence of concepts that are collectively known as Big Data.

What is 'Big Data'?

Big Data (as it is commonly defined) has some core, and increasingly coherent, characteristics. They are:

- volume – the sheer size of datasets that were rarely analysed in great depth just a few years ago;
- variety – many forms and sources of data broadly classified as either 'traditional' or 'new';
- velocity – increasing speed of analysis and the types of insight created that have opened up data 'interrogation' to many more users.

When organisations reach the point where the volume, variety and velocity of data exceeds storage or processing capability, there are some major challenges. Organisations have a Big Data challenge when their data management systems and analysis tools are overwhelmed or when demands to analyse data become too difficult given existing analytic tools.

Big Data has extended traditional quantitative analysis techniques

The practical tasks almost always involve quantification through statistics, business analytics, advanced algorithms, predictive analytics and data mining.

Ultimately, Big Data by itself has little value. Big Data is very discovery-oriented. What matters most is how the data are analysed. Recent Big Data discussions have often focussed on how to better target advertisements or customise customer experiences – all of which makes sense. Yet having the ability to utilise a rich 'back catalogue' of data, and combine it with new streams and interpret it differently, is a huge asset.

Where is it applied?

Big Data is clearly growing in importance. Proponents claim it can transform processes, restructure organisations and help create better products or services. However, a really clear understanding of what it is can be elusive. Misconception and media hype have made it difficult to distinguish fact from fiction.

Our starting point is simply the acceptance that Big Data is used to mean many things: in this chapter we pin down the sources of Big Data as being a combination of 'traditional' business datasets (including marketing and operational data, such as purchasing data, channel usage, advertising awareness, etc.) and 'external' data (primarily digital data including social media, e-commerce, etc.), which is brought together, analysed in new ways and undertaken at rapid speed.

Hence for many data scientists, the basic concept of Big Data is a familiar one that encapsulates several well-known activities – data processing, applying new analytical techniques, seeking new sources of data, providing interpretation and quickly sharing information. In short, doing old activities, but much better.

Amorphous concepts such as Big Data can appear somewhat vague without a thorough understanding of which activities are being carried out. In any recent list of Big Data activities, the four most typical are:[1]

- customer relationship management/consumer analytics (e.g. direct marketing,
- healthcare (e.g. drug development, patient recovery, incident resource planning, etc.);
- retail (e.g. point of sale data and customer loyalty information);
- banking.

What is new, exactly?

- The emergence of new digital content creating 'new' information streams (images, text analytics, sensor data, data downloads, new content formats, geo-location analytics, etc.);
- new e-channels formed out of volume-based sources of data, not least social media;
- the rise of personalised marketing (with advertising messages closely matched to personal behaviours and preferences);
- significant growth in analysing the 'back catalogue' of historic data, including the digitisation of large amounts of pre-digital records (government archives, census, physical libraries, etc.);
- the *consequent* development of analytical capabilities that have been built to create or serve this new market (including cloud-based analytical capabilities that are typically sold to corporate buyers).

There is a clear suggestion that readily-accessible consumer data are the mainstay of current Big Data initiatives. Social media often provides a headline-grabbing context, simply because of the sheer volumes of data generated on a daily basis, and the need to analyse this in ways that never existed just a few years ago. In this context, traditional data mining and predictive analytical tasks have become subsumed into the wider definition of Big Data.

No single institution or industry can claim outright leadership in Big Data. Social media behemoths – Google, Facebook and Twitter – can make leadership claims with the greatest degree of credibility. While some financial services businesses have perhaps the richest view of customer activity, behaviours and, of course, personal wealth; there are many other sector-specific Big Data 'champions' from retailers, telecoms firms, broadcasters, governments and even charities that are analysing new streams of data in ways not feasible a few years ago. Many innovations are being made by smaller firms since the cost to acquire processing technology is modest and the availability of open-source software (such as Hadoop) has enabled initiatives to be easily scaled up.

Signs of leadership in Big Data can be seen in the tremendous growth of cloud computing, which has been crucial in allowing the large-scale collaboration in the construction, organisation and utilisation of major datasets.

There are enormous opportunities to make money, better serve customers and even save lives (as the example later in the chapter, of Cancer Research UK, shows). The upside of major investment in Big Data seems never-ending for many corporations. The implication for many firms is that success with Big Data can or will foster significant change in the way a business operates, and this, of course, directly affects its employees. In fact, some of the greatest successes have reinterpreted the roles of data scientists and marketers.

The downsides of Big Data are largely over-stated

The eventual outcomes of Big Data at a societal level provide critics of the Big Data idea with a fascinating source of 'what if' scenarios. Most of these are unconvincing; there are, however, a few genuine concerns over the potential for abuse of data by institutions with bad intentions, or more likely, the misuse of data.

A reading of the media and subject matter material produced by institutions fostering its development, routinely underplays the potential downsides. Significant new cost is an obvious issue, but even then, the development of cloud computing – which is closely associated with providing the data storage and on-demand processing capability needed by many Big Data initiatives – is regularly put forward as a driver of lower cost data analysis. Beyond the purely financial implications, there are at least three prevalent concerns around the rise of Big Data. They are:

- a loss of privacy (or the loss of choice over personal anonymity);
- transparency, especially the implications of predictive analytics;
- consent over data-management.

These can be condensed into one single question: who ultimately owns the data? Given clarity on ownership, then dialogue over privacy and commercial usage becomes easier to frame, and legal or regulatory control becomes easier for consumers to apprehend.

A minority of consumers have sought to minimise their 'digital footprint' – the kind of people never to have had a Facebook account or fear the influence of some sort of 'Big Brother' that somehow challenges their rights to privacy. Admittedly, remaining completely anonymous online is becoming exceptionally difficult, and there is a rational argument that suggests large and linked datasets could be exploited to identify individuals.

There is also the genuine concern that through the use of wrongly applied analytics, inappropriate or simply incorrect linkages are made. Extensive academic research from Cambridge University[2] has highlighted concerns over undisclosed private information, such as social media users' sexual orientation or their substance-use. The inference, or the identification, of personal characteristics that a person did not wish to share risks becoming a larger concern as more companies include social media profiling within their customer application assessments. Wonga, the British online lending business, includes many hundreds – possibly thousands – of pieces of information, including an applicant's Facebook profile to gauge the suitability of an application.

Mainstream consumers seem to be ignoring such concerns, while regulators have set out to ensure an individual's right to privacy, even if few rarely seek it. Data access and sharing rules are more stringent than many consumers may recognise. Whatever a business's aspirations for using data to identify trends or preferences, they are constrained by compliance and industry regulations.

From a data management perspective, many companies fear the backlash that could result if they wrongly approach digital identity. To avoid this, such businesses apply data collection and storage rules with built-in privacy-preserving characteristics.

There is slight change in the direction of privacy protection, where today's focus on individual consent at the time of collection appears to be shifting, to include making the institutions that hold data more accountable for what they do with it.

Privacy issues are at the forefront of regulators' concerns. Data collection by companies has become a controversial matter in Europe, and regulators are concerned about the way firms such as Google and Facebook make use of people's sensitive personal information as part of their business.

In 2012, European Union regulators asked Google to change its privacy policies or risk fines, as it failed to provide users with adequate information about how their personal data were being used across the group's various platforms.

The balance of who is benefitting has been very much on the side of major corporations. Many consumers do not yet see an overt benefit, or don't even recognise Big Data in everyday life.

How can consumers obtain greater benefit from the growth in Big Data?

Given the vast sums that leaders in Big Data have generated, it appears that monetisation of data is mainly one-way: to the benefit of the institution that has the ability to create value. Of course, a large proportion is reinvested in new products and services, but the linkages for consumers are unclear.

There is a clear lack of tangible 'rewards' for many consumers. The financial value of a person's digital life is clearly hard to estimate, but if that could be achieved, the relationship could become more two-way. The starting point is likely to be a single holistic view of a consumer's digital life that encompasses all aspects of off- and on-line behaviours. Such a 'passport' would need the buy-in from consumers, since it will have the whiff of 'Big Brother'. By allowing institutions access to this passport, users will be creating a market for their own information. Concepts such as 'digital self' indicate that consumers are increasingly aware of the financial value of their digital data.

Offering degrees of 'opt-in', each with a sliding scale of overt benefits may partially offset fears about control. Logically, those willing to share their full personal digital history would maximise their market value. By putting control of the passport in the consumer's hands, they will also have self-determined privacy levels.

Such a move would initially appeal to very few consumers. Few have a clear understanding of which institutions are collecting and using their digital information. Concern over privacy and control should not automatically be interpreted as unwillingness to share, but it may justify the need to reward or compensate consumers differently.

If the market value of the digital passport turned out to be very low, then it risks stumbling at the first hurdle. It would also constitute only a small proportion of the total market, since institutions would still seek to collate data outside of that directly held and managed by the consumer. Estimates of the value of consumers' personal data are still in their infancy, but suggest the total value to be worth several hundred billion euros. On an aggregate level in Europe, the value extracted from European consumers' personal data in 2011 was worth €315bn, and has the potential to grow to nearly €1tn annually in 2020, according to the Boston Consulting Group.[3]

This suggests there are many opportunities to develop new strategies to incentivise data-sharing by consumers – with each other and with institutions. If this could be built alongside consistently applied privacy controls, the barriers to apathy or trust could be overcome significantly.

New sources of insight 1: the rise of crowdsourcing in Big Data

A variety of *systems* has been deployed that use crowdsourcing techniques to support Big Data ventures. Crowdsourcing helps turn unstructured data into actionable insight typically through data collection, tagging or data synthesis roles. It is occasionally applied to actual data analysis. There are hundreds of crowdsourcing initiatives; those with a Big Data application include:

- Amazon's Mechanical Turk platform divides major projects into manageable smaller pieces and then uses crowdsourcing to undertake the work, paying participants for manual tasks that are successfully accomplished. Tasks are varied but typically include writing product descriptions, audio transcription or identifying music performers.
- Since 2004, PatientsLikeMe has collated a substantial volume of health-related information from volunteers and then made it available for medical research. It has helped nearly 200,000 people with over 1,000 medical conditions connect with other patients, doctors and health organisations from around the world.
- The Zooniverse initiative utilises the collective efforts of over half a million volunteer astrologers to classify pictures of the universe to catalogue galaxies. This is citizen science – which broadly encompasses public involvement in science, increasingly in crowdsourcing conditions. Zooniverse is different since many participants are learned scholars.
- TopCoder.com is a community of more than 400,000 coders who compete in programming competitions. Winning is a badge of honour and financially

beneficial. Coders' skills have been applied to hundreds of socially relevant activities including health research.

Crowdsourcing initiatives are successful when there is a shared mutual interest or commitment to a common cause. Their ability to bring a tremendous volume of initial insight and preparation to major Big Data campaigns is unquestioned. They also overcome one of the most common barriers to Big Data: poorly organised underlying information.

New sources of insight 2: gamification

Several commentators have suggested the value that enhancing the game element in any data assessment or classification activity brings to Big Data exercises, particularly for broadening the participation beyond those directly benefitting from the analysis.

The impact of Big Data is also felt in corporate life

The capabilities that Big Data brings are changing the way that companies operate. There is a robust argument to be made for the value of 'good enough' over absolute accuracy that Big Data can bring. For many everyday corporate needs, knowing 'what' not 'why' is still good enough. This is likely to change slowly as barriers to access are removed, particularly for smaller traditional businesses, and as sector-specific Big Data solutions become more common.

It is fair to assume that those institutions that collect lots of data and find valuable uses for it, still have the potential to exploit more applications for Big Data than they currently have deployed. Not least because Big Data often involves datasets so large and complex that legacy IT systems cannot handle them.

Which businesses are ahead and why?

There are some clear corporate winners, including those firms whose unique selling point leverages data analysis, e.g. Amazon, and other corporate heavyweights that have made massive investments in Big Data to build a competitive advantage or just maintain competitive parity, e.g. IBM, Deloitte, Accenture, Google, Tesco and P&G. There are also many institutions applying Big Data techniques outside of these corporate stalwarts:

- Cancer Research UK launched the first-ever interactive website that allows the public to delve into real-life cancer data from research archives and speed up research.[4]
- CERN – the scientific centre based in Switzerland – records enough data from each of its major experiments at the Large Hadron Collider to fill around 100,000 DVDs every year.[5]

- The entire US federal government is involved in the growing Big Data challenge. In March 2012, the Obama administration announced the Big Data Research and Development Initiative to 'greatly improve the tools and techniques needed to access, organize, and glean discoveries from huge volumes of digital data'. The goal is to transform the US government's ability to use data for scientific, environmental and biomedical research, education and national security.[6]

Adoption stages of Big Data

Traditional barriers to uptake appear to be fading. The combination of the affordability of commodity hardware and software, which allows effective management and processing of Big Data, and the relative ease of testing new applications, are driving familiarity and usage. There are four broad stages:

- corporate education – building awareness of relevant 'off-the-shelf' solutions;
- corporate exploration – initial matching of solutions against corporate need or data availability;
- testing – pilot stage of concept definition and business benefits;
- adoption or rejection – initiatives deployed, with measurable return on investment.

The stages will evolve over time, particularly as Big Data becomes a mainstream corporate activity.

Implications for businesses

There will be a significant increase in the volume of data captured, the variety of data and speed of analysis. For many firms – perhaps the majority – Big Data and related technologies remove silos by using fewer but bigger data clusters, which are more economical. This supports better experimentation and ultimately better analysis. Big Data is a game-changer by transforming the way organisations perform an array of business metrics, and those that change with the game gain a scalable commercial advantage.

If Big Data is to quickly extend beyond the usual 'corporate suspects' and into more areas of commerce, a bite-sized approach is likely to be needed. The availability of robust open-source software, plus existing cloud-based data analytics services, is the key to the most likely low-cost solution.

A new 'school' of Big Data is emerging. This is one in which businesses use intuitive, interactive user interfaces to liberate insight from Big Data – and avoid the dependency on small armies of data scientists. This is occurring at the same time as an explosion of interest in infographics, which is fed by a wider interest in the data behind the headlines.

Very few organisations need to manage the full spectrum of capabilities that

Big Data offers. Yet for most businesses, there will be some opportunities to utilise new sources of data and accompanying analytics.

The rate of adoption of Big Data capabilities will be uneven. Larger businesses are likely to find the need is (in part) identified by technology consultants who 'sell in' their Big Data capabilities to firms with the budgets to benefit. In general terms, the mid-market is likely to see slower adoption with longer cycles of concept exploration and pilots. The small business market is too complex and broad to make generalisations, but it will be clear to many small firms that there is real value in better understanding the benefits of Big Data.

There will be set-backs. After the recent financial crisis it has become clear that many banks and rating agencies had relied on analytical models that although used a vast amount of information, failed to reflect the broader financial risks in the wider world. This was the first crisis where Big Data was at its core.

What could hold back growth? The risk of human error or the inflated expectations for what Big Data will actually deliver suggests there's still some way to go before the concept becomes era-defining (and even further to go before it is recognised by many consumers).

Key implications

A critique of the idea of Big Data may suggest that it is not wholly new, and that the need to analyse whole datasets, rather than representative samples (such as in the market research industry), does not necessarily lead to significant improvements.

However, in highly competitive markets, a business tool that offers even a slight improvement in customer understanding and consequent revenues is very likely to overcome barriers. We should expect significantly more applications of Big Data. But like the internet or telephony before it, it may become relatively un-noticed as it simply becomes 'normal' practice.

Implications for consumers

For most consumers, the benefits are not yet fully recognised, since Big Data is not seen in isolation to everyday 'digital' life. There are reasons to be optimistic since many 'Generation Y' consumers are more likely than their predecessors to understand the role of Big Data and demand the benefits it can offer them – financially or otherwise. There will be huge opportunities for consumers, should they be able to tap into the real financial value of their 'digital self' (which is likely to require Big Data to facilitate).

We should remember that the internet is the greatest (and fastest) ever generator of data about human endeavour. There's one simple reason – 2 billion people use it and almost everything they do is recorded – partially or in full – and therefore available for analysis. Big Data will be the defining buzzword for some time to come.

Case study

Making Big Data work for the big society: citizen science and cancer research

Unlocking the value of the citizen workforce to transform our world of information into one of knowledge and intelligence, beginning with cancer research

The word 'revolution' is not too strong a term to compare the reclassification of data analytics with a political or social revolution gone by. The application of the thought process about to be described has the capacity to elicit socio-political change on a global scale, much beyond its current concern.

The world has become saturated with information. Data are collected daily in almost incomprehensible volumes. Some are mined and used by individuals and bodies ranging from governments, corporations and charities to sociologists, anthropologists and marketers. Most of the data sit, awaiting an analyst to make some use of them.

Data are a valuable asset but much like a nineteenth-century counterpart – coal – they must be worked upon extensively in order to draw out their true worth. Coal becomes fuel that begets product. Data become information that beget knowledge.

Despite being centuries apart, the demand for both commodities remains remarkably alike. Factories arose during the industrial revolution when the need for economies of scale utilising skilled labour became prescient. This marked the end of 'cottage industries'. The catalyst for the industrial revolution lay in the advancement of technology and a move to a socio-technical system – the fusion of technology and people in workplaces. This combined skilled labour with unskilled workers in new and profitable ways.

Socio-technical theory as citizen science

In cancer research, there is a search for a similar equilibrium. At the moment, cancer samples are given special stains that highlight certain molecules as part of research. These molecules could reveal how a patient will respond to treatment. But this process is slow and analysis is mostly done by trained pathologists, who are often also cancer researchers.

In 2012, Cancer Research UK discovered entirely new ways to engage consumers in classifying real cancer data and significantly accelerate cures for cancers. In October 2012, it launched the first ever interactive website – http://www.cellslider.net/ – that appeals to the public to explore real-life cancer data from research archives and speed up lifesaving research, outside of the laboratory.

The project marked the first time real cancer data have used technology to present them in a format that can be analysed by the unskilled volunteer. By encouraging as many people as possible to take part, more samples can be analysed faster and more effectively, freeing up scientists to carry out other cancer research.

Professor Paul Pharoah, a Cancer Research UK scientist from the University of Cambridge who helped develop Cell Slider, commented:

> There is information that can transform cancer treatments buried in our data – we just need the manpower to unlock them. We've turned our data into something that can be accessed by anyone – you don't have to be a scientist to carry out this type of cancer research. If we can get millions of people on Cell Slider, we hope to condense what normally takes years of research into months.[7]

Professor Andrew Hanby, a Cancer Research UK scientist from the University of Leeds who also helped develop Cell Slider, said:

> We're being held back by how quickly we can process information on tumour samples. Computers can only go so far – they can pick up obvious trends but only the human eye can spot subtleties that have, in the past, led to important serendipitous discoveries.
>
> Cell Slider makes our data so accessible – it's not just for scientists and computer geeks – everyone can play their part in curing cancer from the comfort of their own homes.[8]

Building a viable ecosystem

Cell Slider is a very early prototype of a larger idea. Initial insight gleaned from 10,000 consumers found that although awareness was limited, appetite was overwhelming. Cell Slider, and citizen science in general, has the capacity to become a method of data analysis stretching far beyond its current remit. While usability from a clinical perspective is still being tested, one thing is for sure: there is real scope for replication and extension, as soon as a full roll-out is approved.

During 2013, KAE, the strategic marketing consultancy, is considering the most important elements of the ecosystem that would underpin the scalability required to cope with the consequences of success: these include conversations and inputs with technology and hardware partners, specialists in bringing gaming and analytics together, representatives from pharmaceutical and bio-tech companies and, most importantly, the millions of people that would transform cancer cures forever.

To revisit the earlier analogy in this chapter, we expect the knowledge revolution to fit the model of the industrial revolution in unexpected but logical ways. Cancer research as it stands is a cottage industry, in modest workshops filled with skilled pathologists. To bring the output – a commodity, product, knowledge – to scale, the next step is to build a factory or in its modern-day incarnation: an ecosystem. This requires a number of variants to slide together at one point.

Demand

Investments of time and money need a *raison d'être*. Proven demand is the primary driver in this 'grand plan' to build a factory to cope with that demand.

Where the knowledge revolution meets cancer research, our principal evidence for demand is the pathology 'bottleneck'. There aren't enough pathologists in the world to deal with the flow of data, let alone a re-examination of all that's been analysed before. Investment of time and money in 'the factory' tends to follow a breakthrough. The breakthrough in the industrialisation process for accelerating cancer cures came in 2012 in the form of Cell Slider.

Clinical efficacy is the proxy for demand: Cell Slider has to work to the satisfaction of the pathologists involved. It's not a new concept: there are some parallels with the breast cancer screening process brought into the UK decades ago. A radiology bottleneck was unblocked by digitising images and sending them around the world to available capacity, first to other professional radiologists and – over time – to technicians. The industrialisation of the screening process began and continues.

An incentivised volunteer workforce

The old adage goes that one volunteer is worth ten pressed men. This originates from the eighteenth century when Royal Navy press gangs roamed the streets 'pressing' able bodied men into service. Those who chose to volunteer benefited from certain privileges and were deemed to be more hardworking and loyal than those who had no choice.

In the healthcare sector, there is a similar widespread agreement that the volunteer workforce plays a valid and valued role in the system.

However, for the volunteer workforce to produce consistent high-quality work, it is necessary to be honest about the natural fusion between volunteered and incentivised labour. The 'Helping Out' survey researched on behalf of the Office of the Third Sector in 2007[9] reported the most common reasons for getting involved in volunteering as being:

- to improve things or help people (53 per cent);
- because the cause was important to the volunteer (41 per cent);
- because they had spare time on their hands (41 per cent).

The most important aspects are the impetus to volunteer and an implicit benefit. While a monetary incentive is omitted from the volunteer model, almost all 'free' labour works for a form of social currency, be it something that is personally delivered (a feeling of goodwill or connection to a particular cause) or one that is harvested (a good reference, investor insights, academic and practical experience).

There is good reason to believe that there is a non-financial price to be exchanged, and a sponsored social currency leading to social rewards, is the most likely route.

A managed and accountable workforce

Socio-technical theory shifted the burden of analysis from the individual to groups and teams. The notion of responsible autonomy was born: a theory of internal supervision and leadership.

When the theory pertains to citizen science, one must consider how to ensure consistent and quality outputs of a voluntary workforce in an ecosystem that finds itself physically annexed from those regulating it. We believe that the self-regulatory qualities of gamification, coupled with the social currency incentive inherent in the workforce, will empower it to produce valuable and reliable results. Responsible autonomy is manifest in an underpinning drive in the workforce to get things right on behalf of both themselves (a high score through gamification) and the project (a higher social currency garnered from their own involvement).

A regular and reliable workforce

The Mackinnon Partnership in 2009[10] published a report entitled 'The hidden workforce: volunteers in the health sector in England'. The findings demonstrate who the volunteer workforce consists of, why they contribute, the size of the workforce and the roles fulfilled successfully by volunteers.

In terms of management theory, it builds upon Charles Handy's theory of a shamrock organisation: one in which three groups work well together for organisational success: a core team of directly-employed professionals, freelancer workers and a marginal fringe of part time, and temporary staff whose numbers ebb and flow. The report suggests an adaptation to this theory, consisting of a directly-employed workforce, contracted staff, and volunteers, with all three contributing to the organisation's goals and all requiring attention by management. It is these 'contracted staff' who will provide a supplementary group to draw upon when the volunteer attendance is not fitting the citizen science model, providing a robust corporate social responsibility initiative for companies to donate employee's time in return for corporate social currency.

Investors and benefactors

There is no greater advocate or beneficiary for this ecosystem than the current UK government. From a social engagement perspective through to tax and employment, the blueprint fits its big society ideology. Healthcare costs are controlled, mainly due to the greater effectiveness of treatments; patients become workers and carers go back to a commercially productive state with wages earned and taxes paid.

With time and investment, this system could form the framework of the government's big society plans to empower local people and communities. Other advocates, such as large pharmaceutical companies, have an undisputed interest in the ecosystem: investment will be rewarded through the therapies produced via this route.

Biotech companies need funding from venture capitalists. The output of the ecosystem will deliver them effective stage 1 or stage 2 clinical trial 'goods outwards', which they can bid for. The money goes back into cancer research, through organisations such as Cancer Research UK who provide the active ingredient to make this all work – predictable, qualified, productive labour.

Conclusion: Big Data for a big society

It is here that the knowledge revolution begins to take hold as a socio-political concept. Policy-makers must look to trends rather than tactics to discuss what implications and opportunities may arise on bringing the ecosystem to scale. Beyond cancer research, beyond citizen science and beyond principles of a big society: the process of unlocking the value of time and resource through technology and organisation is a blueprint that can be applied to multiple industries.

It has the power to release data analytics and scientific research from its highly skilled and costly silo and empower society's under-skilled worker with academic and practicable expertise. It is a global development, a lesson in macro economics and a practical solution to the data bottleneck all in one.

Notes

1 Http://www.kdnuggets.com/polls/2012/where-applied-analytics-data-mining.html.
2 University of Cambridge, 2012. Digital records could expose intimate details and personality traits of millions (http://www.cam.ac.uk/research/news/digital-records-could-expose-intimate-details-and-personality-traits-of-millions).
3 Boston Consulting Group, The value of our digital identity, November 2012 (www.bcgperspectives.com/content/articles/digital_economy_consumer_insight_value_of_our_digital_identity).
4 Http://www.clicktocure.net.
5 *Wired*, Subatomic inferno under the Alps, November 2006 (http://www.wired.com/science/discoveries/news/2006/11/72198?currentPage=all).

6 Office of Science and Technology Policy Executive Office of the President, Obama administration unveils 'Big Data' initiative, March 2012 (http://www.whitehouse.gov/sites/default/files/microsites/ostp/big_data_press_release_final_2.pdf).
7 Cancer Research UK, Charity creates world's first citizen science project to speed up cancer research, October 2012 (http://www.cancerresearchuk.org/cancer-info/news/archive/pressrelease/2012-10-23-worlds-first-citizen-science).
8 Ibid.
9 '"Helping Out", 2007: a national survey of volunteering and charitable giving', Natalie Low, Sarah Butt, Angela Ellis Paine and Justin Davis Smith. Prepared for the Office of the Third Sector in the Cabinet Office by the National Centre for Social Research and the Institute for Volunteering Research.
10 The Mackinnon Partnership, 'The hidden workforce: volunteers in the health sector in England – a report to skills for health', 2009.

9 Innovation, valuation and crisis

Alojzy Z. Nowak and Bernard Arogyaswamy

When asked whether the present economic crisis is already on the wane, experts are uncertain, even vague. Some believe that an extensive intervention launched by final borrowers (i.e. governments and central banks) has managed to control further escalation of loss of liquidity suffered by regular commercial and financial entities (commercial banks, investment funds, insurance funds, etc.) and that this brought more optimism into the real economy that should soon translate into more solid economic growth and a consistent, if slow-paced, process of recovery from the crisis. Others, instead, point out that, first, due to the volume and diversity of financial resources, including toxic assets that remain in circulation, the crisis has in fact only been slowed down a little and the worst is still to come.[1] Second, apart from the USA and some Asian countries, we still face the problem of deteriorating consumer confidence, declining trust in the future, contradictory strategies for development of the global economy as well as that of leading countries and economic/political groups, and, finally, the problem – still observable – of undermined moral principles and ethical codes in business.[2]

It seems that this fundamental discordance of views upon the future of the global economy stems from the fact that the present crisis is not like the previous cases of economic downturns. Thousands of detailed and often incompatible pieces of information, coming from many countries, actually blur rather than clear the picture of transformation occurring in the global economy. What we have to deal with is a mix of positive and negative information, potentially leading to misleading conclusions. In many countries, financial markets increasingly seem to influence the actions taken by political and economic rulers.[3]

Possible roads to recovery

Nonetheless, possible scenarios for the global economy's recovery from the present slow-down assume the following:[4]

- *That a need will emerge for businesses to renew their aging productive capacities precisely because of the downturn.* In effect, demand rises for investment goods such as machines, equipment and new technologies, which fosters inventory replacement or shift. The process is slow but it may already be observed in the real economy. This is especially evident in the USA and in several Asian countries, China in particular. Hopefully, more and more distinct signals of economic stimulation there precede, perhaps even create, an improvement in the climate for investment in the entire global economy.

- *That it will become possible to implement innovations created or introduced during the downturn.* Usually a crisis is also a period when universities and research institutions increase their activities, often subsidized from either state or local budgets so that they can absorb jobless youth and raise their skills. As experience teaches us, this process, combined with a growth in business competitiveness, both of enterprises and their employees, results in increased tendency to innovate and launch state-of-the-art technologies.[5] These include new products such as tablet computers, 3D printing and affordable solar panels, new services such as Zipcar and new business models based on the long tail (customization based on flexible platforms) and "freemium" (where most services are free, the model being viable due to buyers of premium services) strategies.[6] Even in an economy as troubled as Italy's, innovation has proceeded apace albeit in select regional pockets. Fiamm, which produces nickel sodium batteries is rapidly expanding output and exports, as is Interpump, a manufacturer of high pressure pumps for specific industries. Mossi & Ghisolfi, a bioplastics firm, is likewise expanding its already impressive list of global customers.[7]

At the same time, we observe how individual governments undertake all sorts of actions in order to overcome the economic stagnation and its consequences and to give new impulse for development in the area of the real economy. Traditional methods of recovering from the crisis, undertaken by governments, include, on the one hand, budgetary and fiscal discipline, restricted public spending, raised taxes and, on the other hand, stimulating the economy, relieving the fiscal regime and undertaking actions that aim to increase consumption and to reduce unemployment. Injection of an economic stimulus has been tried in different countries with varying degrees of success. The near US$800 billion stimulus in the United States helped, in the view of leading economists, avert a depression but, due to not being large enough, has only succeeded in creating tepid growth.[8] Recent data indicate that the employment situation may be taking a turn for the better, with nearly 250,000 jobs being added in February 2013, and the unemployment rate falling to 7.7 percent, despite the loss of over 350,000 government jobs in the past two years alone.[9] It may well be true, however, that a larger stimulus would have lowered unemployment and fostered innovation more rapidly. A portion of the package (around 20 percent) was directed toward fostering innovation through (1) *direct investment* (e.g. in government-owned labs such as the Energy Research Center in Colorado;[10] (2) *enabling*, accomplished by providing subsidies and support (as in the case of light emitting diode research), for work on robotics in universities;[11] and (3) *facilitation*, exemplified by the Nanoscience Center in Albany, New York, where the government has been instrumental in organizing a research and manufacturing cluster.[12]

What may be observed during a crisis is that some governments go beyond just standard policy prescriptions, and either increase, or at least refrain from restricting, public spending on servicing the needs of certain segments of the population (such as the elderly, college students, those in need of public housing or transport, etc.) particularly in such areas as biomedicine, education, mass transit, health care or social welfare, because these fields could well be potential sources from which new, successful products or innovative technologies might emerge.

Innovation models

The experience gathered so far also seem to affirm that both strategies of anti-crisis action mentioned above are – as intended – meant to yield positive results over a mid-term perspective. Without objecting to whether it is justified or needed to get involved in this sort of actions, it seems that in the long run consistent efforts to raise competitiveness and productivity of a given economy are the key to achieve a more steady economic development.[13]

Accordingly, innovations become, especially during a crisis:

- a driving force of the economy, on the supply and demand sides;
- a vital modernization-promoting factor that increases the economic efficiency;
- a factor that lays down foundations for solid and durable economic growth, reinforces the economic potential; and
- a factor that exerts a crucial influence not only upon development of businesses, but also upon the standards of consumers' lives.

Governments that choose this development model, therefore, aim to:[14]

- broaden and deepen knowledge-based economy and services;
- implement a system of education in which the priority is given to creativity and new skills creation;
- reform universities so that they are more strictly related to needs and challenges of local and global economy thus establishing a launch-pad for creating and releasing intellectual capital;
- support public education where electronic media, the internet and e-learning are capable of playing a vital role in propagating innovative attitudes;
- create the legal and institutional framework for a sound and efficient, innovation policy-friendly state.

Key strategies for successful innovation policies

1   *A shift from the previous model of the innovation policy,* based upon a single company, toward one based on collaboration between a number of companies operating in complementary areas of entrepreneurship. It has become more and more popular to set up new technology clusters or consortia whose

cooperation, based on similar scientific or technological levels, also involves better recognition of a given market, including its cultural aspect. The region increasingly becomes the arena of interaction necessary for modernization processes to emerge. Competencies and specific potential of a given region allow the reduction of the risk involved in innovation, favor the absorption of various segments of knowledge and open the door to interactive learning and expertise exchange.[15] As a result of an increasing complexity and risk involved in innovation, *relationships between various entities, reaching beyond regular market relations*, are going to grow more and more critical. This will include relations held with universities, research labs and providers of counseling and technological services.

2   Small and medium-sized enterprises (SMEs) *are going to enjoy an ever-increasing share in innovation* because it is not only the level of research spending that acts as their principal drive, but it is also creativity and the ability to exploit a high level of development of science that may be used by individuals and relatively minor groups, hence the growing importance of innovative family businesses in the market. As the Kauffman Foundation's study[16] demonstrates, the rate of entrepreneurial startup in the US rose in the years post-2008, in response to the crisis. While part of the uptake in startups may be attributed to necessity entrepreneurship (say, by those who were laid off and by others unable to find jobs), innovation-oriented activities of businesses in the twenty-first century, rather than concentrating purely on maximization of profit, are also going to be increasingly oriented to dealing with challenges and threats to humanity, and to the planet at large. Therefore, new dynamics may be expected in the development of areas such as green technologies, medical advancements, and information, bio- and nanotechnologies. Whole Foods (a large retailer of organic food products), for instance, has fostered an entire ecosystem of farmers, livestock owners, distributors and logistical firms to bring produce from far-flung supply points to its urban stores.[17] Herman Miller, a medium-sized manufacturer of office furniture, has developed a "cradle-to-cradle" system whereby its inputs are drawn largely from recycled material, while its products are almost fully recyclable. The company also sees itself as a designer of working spaces thereby interfacing with ergonomics, illumination, telecommuting and so on.[18]

3   *Demand-based innovation becomes an even more significant method of implementing innovation during a time when economies are slowing down, and uncertainty over the nature of re-employment, if and when it occurs, persists.*[19] Customers, are not, surprisingly enough, becoming more risk-averse. However, the level of excitement and value they expect from the product/service and the firm offering it has tended to grow. User-driven innovation, particularly where usage conditions and user needs could vary within a market segment, has become more widespread. Mountain bikes, hiking boots, surgical tools and software bought off-the-shelf are instances of products where users often modify products to suit their specific needs, probably because the supplier would charge too much to customize them. Companies that track

customer use stand to gain by incorporating the necessary changes especially if the modifications are common to a large slice of the target segment. 3M, for example, in tracking the use of its masking tape, found most users modified the tape before use so that it adhered better. The company decided to incorporate the fix itself. 3M also focuses on lead-users (those working under the most exacting conditions) to develop the most robust product possible. User innovation could see even more explosive growth as social networking combines with "democratic" production techniques such as 3D printing (made by layering material to the required shape, rather than reducing it) and the introduction of carbon fiber and nanotubes to give rise to what is being called the age of "social manufacturing."[20] Innovation truly is being democratized at an accelerating pace.

4   *Cultural factors, traditions, organizational cultures, and competing models of economic development* are going to be even more influential upon the innovativeness of businesses and economies.

The experiences of two very different countries, the USA and Japan, concerning the level and nature of innovation may be used as empirical evidence to show that there are no ready-made, identical recipes for achieving the principal driving forces, on which the successful achievement of innovation potential depends. Both countries in question often seem to feature different conditions and mechanisms for unleashing innovation to generate economic development.

Case of the USA

- Americans are interested in achieving success and taking business risk.
- Bankruptcies are perceived as positive events and seen as a new business experience and an opportunity to heal the company.
- Protection of intellectual property has been regarded as one of foundations for development for as long as the country has existed. (The first patent was awarded in the USA as early as 1790.)
- The tax system favors innovation.
- Foundations are established at both federal and state level to support entrepreneurship and innovation.
- Extensive investments (both private and public) in research and development (R&D), in particular in information technologies, nanotechnology and biotechnology, are supported by technological universities, often with governmental backing.
- It is quite common for SMEs to become initiators of entrepreneurship development and for high-risk business.

The case of Japan

- *Collectivist culture*, in which a group is of superior importance to an individual, has been emphasized for centuries and belonging to networks of social ties is seen by members of the society as a source of identification and sense of safety, otherwise provided by the relationship between an individual and corporation.[21]

- *Kaizen*, i.e. perfection of work done, has been a central element in the Japanese model of management. It creates an atmosphere in which companies may solve their inner problems avoiding major conflicts. What counts are incremental improvements introduced without disturbing the working system or social status quo. *Adaptability, team work, close attention to detail and a continuous process of small adjustments sum up the approach to innovation.*
- *Partnership* between large companies and SMEs is often not only based upon economic premises and tendency to maximize profit, but also on the omnipresent spirit of cooperation and mutual trust.
- *The government supports and initiates creation of scientific consortia*, horizontal cooperation networks, clusters, etc.

The Japanese, thanks to the above-mentioned cultural background, idiosyncratic solutions and their approach to searching for new technologies, are able to offer products featuring an almost perfect level of manufacturing quality and it is not by chance that they enjoy a long-standing reputation for being among the leaders in all sorts of innovation rankings. In 2010 Japan ranked first in the world with 295,315 patents applied for domestically. Japan, in response to its nuclear meltdown and lack of natural resources, has developed a way to source methane hydrate gas 3,300 feet below sea level and is further developing this new source of energy, which is also environmentally clean. Interestingly, other Asian countries, including Singapore, Hong Kong and China also secure top places in this line-up.

It is undeniable that a high level of innovativeness in a given country largely depends on whether the government, various sectors of industry and services, and scientific and academic circles come together to create a system of complementary relationships. The shared search for new sources of knowledge and technology rest on a set of supportive values and norms, and draw sustenance from the appropriate institutional and legal infrastructure. In addition, the willingness of buyers to purchase new products and services, and for investors to fund startups and newly developed products is critical to innovation during hard times.

Creation of new, original knowledge and its dissemination is, in part, dependent on substantial outlays being made, both public and private, in R&D, as a gross domestic product (GDP) percentage (that is, R&D intensity). The present experience indicates a clear relationship between R&D spending, the number of patents, especially those applied for abroad, and share of high-technology goods in a country's export.

Table 9.1 shows there is a relationship between a level of R&D intensity and the share of high-technology goods in export. Countries such as Israel, Japan, the United States, Germany, France, the United Kingdom and the Netherlands are leaders in the export of advanced technology goods – and most often these are also goods patented abroad. China is a part-member of this group with its 31 percent share of high-technology goods in export. However, while China is becoming a country

Table 9.1 Innovation ratios in selected countries in 2010

Item	Country	Public outlays on R&D (as % of GDP)	Number of patents applied for abroad	Number of patents applied for domestically	Share of high-technology goods in total export (%)
1	Israel	4.86	5,387	1,387	23
2	Japan	3.44	53,281	295,315	20
3	USA	2.82	231,194	224,912	23
4	China	—	85,477	229,096	31
5	Germany	2.72	11,724	47,859	16
6	Sweden	3.75	306	2,549	17
7	Finland	3.46	127	1,806	18
8	France	2.02	1,809	14,295	23
9	United Kingdom	1.88	6,480	15,985	23
10	Denmark	2.72	131	1,518	18
11	Netherlands	1.63	53	908	24
12	Austria	2.66	292	2,263	11
13	Czech Republic	1.47	92	789	16
14	Spain	1.34	207	3,596	5
15	Italy	1.18	903	8,814	8
16	Russia	1.03	12,966	25,589	9
17	Croatia	0.90	68	250	12
18	Poland	0.61	242	2,899	5
19	Romania	0.59	37	1,054	10
20	Slovakia	0.47	63	176	5

Source: The author's own calculation is based on: World Development Indicators, 2013, http://databank.worldbank.org/data/download/WDI-2013-ebook.pdf.

exporting more and more sophisticated technologies, not only to so-called Third World countries, but to developed Asia, USA and Europe as well, the technologies concerned are more likely to be of foreign origin than home-grown. The incentives offered by the government to file and obtain patents has resulted in a high number of patents registered in China (in fact, in excess of that in the US), but only about 5 percent are also registered abroad, the corresponding figures for the US and Europe being 27 percent and 40 percent respectively.[22]

It is evident China has embarked on a shift from imitation of technologies developed elsewhere to expanding its presence in global markets by offering goods and services increasingly based upon original and innovative solutions. Conversely, countries ranked near the bottom end of Table 9.1, such as Poland, Romania or Slovakia, also serve well to illustrate how a low level (as GDP percentage) of spending on research translates into a very weak percentage share of high-technology goods in their exports. The table also provides an insight into why it was Budapest in Hungary rather than Wrocław in Poland that was chosen as a seat of the European Institute of Innovation and Technology. The share of high-technology goods in Hungarian export in 2010 amounted to an impressive 26 percent of the country's total exports, while in Poland it was as little as 5 percent. If Poland suffered the consequences of the global crisis to a comparatively lesser extent, it was also – and paradoxically – thanks to the relative technological underdevelopment of its banking sector, and a proportionately minor share in transactions conducted in global financial markets. As far as innovativeness is concerned, Poland continues to face challenges in shifting from its present stage of development to the next level of persevering in the search for new sources of knowledge and technology that address market needs.

R&D value: China and India

Reverting to China, whose R&D effort has spiked sharply over the past decade, it may be noted that its spending on technological development has far outstripped that of India's whose spending on R&D barely is a little over 1 percent of GDP. It is noteworthy, however, that, since the global economy imploded in 2007, the two Asian giants combined to contribute 20 percent of R&D expenditure worldwide.[23] While China's share is about two-thirds of this amount, India's spending on this account has doubled in the past five years. Both countries' efforts to stimulate innovation are driven by generous incentives, subsidies and even outright investment to "jumpstart" the innovation society. Since consumption is only around one-third of GDP in China, the innovative effort is more dependent on government spending than in India, whose consumption share of the economy is nearer that of developed nations (that is, around 70 percent).

China's model of "state capitalism" has served the country and its people well, raising living standards, creating a solid infrastructure and putting in place a sound technological base. Whether the intense focus on achieving technological leadership in an innovation-driven world continues remains to be seen.[24] The ability to bridge the so-called "valley of death" (the leap from technology to the market),[25] overcoming the bureaucracy that goes with state funding, governmental interference in the market-driven process, and the "too big to fail" syndrome that might bedevil firms and their governmental sponsors in countries such as China (as well as Brazil and Russia), as they attempt to parlay state power into technological prowess and market acceptance, are elements that could imperil the drive to foster innovation with the state as prime mover. The "stickiness" of users' knowledge[26] and experience, that is, the difficulties involved in communicating their needs to technology developers and product designers, and the possible lack of absorptive capacity (which could include the ability to understand and satisfy customers' expectations, creating new competencies if necessary) on the part of the product/service innovators, make the valley of death a chasm that requires more than money or authority to cross.

Another look at Table 9.1, this time at the Scandinavian nations, might indicate that high R&D intensities do not always result in large numbers of patents nor does patenting on a large scale necessarily result in a proportionate level of innovation (as noted earlier in the case of China). The combined GDP of Denmark, Sweden and Finland come to around US$1 trillion, while China's is eight times that, with Japan and the US coming in at around US$6 trillion and US$16 trillion respectively. Apart from the actual amount invested in R&D and the state's role in the activity (which is comparatively low in the cases of the three Scandinavian countries), a broader point is that these three northern European nations (and Norway) have undertaken innovation that goes beyond the realm of the market. They have innovated socially, politically and culturally as well creating a version of capitalism that is uniquely theirs. While they remain states that provide welfare benefits to their citizens, the Nordic countries have lowered taxes, including those on corporations. (Sweden's corporate taxes are being reduced by over 16 percent.) Finland's Nokia-centered economy has given way to one in which entrepreneurship is being stimulated, with venture capitalists and angel investors ready to provide funding. Across the region, startups are being encouraged and helped to bring more ideas from universities and incubators to the market. In Denmark, while employers can close businesses and lay off labor with relative dispatch, the government steps in with programs to help these employees find work again. Government spending is being cut with the help of innovative social measures. Parents can send their children to schools of their choice with the state offering vouchers to help with the tuition. Health care in Sweden is provided by a combination of state-run and private providers. Politically, governments are opting for transparency and easy access to all services by electronic means, including paying taxes by SMS. The outcomes in terms of gender equality, social mobility and low income disparity offer a vision of a different type of society based on this Nordic capitalism.[27]

Conclusion

As the world seeks to find more effective ways to cope with the economic crisis, the conviction that innovation is a crucial component of the solution has become widely accepted. However, depending on the nature of the institutions prevalent in a society and its most pressing needs at the time, the approach to innovation and how it is implemented is likely to vary considerably from one country to the other.

Notes

1. Kołodko, G. (2012), Ekonomia kryzysu, czy kryzys ekonomii (Economy of crisis or the crisis of economy) in: *Kryzys i co dalej? (Crisis . . . and What Next?)*, I. Lichniak (ed.), Warsaw: Warsaw School of Economic Publishing.
2. OECD (2010), *The OECD Innovation Strategy. Getting a Head Start on Tomorrow*, http://www.oecd.org/innovation/strategy/, Paris: OECD.
3. Legrain, Ph. (2010), *Aftershock: Reshaping the World Economy after Crisis*, London: Little Brown; Yin, E. and Williamson, P. (2011), Rethinking innovation for a recovery, *Ivey Business Journal*, May/June.
4. Taplin, R. and Nowak A.Z. (eds), (2010), The financial crises, intellectual property and prospects for recovery: the case of Poland and Central and Eastern Europe in: *Intellectual Property, Innovation and Management in Emerging Economies*, London: Routledge.
5. Prahalad C.K. and Krishnan M.S. (2010), *Nowa era innowacji* (The new age of innovation), Warsaw: PWN.

6. Osterwalder, A. and Pigneur, Y. (2010), *Business Model Generation*, Hoboken: Wiley.
7. Jewkes, S. (2013), Italian firms innovate to fight recession, www.Reuters.com/article/2013/02/22.
8. Krugman, P. (2012), *End this Depression Now*, New York: Norton.
9. Straw, W. and Pratt, A. (2009), Recovering innovation, innovating to recover, www.scienceprogress.org/2009/01.
10. Jaffe, M. (2012), Colorado renewable energy collaboration lands $37 million in funds, *Denver Post*, May 8.
11. Northeastern University (2013), University–government relations, www.northeastern.edu/governmentrelations/research.
12. Vielkind, J. (2011), Poised to ride the tech wave, *Times Union*, September 28.
13. Oleksiuk, A. (2012), *Uwarunkowania i mechanizmy tworzenia innowacji jako czynniki rozwoju gospodarczego* (*Pre-conditions and Mechanisms for Creating Innovation as Factors of Economic Development*), Olsztyn: University of Warmia and Mazury Publishing.
14. Edvinsson, L. (2012), Universal networking, intellectual capital in: *European Integration Process in the Regional and Global Settings*, E. Latoszek, I. Kotowska, A.Z. Nowak, A. Stępniak (eds), Warsaw: University of Warsaw, Faculty of Management Publishing.
15. Cooke, P. (2002), *Knowledge Economies: Clusters, Learning, and Cooperative Advantage*, London: Routledge.
16. Florida, R. (2010), Start-ups surge in the Great Reset, http://www.theatlantic.com/business/archive/2010/05/start-ups-surge-in-the-great-reset/57052/.
17. Harasta, P. and Hoffman, A. (2010), Whole Foods market in: *Strategic Management*, C. Hill and G. Jones, Mason, OH: Southwestern.
18. Shipper, F., Adams, S., Manz, K. and Manz, C. (2010), Herman Miller: a case of reinvention and renewal in: *Strategic Management*, C. Hill and G. Jones, Mason, OH: Southwestern.
19. Research International (2009), How to drive successful innovation in a recession, http://www.wpp.com/~/media/SharedWPP/Marketing%20Insights/Hot%20Topics/Downturn/ri_innovate_in_a_recession.pdf.
20. Markillie, P. (2012), A third industrial revolution, The *Economist*, April 21, pp. 3–20.
21. Hofstede, G. (2000), *Kultury i organizacje: zaprogramowanie umysłu, (Cultures and Organizations: Software of the Mind)*, Warsaw: PWE.
22. Liu, J., Baskaran, A. and Muchie, M. (2011), Global recession and the national system of innovation in China: a blessing in disguise?, Aalborg University working paper.
23. The *Economist* (2013), How innovative is China? *Valuing Patents*, January 5.
24. Wooldridge, A. (2012), The visible hand, The *Economist*, January 21, pp. 3–18.
25. Van Hippel, E. (2010), *Technology and the Market*, Kindle Books.
26. Ibid.
27. Woodridge, A. (2013), Northern lights, The *Economist*, February 2, pp. 3–16.

Index

Relevant figures and tables are indicated by *italic* type. Where capitalisation, hyphenation or spellings differ between chapters, the majority usage has been followed.

Abe, Shinzo 11–12
Aboody, David 78
Accenture, USA 154
Accentus, UK 25
accounting: Amoeba Management 9; dynamic added value taxation 101–2; law of energy conservation 84; R&D reporting requirements 73, 74–7
Acer, Taiwan 39
Aconchego Program, Portugal 64
Acorn Computers, UK 26
added value, socio-economic system 84–5, 86–7, 95–7
added value taxation 85; dynamic 19–20, 85, 86, 98, 99–111, *102*, *105*, *107*
Addenbrooke's Hospital, Cambridge, UK 58
Ad Words/Ad Sense, Google 34
agriculture: food biomass production 89–91, *91*, 93; food energy carriers 96, 97–8, *98*
aircraft sector 125, 138
Allum, Stephen xv, 2, 11, 113–34
Amazon, USA 3, 29, 30–2, 35–7, *36*, 153, 154
Amazon Web Services (AWS) 32
'Ambulatory ICU' approach, USA 61
Amoeba Management 9
Anderson, Chris 43
Android operating system 33
Andromo 145
AppBuilder, UK 145
Apple, USA 3, 40; Apple/Samsung disputes 3–4, 5, 6–7, 10
application software: mobile apps and consumer creativity/invention 16–18, 139–46; open source 29, 150

Appmakr 145
AppStori/AppsFunder 17, 144
ARM Holdings, UK 26–7
Arogyaswamy, Bernard xv, 20, 163–71
art valuation 1–2
asset-backed securitisation, music industry 25–6
asset markets, dysfunctional 126–7
asset valuation, maritime sector 2, 122–7, *124*, 129–34; and residual value risk/insurance 120–2, 127–9, 133–4
Australia 11, 55, 68, 115
Austria, innovation ratios *169*

Baltic and International Maritime Council (BIMCO) 116
Baltic Dry Index 115
Baltic Exchange 123
bankruptcies 3, 8, 127, 167
Bartenev, Victor xv–xvi, 19–20, 84–111
BCG/*Businessweek* Fund 13–16, *14–15*
'Bell-Mason' framework 61
'Best Doctors' programme 55
'best use' concept, asset valuation 126
BHP Billiton, Australia 115
Big Data 148–51, 161; benefits/implications for consumers 19, 152–3, 156; contribution to big society 157–61; gamification 154, 160; impact/implications for businesses 154–6; privacy issues 19, 151–2; rise of crowdsourcing 153–4
big society, contribution of Big Data 157–61
biotech companies, patenting 29
BlackBerry 3, 7
'black swan events' 24

blogs 140
Blood Sprint 144
'blueprint' scenario, Shell 23–4
Boston Children's Hospital, USA 55
Boston Consulting Group *see* BCG/*Businessweek* Fund
Bowie, David 25–6
brand, and value 5, 6
break-through innovation 24
Broad Institute, MIT, USA 44
BTG, UK 25
Buckley, Peter 79
Buddhism 9
Bunt, Laura 61
business method patents 29–37, *36*
business model open innovation 45–6
business models 164

Canada 64–5
cancer research, and Big Data 154, 157–61
Cancer Research UK 154; Cell Slider 157–8, 159
capitalisation of R&D 8, 73, 75, 76–7, 78–81
carbon reduction strategies 65
Cargo Innovation Challenge, Lufthansa 138
Casson, Mark 79
Caves, Richard 79
Cazavan-Jeny, Anne 79
Cell Slider 157–8, 159
Centrelink agency, Australia 68
CERN, Switzerland 154
charterers' default insurance 122
Chesbrough, Henry 8, 27
China 39, 40, 49, 54–5, *92*, 168–9, *169*; Diaoyu (Senkaku) Islands dispute 11–12; R&D value 170; and sea freight 114–18, *116–17*
Christensen, Clayton 39
Cisco, USA 28
citizen science 153, 157–61
cloud computing 150, 151
co-creation *see* consumer creativity/invention
'Collaboration Kitchen', Kraft 137
collaborative protocols/agreements 49–50
'collaboratives', health care, UK 64
collateralised debt obligation (CDO) 120
collectivist culture, Japan 167–8
Comedy School, London, UK 55
commoditisation of knowledge 39–41

Community Health and Learning Foundation, UK 58
community support, mental health 58
Compaq, USA 39
Compass Maritime, USA 123
competition law 10–11
competitive advantage, and innovation 13
computers *see* information and communication technology (ICT)
Connect + Develop approach, P&G 27, 28
consumer creativity/invention 135–6, 166–7; consumers as entrepreneurs 138–9; involvement in mobile app creation 16–18, 139–46; technology as enabler 136–8, 144
consumers, benefits/implications of Big Data 19, 152–3, 156
container shipping 115–18, *116–17*; *see also* maritime sector
co-production, health care 68
copyright, decline of 3, 41–3
Corna, Valeria xvi, 16–17, 135–46
Corporate Lego 46–8
creative commons/open source movement 7–8, 28–9, 41, 47, 50, 66, 150
creativity: globalisation of talent 12–16, *14–15*; music industry 42; *see also* consumer creativity/invention
credit crunch *see* financial crisis
Croatia, innovation ratios *169*
crowdfunding, mobile apps 144–5
crowdsourcing: and Big Data 153–4; citizen science and cancer research 157–61; *see also* idea crowdsourcing
cultural factors 5, 20, 167; family-owned businesses, Asia 7, 10; Japan 8–10, 167–8; and open knowledge 7–8; Western and Asian linkages 10–11
customer-centricity, Amazon 32
Czech, Marcin 18
Czech Republic, innovation ratios *169*

data integration 47
data management/datasets *see* Big Data
decentralised organisations 46–8
default risk, maritime sector 126
Dell Idea Storm 136, 137
Dell, USA 39
Deloitte, UK 154
demand-based innovation 166–7
democratisation of innovation 167; mobile app development 17, 145–6

Denmark *169*, 170–1
diabetes problem 18
Diaoyu (Senkaku) Islands dispute 11–12
differentiated knowledge 39–41, 47
digital data: integration of 47; *see also* Big Data; information and communication technology (ICT)
'digital nomads' 48–9
digital replication (3D printing) 42–3
'digital self' concept/digital passports 152–3
discounted cashflow (DCF) 124
disruptive innovation 24
downloads 16–17, 140–1
drugs *see* pharmaceutical industry
dry bulk freight market 115
DSM 28
dynamic added value taxation (DAVT) 19–20, 85, 86, 98, 99–111, *102, 105, 107*

earning power, ships 132
earnings-management, and R&D 79
Eastman Kodak, USA 3
economic models, Western/Asian 10–11
economic theories/analysis 11
education, and innovation 17, 30, 34
efficiency: ecological 90; economic 86–8, *87*, 91–4, *92–4*, 95
Ekuban, Andrew xvi, 8, 73–81
electricity prices, USA 87, *87*, 93, *93*
electronics *see* information and communication technology (ICT)
employees: benefits of social innovation 66–7; 'Montessori mafia' 17, 30, 34; project-by-project 48–9; rights to compensation 4–5; and social value 65; *see also* talent
empowerment, health care 57, 68
end of life care 59–60
energy carriers 96, 97–9, *98*
energy conservation, law of 84
energy sources, world economy 88–94, *88–9, 91–4*
energy–value interrelationship *see* physical macroeconomics
Enterprise 2.0 47
entrepreneurs 12–13; consumers as 138–9; and financial crisis 166; young people as 17–18
equilibrium: living systems 108–10; markets and DAVT 104–6, *105*
e-readers, Amazon Kindle 32, 35
European Patent Convention 30

European Union (EU): accounting standards 73, 74–7; efficiency and energy consumption *92*, 93

Facebook 19, 151–2
fair market value (FMV) 123, *124*, 125
family-owned businesses, Asia 7, 10
family support, young people's innovation 17–18
feedback, living systems and taxation 85, 86, 104, 106–7, 108
Fiamm, Italy 164
Financial Accounting Standards Board (FASB), USA 78, 80
financial crisis 163, 171; impact of credit crunch on maritime sector 113–19, *115–17*; and innovation models 165; key strategies for innovation policies 165–70, *169*; and R&D value 170–1; scenarios for global recovery 163–5
financial reporting, signalling effects of R&D 8, 73–81
Financial Reporting Standards (FRS), UK 74
Findlay, Michael 1–2
fine art valuation 1–2
Finland *169*, 170–1
fishing industry 91, 97
FLAG, UK 57
Flipboard 141
food biomass production 89–91, *91*, 93
food energy carriers 96, 97–8, *98*
Foote Hospital, USA 67
foresight *see* futures thinking/foresight/scenarios
Foucault, Michel 68
France, innovation ratios *169*
free energy 84–5, 86, 95, 98, 108–9
freelance talent 48–9
'freemium' strategy 164
Friedman, Thomas 39
FRS *see* Financial Reporting Standards
Fry, Adrian xvi, 19, 148–61
FTSE 13, 15
Future Agenda programme 22, 38, 41, 46, 47
future of innovation and IP 38–9, 51–2; big collaboration 49–50; business model open innovation 45–6; Corporate Lego 46–8; differentiated knowledge 39–41, 47; the end of IP 41–3; and failed drugs 43–5; projects worth working for 48–9

futures thinking/foresight/scenarios 22–4; link with innovation 24–5; 'open foresight' concept 37–8; *see also* future of innovation and IP

gamification, Big Data 154, 160
Garcia-Manjon, Juan 78
General Accepted Accounting Principles (GAAP), UK and USA 74, 77
Generics Group, UK 25
Germany 56, 124, 125, 138, *169*
goodwill 5, 74–5
Google, USA 3, 30–1, 32–7, *36*, 145, 152, 154
government bureaucracy, Japan 10
government strategies, financial crisis 164–5
GPs (general practitioners), UK 55
'grain basket': price 97–8, *98*; world production 90–1, *91*
gross domestic product (GDP) 85, 86, 87, *89*, *92*, 93, 108, 168, *169*, 170; energy and information components 95–7

Hailo 17, 142
Hall, Justin 140
Hamburg Shipbrokers Association (HSA) 124–5, 126
Hanby, Andrew 158
Handy, Charles 160
harmony, living systems 108–10
health: and Big Data 153, 154, 157–61; Blood Sprint app 144; diabetes problem 18; *see also* social innovation, health care
Heartland Health, Missouri, USA 65
'Helping Out' survey, UK 159
Herman Miller, USA 166
Hewlett Packard (HP), USA 39
'Homeless World Cup' 57
Homeshare International 55
hospice care 59–60
hospital passports 58
household energy carriers 96
HTC, Taiwan 7, 39
Huawei, China 3, 7, 49
Hungary 169
Hyundai Heavy Industries, South Korea 114

IAS *see* International Accounting Standards
IBM, USA 23, 28, 154

idea crowdsourcing 136–8, 144–5; consumers as entrepreneurs 16, 138–9
IdeasProject 17, 144
Idea Storm, Dell 136, 137
IFRS *see* International Financial Reporting Standards
Inamori, Kazuo 8–10
income, and greed 109–10
income method, asset valuation 124
income-smoothing, and R&D 79
incremental innovation 24
India 39, 40, 49, 64, 170
inflation 95, 114
information ('negative entropy') 95–6, 108
information and communication technology (ICT): blogs 140; and business method patents 29–37, *36*; consumer involvement in mobile app creation 16–18, 139–46; and copyright decline 41–3; and death 60; downloads 16–17, 140–1; as enabler of consumer creativity/innovation 136–8, 144; as enabler of consumer entrepreneurship 138–9; and health 57–8; open source/creative commons movement 7–8, 28–9, 41, 47, 50, 66, 150; patent pools/standard sharing 25, 26–7; *see also* Big Data
Infosys 39
Innovation Leaders Fund (ILF) 13–16, *14–15*
insight generation *see* Big Data; futures thinking/foresight/scenarios
insourcing 12
insurance, maritime sector 122; residual value insurance 122, 127–9, 133–4
intangible assets 3; financial reporting of 74–7
Intel, USA 28
Intellectual Ventures, USA 3
internal profitability 100–6, *105*, 110–11
internal reputation managers 47
International Accounting Standards (IAS), EU 74–7
International Financial Reporting Standards (IFRS) 74–7, 79, 80
internationalisation theory, M&As 79
International Society of Transport Aircraft Trading 125
Interpump, Italy 164
inventors: employees' rights to compensation 4–5; globalisation of talent 12–16, *14–15*; and patents 4

investment: crowdfunding, mobile apps 144–5; and innovative companies 13–16, *14–15*; *see also* research and development (R&D)
IP development companies 25
iPhones *see* smartphones
IP licensing companies, ARM Holdings 26–7
Isis Innovation, UK 25
isomorphism, living systems 86
Israel, innovation ratios *169*
Italy 164, *169*

Japan 7, 11, 11–12, 57, 168, *169*; cultural factors 8–10, 167–8; efficiency and energy consumption 91, *92*, 93; Nakamura Shuji case 4–5; Senkaku (Diaoyu) Islands dispute 11–12
Japan Airlines (JAL) 8–10
Jeanjean, Thomas 79
Jones, Tim xvi, 7–8, 13–16, *14–15*, 22–52

KAE, UK 158
kaizen, Japan 168
Kawalec, Pawel 18
Kickstarter, USA 139
Kindle, Amazon 32, 35
knowledge and know-how sharing/transfer 25, 45–6, 49, 50; developing economies 39–41; and social innovation 64
knowledge, differentiated 39–41, 47
Kodak, USA 3
Koh, Judge Lucy 5
Kommanditgesellschaft (KG) funds, Germany 124
Kotter, John 61
Kraft, USA, 'Collaboration Kitchen' 137

Laing, R.D. 68
law: competition law 10–11; rule of law 11–12
law of energy conservation 84
lawsuits: Apple/Samsung 3–4, 5, 6–7, 10; *Mayo v. Prometheus* (2012) 29; Nakamura Shuji case 4–5
Leadbeater, Charles 61
lease encumbered value 125
lease financing, maritime sector 2, 119–22
Lenovo, China 39
Lev, Baruch 78
life expectancy/saleability risk 130, 132, 133
light displacement tonnage (LDT), ships 131

Linux operating system 29
literacy, and health 58
living systems *see* physical macroeconomics
loan-to-value (LTV) ratio 123
long tail strategy 164
long-term asset value (LTAV) 124–5
Lufthansa, Germany 138

Mackinnon Partnership, UK 160
maritime sector: asset valuation 2, 122–7, *124*, 129–34; impact of credit crunch 113–19, *115–17*; lease financing and residual value risk 2, 119–22; residual value insurance 122, 127–9, 133–4; and rule of law 11–12
Maritime Strategies International, UK 128
Markarian, Garen 79
market equilibrium, and DAVT 104–6, *105*
Massachusetts Institute of Technology (MIT), USA 40, 44, 145
Maven Research, USA 40–1
Mayo v. Prometheus (2012) 29
Mechanical Turk (MTurk), Amazon 153
Medical Research Council, UK 44
Medic Mobile, India 64
mental health 58, 68
mergers and acquisitions (M&As) 77–8, 79
Meyer, Chris 40
mGraffiti 144
Microsoft, USA 19, 23, 28, 39, 48
MIT *see* Massachusetts Institute of Technology
MIT App Inventor 145
mobile applications (apps), consumer involvement 16–18, 139–46
monopolies, and patents 4
'Montessori mafia' 17, 30, 34
moral obligation, and Japan Airlines 8–10
Mossi & Ghisolfi, Italy 164
motivation, intrinsic/extrinsic, customer innovation 137
MTurk, Amazon 153
music applications (apps) 143
music industry 25–6, 42
'My Starbucks Idea' 136–7

Nakamura Shuji case, Japan 4–5
NASDAQ 13, 15
National Center for Advancing Translational Sciences (NCATS), USA 44

National Health Service (NHS), UK 18, 54, 65
'negative entropy' (information) 95–6, 108
nemawashi 9
Netflix Prize 137–8
Netherlands, innovation ratios *169*
networks: and Corporate Lego 46–8; social media/networking 19, 47, 143, 145, 150, 151–2, 167; of talent 49
NHS *see* National Health Service
Nichia Corporation, Japan 4–5
Nike Plus/Nike Fuel Band 143–4
Nordstrom, Kjell 48
Novartis, Switzerland 28
Nowak, Alojzy Z. xvi–xvii, 20, 163–71

Ocado, UK 142
OECD *see* Organisation for Economic Co-operation and Development
oil prices 98–9, *99*
online communities: consumer entrepreneurship 138–9; consumer innovation 17, 136–8, 144
online shopping 142; Amazon 3, 29, 30–2, 35–7, *36*, 153, 154
'open foresight' concept 37–8
open innovation movement 8, 27–9; business model open innovation 45–6
openness, living systems 86
open source/creative commons movement 7–8, 28–9, 41, 47, 50, 66, 150
Organisation for Economic Co-operation and Development (OECD), definition of R&D 75
outsourcing 39, 46–8

Page Rank algorithm, Google 33
palliative care 59–60
P&G *see* Procter and Gamble
Paragon Shipping, Greece 119
patent infringements 7; Apple/Samsung disputes 3–4, 5, 6–7, 10
patents 168–9, *169*; and biotech companies 29; business method patents 29–37, *36*; good and bad 3, 3–7; patent pools 25, 26–7; and 3D printing 42–3
PatientsLikeMe 153
Patterson, Henry 18
Pawprints, Boston Children's Hospital, USA 55
payday loan companies 19
peer learning, health issues 59

pharmaceutical industry 29, 39; failed drugs 43–5
Pharoah, Paul 158
physical macroeconomics 84–5; and dynamic added value taxation 19–20, 85, 86, 98, 99–111, *102*, *105*, *107*; economic efficiency 86–8, *87*, 91–4, *92–4*, 95; economy and general living system principles 85–6, 108–10; energy and information components of GDP 95–7; energy sources, world economy 88–94, *88–9*, *91–4*; symmetry and harmony in the economy 108–10
Poland *169*, 169–70
portfolio careers 48–9
Portugal, Aconchego Program 64
power *see* empowerment
premise, valuation 126–7
Priceline, USA 29
prices: 'grain basket' 97–8, *98*; shares 13–16, *14–15*; *see also* prices, maritime sector
prices, maritime sector 116, 118, 130–4; and residual value risk 2, 120–2; *see also* asset valuation, maritime sector
privacy issues, Big Data 19, 151–2
Procter and Gamble (P&G), USA 23, 27, 28, 51, 154
profitability, and DAVT 100–8, *102*, *105*, 110–11
project-focused talent 48–9
public energy carriers 96
public relations 5, 47; and Apple/Samsung disputes 6–7
Pyykkö, Elena 79

quantitative analysis, Big Data 149

radical innovation 24
Rankin, David xvii, 19, 148–61
Reckitt Benckiser, UK 51
Reeder, Neil xvii, 18, 54–69
religion, and health 57
renewable energies 88–9, *88–9*
replacement cost valuation/risk, maritime sector 123, 130–1, 132
research and development (R&D) 3, 170–1; alternative uses for failed drugs 43–5; ARM Holdings 26–7; and open innovation movement 8, 27–9, 45–6; and open source/creative commons movement 7–8, 28–9, 41, 47, 50, 66, 150; signalling effects of R&D reporting 8, 73–81; *see also* patents

Index

Research in Motion, Canada 3
residual value insurance (RVI) 122, 127–9, 133–4
residual value risk 2, 120–2
'Re-think Mental Illness' user groups, UK 59
Ridderstrale, Jonas 48
risk management 47; residual value insurance/risk 2, 120–2, 127–9, 133–4
Roche, UK 44
Romania, innovation ratios *169*
Romero-Merino, M. Elena 78
royalties, music industry 25–6
RPX Corporation, USA 3
RSM, UK 59
rule of law 11–12
Russia, innovation ratios *169*

Samsung, South Korea 3, 51; Samsung/Apple disputes 3–4, 5, 6–7, 10
S&P *see* Standard and Poor
San Patrignano community, Italy 59
Scandinavia *169*, 170–1
scenarios *see* futures thinking/foresight/scenarios
Scipher, UK 25
'scramble' scenario, Shell 23–4
scrap values, maritime sector 131–2
SeaChange Maritime LLC 125
search engines, Google 3, 30–1, 32–7, *36*, 145, 152, 154
securitised value 125
self-interest, and creativity 12
semiconductor industry 26–7
Senkaku (Diaoyu) Islands dispute 11–12
service-level agreements (SLAs) 47
SFAS *see* Statement of Financial Accounting Standards
shamrock organisations 160
share prices, and innovative companies 13–16, *14–15*
Shazam 143
Shell, 'blueprint' and 'scramble' scenarios 23–4
Sherbertpip.co.uk 18
Shin, J.K. 6
shipping *see* maritime sector
Shitara, Judge Ryuchi 4–5
Siemens, Germany 23
signalling effects, R&D reporting 8, 73–81
Slovakia, innovation ratios *169*
small and medium enterprises (SMEs) 12–13, 166, 168

smartphones 26; Apple/Samsung disputes 3–4, 5, 6–7, 10; consumer involvement, mobile apps 16–18, 139–46
smoking 18, 54–5
social innovation, health care 54–6, 69; creating and growing value 60–4, *60*, *62–3*; for differing levels of health need 56–60, *56*; providing wider value 18, 64–5; recipients of value 66–8; resources and pathways 62–4, *63*
social innovation, stages of *60*
'social manufacturing' 167
social media/networking 19, 47, 143, 145, 150, 151–2, 167
social relationships, and health 54, 57
Social Value Act (2012), UK 65
social value: Big Data and the big society 157–61; and employment 65; new applications for failed drugs 44
society, role in socio-economic processes 95–6
socio-economic system, and added value 84–5, 86–7, 95–7
software: open source/creative commons movement 7–8, 28–9, 41, 47, 50, 66, 150; software costs 78
Software Publishers Association (SPA), USA 78
solar energy consumption 88–91, *89*, 93
SoundHound 143
South Korea 114, 142; Samsung/Apple disputes 3–4, 5, 6–7, 10
Spain, innovation ratios *169*
sport, and health 57
Spotify 143
SSAP *see* Statement of Standard Accounting Practice
stability theorem 103–4, 110–11
staff *see* employees; employment
Standard and Poor (S&P) 13, 15
standard sharing 25, 26–7
Starbucks, USA, 'My Starbucks Idea' 136–7
Statement of Financial Accounting Standards (SFAS), USA 77, 78
Statement of Standard Accounting Practice (SSAP), UK 74, 75, 76
steady state, living systems 86
steel scrap prices 131–2
subprime mortgage market, USA 113–14
Survivors' Poetry, UK 59
Sweden *169*, 170–1

symmetry principles, living systems 108–10

tablets 26; consumer involvement, mobile apps 16–18, 139–46
Taiwan 39
Taleb, Nassim Nicholas 24
talent: globalisation of 12–16, *14–15*; 'Montessori mafia' 17, 30, 34; project-focused 48–9; *see also* consumer creativity/invention
tangible assets, valuation of 1–2
Taplin, Ruth xvii–xviii, 1–20
taxation: Amazon's avoidance of sales tax 31–2; dynamic added value taxation 19–20, 85, 86, 98, 99–111, *102*, *105*, *107*
technologies: and the financial crisis 164; patents and exports 168–70, *169*; *see also* information and communication technology (ICT); research and development (R&D)
technology clusters/consortia 165–6
telemetry devices, health care 59
Tesco 154; Tesco Home Plus 142
Thatcher, Margaret 11
TheAppBuilder, UK 145
thermodynamic free energy 84–5, 86, 95, 108–9
Threadless, USA 138
3D printing 42–3
3M, USA 167
Tokyo District Court 4–5
TopCoder.com 153–4
Translational Clinical Research Center, Roche 44
Trans-Pacific Partnership 10
transport fuel as energy carrier 96, 98–9, *99*
Tse, Chin-Bun xviii, 8, 73–81
Tsinghua University, China 40

uncertainty: of intangible assets 75, 76–7; skills needed to deal with 61–2, *62*; residual value risk 2, 120–2
United Kingdom (UK) 44, *169*; ARM Holdings 26–7; citizen science, Big Data and cancer research 154, 157–61; and health care 18, 54–5, 55, 57, 58, 59, 63, 64, 65, 154, 157–61; and R&D reporting 74, 75, 76, 77, 79, 80; Social Value Act (2012) 65
United States (USA) 28, 39, 40, 44, *89*, 167, *169*; Amazon 29, 30–2, 35–7, *36*, 153; Apple 3–4, 5, 6–7, 10, 40; and Big Data 155; consumer involvement initiatives 136–8; efficiency and energy consumption *92*, 93, 94, *94*; electricity prices 87, *87*, 93, *93*; Google 30–1, 32–7, *36*, 152; health care 54–5, 58, 61, 63, 65, 67; innovation strategies 164; and R&D reporting 74, 77, 78, 80
United States Patent and Trademark Office (USPTO) 30
universities as knowledge hubs 40
'useful energy', commodities 95, 98–9, *99*

valuation of assets, maritime sector 122–7, *124*, 129–34
valuation standards, assets 123–5, *124*
value added tax (VAT) 99–105, *102*, *105*, 106–8, *107*, 110–11; *see also* added value taxation
value creation, and R&D 73–4
value–energy interrelationship *see* physical macroeconomics
value-relevance, R&D reporting 79–80
Vanderbilt Children's Hospital, Tennessee, USA 58
Viafo, Blood Sprint 144
video technology, and death 60
volunteer workforce, health care 159–60
von Hippel, Eric 42
VW, Germany 51

weapons as energy carriers 96
Whole Foods, USA 166
Wikipedia 29
Wine Foundry, USA 139
Wise, Sarah 68
Wonga, UK 151

Yapp 145
young entrepreneurs 17–18
Young, Michael, Lord Young of Dartington 64

Zamzee 68
Zooniverse 153

Taylor & Francis
eBooks
FOR LIBRARIES

ORDER YOUR FREE 30 DAY INSTITUTIONAL TRIAL TODAY!

Over 23,000 eBook titles in the Humanities, Social Sciences, STM and Law from some of the world's leading imprints.

Choose from a range of subject packages or create your own!

- ▶ Free MARC records
- ▶ COUNTER-compliant usage statistics
- ▶ Flexible purchase and pricing options

- ▶ Off-site, anytime access via Athens or referring URL
- ▶ Print or copy pages or chapters
- ▶ Full content search
- ▶ Bookmark, highlight and annotate text
- ▶ Access to thousands of pages of quality research at the click of a button

For more information, pricing enquiries or to order a free trial, contact your local online sales team.

UK and Rest of World: online.sales@tandf.co.uk
US, Canada and Latin America:
e-reference@taylorandfrancis.com

www.ebooksubscriptions.com

A flexible and dynamic resource for teaching, learning and research.